WS/H
0623

Less Time
for
Meddling

FRANCES GRIFFIN

Less Time
for
Meddling

A History of
Salem Academy and College
1772-1866

JOHN F. BLAIR, Publisher
Winston-Salem

Copyright © 1979 by Salem Academy and College
Library of Congress Catalog Card Number: 79–20697
ISBN 0–89587–012–6
All rights reserved.
Printed in the United States of America

Library of Congress Cataloging in Publication Data

Griffin, Frances.
    Less time for meddling.

    Bibliography: p.
    Includes index.
    1. Salem Academy and College, Winston-Salem, N. C.—
History. 2. Moravian Church—Education—North
Carolina—History. 3. Education of women—North
Carolina—History. I. Title.
LD7251.W782G74   373.756′67   79–20697
ISBN 0–89587–012–6

To parents of all time, especially my own,
who have given of themselves that their
daughters might have an education.

Acknowledgments

ANYONE WHO UNDERTAKES TO WRITE OF THE EIGH-
teenth and early nineteenth century Moravians in North Carolina
becomes immediately and remains eternally grateful not only to those
methodical Brethren, who recorded the day-to-day happenings of
their time and place, but also to their descendants, who have so con-
scientiously preserved these records. The wealth of primary material
at my disposal in the preparation of this book was truly a historian's
pot of gold. But I could never have found my way to the many nooks
and crannies of this treasure without the guidance of Susan Smith
Taylor of the Salem College Library and Mary Creech of the
Archives of the Moravian Church in America, Southern Province,
and I am indebted to both of them for their assistance and forbearance throughout the years of my research.

Others also responded generously to my calls for help in locating
bits and pieces of information needed for an accurate presentation of
this history: Anna Cooper, former Salem College librarian; the Rev.
Vernon Nelson, Moravian archivist at Bethlehem, Pennsylvania;
Richard Träger of the *Archiv der Brüder-Unität* in Herrnhut, East
Germany; Claramae R. Hamilton of the Moravian congregation at
Gnadenhütten, Ohio; Harriet J. Quin and Frances Rainey of the
James K. Polk Auxiliary in Columbia, Tennessee; Patricia Clark of
the University of Tennessee; and Margaret Patterson Bartlett of
Greeneville, Tennessee. I am grateful to them all. And equal thanks
go to William Ashe of the Wake Forest University Library staff and
Robert Woerner, Salem College librarian, for making it so con-
venient for me to study microfilms.

For sharing some of the fruits of their own research, Mary Jane
Whalen, Alice Henderson North, Betty Ring, and Stuart Wright have
my sincere appreciation. Had it not been for the translations of the
late Rt. Rev. Kenneth G. Hamilton, Dr. Frank P. Albright, and Mary
Creech, I could never have penetrated the language barrier to reach
much of the information so important to this history. And although
their work was not done for my particular benefit, the research
material compiled by Frank L. Horton and filed in the offices of Old
Salem, Inc., and the card index of all Salem Academy and College
students prepared by Elizabeth Zachary Vogler and Anna Perryman
were invaluable.

The production of this book was a project apart from my responsibilities as director of information at Old Salem, Inc. But I am grateful for the support of the three men who served successively as president of Old Salem, Inc., during the book's progress: James A. Gray, Gardner Gidley, and R. Arthur Spaugh, Jr. I am deeply appreciative, too, of the patience of those who served as president of Salem Academy and College during this time: Dr. Merrimon Cuninggim, Dr. John H. Chandler, and especially Dr. Dale H. Gramley, who had faith enough in me not only to assign me to this task but also to hold his peace while the project dragged on far longer than either of us had anticipated.

The encouraging words of my friend and favorite teacher, Lois Johnson, who read portions of the manuscript from time to time, helped me enormously in "keeping the juices flowing." The suggestions and approval of Margaret Blair McCuiston and Mary Creech of the Moravian Archives reading committee were both helpful and gratifying. And my thanks certainly extend to Jane Kelly and Mary Scott Best for their enthusiastic support of the finished product and to John Fries Blair, who painstakingly removed the excess commas, supplied the missing apostrophes, and performed all the other tedious chores needed to make a raw manuscript acceptable for publication.

Finally, I am thankful to have been able to share the ups and downs of this venture with Elizabeth Trotman. "Liz's" buoyant support— given with the warmth and understanding and openheartedness that were so much a part of her—will remain a cherished memory.

Contents

Foreword

OF THE HUNDREDS OF SCHOOLS WHICH THE MISSION-minded Moravians established on four continents and various islands of the sea in the eighteenth and nineteenth centuries, Salem is one of the very few in operation today. It entered its third century of service in 1972. It survived its childhood and adolescent years, as Frances Griffin tells us so beautifully in this volume, because it met a need, first for girls of the Salem village and then for those of families over a wide area of the sparsely-settled Southeast.

The institution survived also, perhaps more significantly, because those devoted to its operation never surrendered to the difficulties and vicissitudes they encountered. Included were epidemics, the problems of finding qualified teachers, slow and inadequate communication with parents, and the hardships of the Civil War. During this conflict the head of the school spent much of his time scouring the countryside for food to sustain an overcrowded student enrollment. Salem indeed was a place of refuge during those agonizing years.

Although the school for girls that opened in April, 1772, was strictly parochial, its character changed forever when boarding pupils were accepted, starting in 1804. Throughout the years since that date, the institution has served preponderantly the daughters of non-Moravians. Attempts to proselytize were never considered and never practiced. The clergy who administered the school, the church boards which authorized and encouraged its operation, and the Single Sisters who taught and lived with the pupils did so with devotion. They kept the school operating. In a sense, the Single Sisters provided "endowment" support. The institution is in existence today largely because of their sacrificial service. They apparently kept their minds busy, their hearts warm, and their days fully occupied. They obviously had little time for meddling in community or church affairs.

As the author's story implies, the school succeeded through the decades despite the fact it had no academic dean, no dean of students, no director of admissions, no comptroller, no director of development, no public relations coordinator, no alumnae secretary, no superintendent of buildings and grounds. The Inspector, in his wisdom or lack of wisdom, provided services in all these areas.

Nor was there an accrediting association to satisfy every ten years, and obviously no complicated regulations by HEW, the State Department of Public Instruction, and the Supreme Court. Surveys and questionnaires were unknown. Student petitions were unthinkable. Still the operation of the school was in its way complicated and difficult. Financial support then, as now, was a continuing problem, although the school in some years yielded a surplus. This was used on occasion to help support the Salem Boys' School and other church agencies. And as late as 1860 a gift of $1,000 was sent to Bethlehem, Pennsylvania, to help support Moravian College and Theological Seminary in that community. But when the Civil War ended, the school's iron boxlike safe was filled with worthless Confederate money. A new start had to be made. More problems lay ahead. This story still remains to be told.

Frances Griffin was asked to undertake this history of the early years not only because of her widely recognized research and writing skills, but also because she is not a Salem alumna. This meant that she would be less sentimental and more objective. But one has to conclude, after reading the volume, that Frances Griffin came to love her task, the school, and all the people involved. She developed rapport with the administrators, empathy for the often ill-prepared teachers, and loving acquaintance with the young boarding students away from home and family for extended periods of time. The text indicates that the author suffered through the measles epidemics, the homesickness, the Spartan life of her subjects. She undoubtedly would have meddled sufficiently to improve conditions if she could have gone back in time and done so.

Miss Griffin ends her story with the passage in 1866 of an act of incorporation of the school by the General Assembly of the State of North Carolina. This provided legal authority for the trustees to adopt appropriate by-laws and subsequently to offer college-level courses and award degrees. The first degrees were conferred in 1890. The next significant development was the organization in 1911 of a board of trustees including others than the members of the central administrative Provincial Elders' Conference of the Moravian Church, and then the gradual expansion of this board to include non-Moravians and alumnae.

The removal in 1931 of Academy students to new facilities on the eastern area of the campus served to stimulate the subsequent growth and strength of both the Academy and the College. Except for the

president, the comptroller, the director of development, and the
maintenance superintendent, the two major units of the corporate
whole have their own personnel. They have their own endowment
funds and their own operating budgets. They make common use of
the Fine Arts Center, the gymnasium, and the playing fields, and
share the wintertime comfort provided by the steam plant. They also
experience a sense of companionship with the past as provided by
six campus buildings over one hundred years in age and by the Old
Salem restoration.

Simple though the organization of the institution was in the years
covered by Miss Griffin's account, it is today somewhat complex. In
addition to the four-year college preparatory program offered for two
hundred students at the Academy and the B.A., B.S. and B.M. degrees
offered for an enrollment of more than six hundred students at the
College, the Board of Trustees maintains a School of Music with
separate individualized and group instruction for children, a Lifespan
Center for women of the community, and a Center for Special Education to serve children and adults who have serious reading problems.
A total of over fifteen hundred are enrolled by Salem for all programs
in 1979 in twenty-five buildings on fifty-six acres of land. In the best
sense, the institution continues its tradition of serving the needs of
the society of which it is a part.

Students at both the Academy and the College encounter more
distractions today than was the case during the years covered by the
author's account. Yet they find more time for meddling—in con-
structive, cooperative and contributing ways. Salem was one of the
first educational institutions in North Carolina to encourage the
organization of a Student Government Association and the adoption
of an Honor Code. The right of petition for redress of grievances or
for changes of varied sorts has long been a cherished prerogative
of students. And as a women's institution, all rights, privileges, and
responsibilities have centered in the female sex. Equal rights have been
the only rights.

That Salem intends to continue its devotion to the education of
women is obvious. Its Board of Trustees was not even tempted to
change the institution's basic purpose to a coeducational one during
the decade leading up to the bicentennial anniversary in 1972. This
was a period which saw many single-sex preparatory schools and

colleges become coeducational as the competition for students heightened and efforts to balance operating budgets brought changes. Modern-day Salem continues in its long-held conviction that women's institutions do a superior job of training women for leadership roles in society. As the oldest women's school in continuous existence in its original location in the United States, Salem looks ahead with as much trepidation as other church-related institutions do, but with high hopes that the importance of its purpose and the quality of its programs will attract students and financial support commensurate with its needs.

Salem also cherishes its continuing relationship with the Moravian Church, which conceived it, nourished it through trying years, and provided its campus acreage. As the institution's fifteenth president, Merrimon Cuninggim, put it in late 1978: "Salem's primary values are the same as those that informed and motivated the Moravians who founded it: honorable dealings, a free and inquiring spirit, loving and caring human relationship, a desire to serve, a tolerant disposition, faith in God. Salem is proud to be related to the Moravian Church and shares its ecumenical attitude. True to its Christian heritage, Salem works at making its values manifest in the daily life of its campus community."

Present and recent students of both the Academy and the College, accustomed as they are to refinements and conveniences made possible by electricity, the automobile, the airplane, the telephone, radio and television, indoor plumbing and central heating, may have to sharpen their imaginations to understand the hardships of the early years at Salem. But they seem to appreciate the twentieth century setting: the beautiful buildings, the distinctive atmosphere, the meaningful traditions. They are well aware of the fact that others were on campus before they arrived.

Students, alumnae, and all other friends of Salem Academy and College are indebted to Frances Griffin for her faithful recording of Salem's first 94 years and for keeping all of us from emptiness of mind as we read her factual and tender story.

—DALE H. GRAMLEY

Why then should we merely dismiss them [women] with the ABC and drive them away from books: Are we afraid of their meddling? The more we introduce them to mental occupations, the less time they will find for meddling, which comes from emptiness of mind.

—JOHN AMOS COMENIUS (1592–1670)

Less Time for Meddling

I

Heritage of Education

I N THE MIDDLE OF MAY, 1804—ABOUT THE SAME TIME
that the Messrs. Lewis and Clark were hoisting sail at St. Louis for
their historic expedition to the Pacific—a merchant set out from Hillsborough, North Carolina, on a journey that was to weave its own
small thread into the fabric of history.

His name was William Kirkland, and traveling with him were
three little girls: his own two daughters, ages ten and eight, and the
ten-year-old daughter of Major William Francis Strudwick, a Hillsborough planter and justice of the peace. They headed their horses
westward toward the sparsely settled "backcountry" of the state.
Though the distance they were to travel was less than a hundred miles,
the roads of that time were rough and the stamina of the travelers
limited; it must have taken them nearly a week to complete the trip.
Precisely when they did reach their destination is not clear in the
records, but the strongest evidence indicates that Kirkland and his
three young charges arrived in the Moravian congregation town of
Salem on Tuesday, May 15, 1804.

They had come from an area strictly English in character, and for
the little girls, at least, this first sight of Salem must have been rather
awesome. For the Germanic Moravian settlers had built their town
in the architecture of their homeland, and its imposing, medieval-
looking buildings surely were like nothing the girls had ever seen
before. They were probably a bit frightened, too, by the strange, gut-
tural accents of the men and women who came out to greet them. But

there was no mistaking the genuine warmth of the welcome accorded the weary, dusty travelers. The Moravians were by nature hospitable people. Also deeply devout, they were never happier than when they were answering a call to Christian service, and, in their minds, the arrival of the Hillsborough party represented the beginning of just that sort of mission.

Since shortly after the American Revolution, visitors passing through Salem—some of them distinguished men of the South—had been urging the Moravians to open a boarding school for girls. From time to time over the past decade, the Brethren and Sisters of the congregation had considered the matter in their various conferences and had spoken to the Lord about it in their prayers. The more they considered and the more they prayed, the more convinced they had become that here indeed was another means by which they could fruitfully serve both the Lord and their fellowman. So being methodical as well as conscientious people, they had appointed a committee to draw up plans for a school building, had tapped one of their ministers for the position of "inspector" (principal) and had proceeded to work out, one by one, such details of equipment and staff as were necessary for the feeding, lodging, and teaching of girls.

In this spring of 1804, the school building was still a year away from completion, but other preparations were so far along that the Moravians had decided to go ahead and accept a limited number of boarding pupils, housing them temporarily in the *Gemein Haus* (Congregation House). Just how word of that decision found its way so quickly to Hillsborough is not clear, but as early as March, William Kirkland and Major Strudwick had applied for the admission of their daughters to the new school. The girls were among the first applicants to be accepted, and they were the first of those accepted to arrive in Salem. So it happened that Elizabeth Jane Strudwick and Ann and Elizabeth Kirkland led the procession of the hundreds and then thousands of girls whose health and happiness, along with their education, were to be entrusted to the Moravian Brethren and Sisters in this small and, in many ways, unusual town. And if all the congregation did not personally turn out to greet them on that Tuesday in May, the entire town soon knew that they had come and hailed the occasion with genuine joy and thanksgiving.

Even so, we can imagine the uneasiness that must have crept over the three little girls now that the excitement of the trip had waned. They were a long way from home. The prospect of being left in this strange town, among these strange people, must have been almost more than a ten-year-old was prepared to face. And one may well wonder how the fathers of the little girls—even less, their mothers— had had the heart to subject them to it.

The truth is, the condition of education in the South at that time left them, and other parents like them, little choice. During the years following the Revolution, academies for boys had sprung up through-out the Southern states—many of them good classical schools which, like the one in Salisbury, North Carolina, purported "to teach young men the first rudiments of language and science, and so to prepare them for a more complete education at the University."[1] But for Southern girls in the late eighteenth and early nineteenth centuries, there were virtually no opportunities for an education of any kind, classical or otherwise, the only girls' boarding school of any con-sequence in all of the South being the Ursuline Convent in New Orleans. To men of standing in North Carolina, South Carolina, Vir-ginia, Georgia, and Tennessee, this was an acutely distressing situa-tion. Not only were their daughters growing up with little or no formal education, but living as they did in small towns or on widely scattered plantations, they also were cut off from cultural and social contacts of almost every kind.

It is small wonder, then, that news of the opening of a boarding school for girls in Salem spread quickly. Here at last was a chance for Southern parents to give their daughters the education hitherto denied them. And it is easy to understand how mothers, along with fathers, would rush to take advantage of it—even though in the doing, little girls would be uprooted from familiar, often spacious surround-ings and sent hundreds of miles away to a place where living condi-tions bordered on the Spartan, where discipline was strict and religion dominant, and where English was spoken only through a curtain of thick German accents. From a parent's point of view, at any rate, the miseries of homesickness must have seemed a small enough price to pay.

Yet the question remains: Why the Moravians? Why in this predominantly English region was it left to a small group of Germanic people, long isolated from others by choice, to be the first to respond to the desperate need for girls' education? Why, for that matter, would outsiders urge them so persistently to do so?

To answer that, one must first travel back through the history of the Moravians themselves. For the residents of Salem in 1804 were an unusual group of people whose character and way of life had been shaped by tenets and traditions that stretched across two continents and three centuries. These roots can no more be separated from the boarding school that opened in Salem than a man can be parted from his own bloodstream.

Oddly enough, the Moravians of Salem were not, on the whole, highly educated people. They were literate, perhaps to a greater degree collectively than the residents of most towns in the South at that time. But essentially they were artisans—men who worked with their hands to produce fine linsey-woolsey and tinware, pottery and shoes, saddles and guns, houses so solid that many would still be standing two hundred years later. Yet embedded in the very marrow of their faith was a high regard for education. They believed, as wholly as the Brethren for three centuries had believed, that in the Scriptures lay the supreme law under which all men and women must live and work. Unless one could read the Word for himself, how could he fully comprehend its teachings, much less dedicate his life to them? Moreover, from the founding of the faith, the Brethren had been led by men whose education stemmed from the great universities of Europe. Both the example and the teaching of these educated leaders had lifted the standard of Moravian schools more than a few notches above the ordinary levels of their time, and, over the centuries, had helped to build a tradition of education among the Moravians so strong, so ingrained in their congregation life, that it was a part of their baggage no matter where they traveled or what hardships they encountered on the way.

John Hus, the Bohemian martyr who sowed the seed of the Moravian faith back in the fifteenth century, was one of the most learned men of his time, having been both dean of the philosophical faculty and rector at the University of Prague. Hus ran afoul of Rome when he preached that the Scriptures were a higher law than the canons of the Church, and in 1415 he was burned at the stake for heresy. But his teachings survived the angry flames. After Hus's death his followers formed a separate society, the *Unitas Fratrum* (Unity of Brethren), ordaining their first ministers in 1467—half a century before Martin Luther posted his "ninety-five theses" on the church door at Wittenberg.

No less than other Protestant groups at that time, the Unity had its troubles with Rome. But there were stretches during the next two hundred years when the religious front in Europe was relatively quiet, and in those periods, the Unity flourished, congregations springing up throughout Bohemia, Moravia, and Poland. Wherever there was a congregation, there was also a school and often a printing press as well. Indeed, out of the ranks of the early Brethren came a man, John Amos Comenius, who later was acclaimed "the father of modern education."

A native of Moravia forced by the Counter Reformation into exile in Poland, Comenius advanced the then-revolutionary idea that schools need not be torture chambers in which the young sit in mortal fear of the masters, but rather a place where they find joy in learning. "Let the teacher not teach as much as he is able to teach," he said, "but only as much as the learner is able to learn."[2] Through his writings, he argued that children should be taught in their mother tongue rather than across the formidable barrier of Latin; that textbooks should include illustrations to help the child understand; that unless a child is to be sent to school "like something flung from a shovel,"[3] his education must begin at home.

And the case for women's education made by Comenius more than three centuries ago may since have sprung a few laughs, but it still holds a lot of water:

No reason can be shown why the female sex . . . should be kept from a knowledge of languages and wisdom. For they are also human beings, an image of God, as we are; they are also partakers of the mercy and the kingdom of the future life; in their minds they are equally gifted to acquire wisdom; indeed, in gentleness of understanding they are often more endowed than we. The Lord God likewise employs them sometimes in large affairs (to manage people, lands, estates, and even whole kingdoms; also to give special advice to kings and princes; also to practice the art of medicine and to care for fellow human beings; even to function as proph-

ets and to aid priests and bishops in giving instruction and chastisement).
Why then should we merely dismiss them with the ABC and drive them
away from books: Are we afraid of their meddling? The more we introduce them to mental occupations, the less time they will find for meddling,
which comes from emptiness of mind.[4]

Neither Comenius nor other leaders of the Brethren had the freedom to teach, or to preach, for long, however. In the mid-seventeenth
century, the enemies of Protestantism finally succeeded in destroying
the Unity's churches, schools, and towns and in scattering its members, Comenius himself being driven to seek refuge in Holland, where
he died in 1670 without ever seeing his native Moravia again. It was
a full half-century after his death before remnants of the Brethren in
Moravia, forced for years to keep their faith secret, finally found a
place where they could worship openly again and where the frayed
strings of the old educational tradition could be rewoven into a new
pattern of life.

Their haven was the estate of a wealthy Saxon nobleman, Nicholas
Lewis von Zinzendorf. A deeply religious man, Count Zinzendorf
had been moved by the plight of these courageous people who, despite the perils of persecution, refused to let go of their faith. He had
offered them sanctuary, and at the risk of their lives, they had come—
a few at a time at first, and then in a steady stream until by the mid-
1720s they had built a whole town on Zinzendorf's lands, naming it
"Herrnhut" ("Lord's Watch").

Although Zinzendorf never intended that they should come in such
numbers or sink such permanent roots, he nevertheless was impressed
by their sincerity and surprised to find that their theology so closely
matched his own. Soon he found himself taking a leading role in their
affairs. Being himself a scholar—educated at Halle and Wittenberg—
the Count saw to it that schools, from nurseries on up to a theological
seminary, were among the earliest institutions to be established in
Herrnhut.

At first, the Brethren had worshiped at the Lutheran church on
Zinzendorf's estate. But eventually, with Zinzendorf's blessing, the
old *Unitas Fratrum* as a separate, cohesive Protestant society was re-
born, drawing to its ranks other religious refugees and other men who,
like Count Zinzendorf, had been educated in the renowned universi-

John Amos Comenius (1592–1670)

Nicholas Lewis von Zinzendorf (1700–1760)

ties of Central Europe—among them, August Gottlieb Spangenberg, a former professor at Halle, who was to lead the first Moravian colonists to America.

It was at Herrnhut that the Brethren's tradition of music, begun in Bohemia with the publication of the first Protestant hymnal, burst into new flower. Orchestras, bands, and choruses were formed; children were taught music at an early age; the congregation's music collection included the works of Handel, Bach, and other leading composers in Europe at that time. It was here, too, that the popular name "Moravians" came to apply to all members of the Unity, though many had come from places other than Moravia. And it was at Herrnhut that the Moravians absorbed the strong Germanic flavor and developed the unusual pattern of living that would set them apart from the mainstream of America for more than a century.

The Brethren in Herrnhut were a tightly-knit group, made so by design as well as by circumstance. For theirs was a practical sort of religion, grounded on the premise that the work of a man's hands was every bit as direct an expression of the will of God as the words spoken by the preacher in the pulpit. Whatever a man did, in fact— whether it was in his work, his financial affairs, his household arrangements, his association with others, even his choice of a wife— was subject to the Lord's will. And if he himself was not always able to determine just what direction the Lord willed him to take, the congregation leaders were only too ready to guide him on his way. Those who could not, or would not, accept such assistance were kindly but firmly invited to leave.

The Moravian congregation lived, in effect, much as one large family, each member with his or her own place and responsibilities but all subject to the same somewhat rigid paternal oversight. And in order to promote further Christian growth and activity, members were divided into "choirs" according to age, sex, and marital status: Married People, Single Brothers, Single Sisters, Widows, Widowers, Older Boys, Older Girls, Children. Each choir had its own special religious "festival day" set aside on the calendar; the adult choirs had their own leaders, and in the cases of some—Single Brothers, Single Sisters, and often Widows—members worked, ate, and slept together in their own choir house.

Because the Moravians in Herrnhut followed a pattern of living so

August Gottlieb Spangenberg (1704–1792)

parochial in nature, so different from that of their neighbors, the community became suspect, even among other Protestants. And it was partly to establish an alternate base, in case of outright persecution, that they decided in the early 1730s to establish a settlement in the New World. Also, buoyed by their own spiritual revival, the Brethren were eager to spread the Gospel to the heathen—in this case, to the American Indians.

Consequently, Spangenberg led a small group to Oglethorpe's colony in Georgia in 1735, and within a few years they had completed a school for Indian children, "Irene," on an island not far from Savannah. But the conscience of the Moravians would not let them bear arms. So when war broke out between the English and the Spanish, they were caught in an intolerable position. Although back in England the trustees of the Georgia colony had promised them that they would not be asked to go against their conscience in this matter, their fellow colonists chose to ignore any such dispensation, insisting that they take their turn at military service along with everyone else. Their refusal stirred up antagonism on all sides. Moreover, the Moravians, unaccustomed to the climate in Georgia and to the stresses of frontier life, had been plagued with sickness almost from the time they landed. This, together with the growing antipathy around them, finally pushed them to the decision to leave Georgia altogether. And in 1740, the entire Moravian contingent moved to Pennsylvania.

In Pennsylvania, the towns built by the Moravians—Bethlehem, Nazareth, Lititz—all patterned after Herrnhut, flourished. Spangenberg, appalled that "in the whole country [Pennsylvania] there are few schools and there is almost no one who makes the youth his concern,"[5] saw that schools were started immediately in the Brethren's communities. The first one, begun in 1742, was, in fact, the first Protestant school for girls in America. In the hands of the fine Moravian craftsmen, who had learned their skills from master artisans in Europe, the Brethren's industries—particularly those in Bethlehem—prospered. Within a short time, the Moravians had earned such a wide reputation as reliable colonists that John Carteret (Earl of Granville), son of one of the original Lords Proprietors, urged them to purchase some of his land in Carolina and begin a settlement there. And in 1752, Spangenberg led a small exploring party south from Pennsylvania to select a site.

It was an arduous expedition. For in order to find enough vacant, contiguous land to accommodate a whole new settlement, the explorers had to push toward the back, or western part of the colony, where the hilly terrain was rugged and where often the only trails were those left by buffalo. The location eventually selected was a tract of nearly a hundred thousand acres in what is now Piedmont North Carolina. It reminded Spangenberg of the ancestral Zinzendorf lands in the Wachau valley in Austria. And so they named the tract "Wachau," which later was Anglicized to "Wachovia."

In early October of 1753, the first group of Moravian settlers set out from Bethlehem to begin a new life in this raw backcountry of Carolina. Each had been chosen for the mission because of his individual skill—doctor, minister, shoemaker, business manager, baker, carpenter, tailor, gardener, farmer—for they were headed toward virtual wilderness land, and if the settlement were to survive the rigors, it had to have men who could provide for all its basic needs. The journey took them six weeks. Finally, on November 17, 1753, they crossed the northern boundary of Wachovia, and because the day was growing dark and the weather was bitter cold, they took shelter in an abandoned log cabin.

Although from the first, the plan had been that the chief town in Wachovia would be a commercial center, a place where the skilled Moravian craftsmen could ply their trades, more than twelve years were to pass before they felt they could begin such a task. First, rough shelters had to be raised; land had to be cleared and fields planted; the doctor had to begin growing herbs for his medicines; workmen had to provide the basic necessities for everyday living: plows, clothing, shoes, pots for cooking, millstones for grinding wheat and corn. So the Moravians simply "dug in" where they had first stopped, knowing full well that the settlement was temporary, but, at the moment, having no choice. Because the settlement was temporary, they called it "Bethabara," meaning "House of Passage."

As the years passed, other Moravians made their way to Bethabara: married couples, Single Brothers whose special skills were needed, visiting church leaders such as Spangenberg, who spent ten months there directing affairs and helping to found another small Moravian settlement, Bethania, nearby. Roads were cut, additional buildings constructed, and shops equipped. Crude though it was, Bethabara soon came to represent an oasis of civilization in a primeval land where panthers often prowled, wolves howled, and the smoke of Indian campfires could be seen curling off the not-too-distant mountains. Other settlers, some from miles away, came seeking the wares of the craftsmen, treatment by the doctor, and later, when the threat of warring Indians moved closer, protection inside the log palisade that had been built around Bethabara.

The first married couples who came to Wachovia had left their children in the Brethren's nurseries or boarding schools in Pennsylvania. So the first school started by the Moravians in North Carolina was not at Bethabara but in the neighboring settlement of Bethania, where some of the residents were families of that area who had affiliated themselves with the Moravians. By and by, though, children were born to the couples in Bethabara. And when they were old enough, the congregation leaders, despite the heavy demands of frontier living, made sure that the little girls as well as the little boys learned to read and write.

Still the central town had not been started, and several among the Brethren began to question whether, after all, another town was needed. But most clung to the belief that it was the Lord's will for such a town to be built, and the arrival of one of His ordained ministers, Frederic William Marshall, in the fall of 1764, provided the impetus to begin.

Marshall, who had been appointed *Oeconomus* (chief executive) of Wachovia, was another in the succession of scholarly leaders in the Unity of Brethren, having been educated at the university at Leipzig. Under his forceful guidance, a site for Salem was selected near the center of the Wachovia tract. Christian Reuter, a Moravian and a trained surveyor, surveyed the land and drew detailed plans for the layout of the town. Finally, on January 6, 1766, "a dozen Brethren, partly from Bethania, partly from Bethabara, took a wagon and went to the new town site where in the afternoon they cut down the trees on the place where the first house was to stand, singing several stanzas as they worked."[6]

The question of the new town nevertheless had been submitted to the Unity's directing board at Herrnhut for confirmation, and late in January, 1766, the answer was delivered by a party of Single Brothers who arrived in Bethabara from Europe: ". . . the Saviour wills that

Salem shall be the town in Wachovia for trade and the professions, and they shall be moved thither from Bethabara."[7]

So, one by one, the houses were staked out. Stones for the foundations were pulled from the frozen earth and hauled to the building sites, where strong arms and backs stacked them intricately one on the other. Heavy timbers for thick walls were hewed and fitted together, and tiles for the roofs were shaped out of clay dug from the bottomland. Tools were crude, and the workmen, though willing, were few.

The building itself was hard enough, but soon the task became even harder as unrest in the colony filtered into the backcountry. Neighboring settlers, rankling under what they believed to be injustices by officers of the Crown, joined the marauding "Regulators," and often the peace-loving Moravians were harassed by their threats and abusive language.

Even Marshall himself, devout minister and effective leader that he was, must have been a bit unnerved by the sheer magnitude of the task at hand. "The present building of Salem," he wrote in a report to Herrnhut, "is an extraordinary affair, which I would not have undertaken had not the Saviour Himself ordered it. I verily believe that the rich city of London could not do that which we must accomplish—move the entire town and its businesses to another place."[8]

For six years, the workmen toiled, sleeping in crude shelters at the building site during the week and returning to Bethabara for worship services on Sundays. As the modest dwelling houses were completed, married couples in Bethabara packed up their tools and other meager belongings and moved to the new town permanently. Late in 1769, the Single Brothers set up housekeeping in their new choir house. Two years later, there were enough communicants living in Salem that one of the ministers began to hold services there. But it was not until the spring of 1772 that all of the major buildings were ready for occupancy. Then it was the Single Sisters' turn to move, the unmarried women taking up residence in the *Gemein Haus*. And about that same time came Frederic William Marshall and his wife—bringing with them, in effect, the government of Wachovia.

By mid-April, only the handful who would maintain Bethabara as a small rural community remained in the old settlement. The citadel of Moravian life in North Carolina was now a totally new town—the town called "Salem," from the Hebrew word for "peace."

Moravian Archives, Winston-Salem, North Carolina

Frederic William Marshall (1721–1802)

2

The School for Little Girls

BY 1780, OTHER MORAVIAN CONGREGATIONS HAD been established in Wachovia: Friedberg in the southwestern section of the tract, Friedland in the southeastern part, and Hope near the Yadkin River. But these, like Bethabara and Bethania, were essentially rural communities. The commercial center of Wachovia, as had been ordained, was Salem, and as such, it had the largest congregation and the most sophisticated system of government.

Salem was operated as a *Gemein Ort* (Congregation Town), which meant, according to Unity principles, that only members of the congregation were allowed to live and work there and that civic and material affairs as well as religious matters were subject to rigid controls. These controls were in the hands of four governing bodies, all of which in later years would figure prominently in the founding and development of the Girls' Boarding School:

(1) The Congregation Council, composed of all adult communicants in Salem, which decided matters of general community interest such as new roads, major construction projects, and church fees.

(2) The *Aeltesten Conferenz* (Elders' Conference), which was made up of ministers, their wives, and other church officials and which was the arbiter of all moral and religious matters.

(3) The *Aufseher Collegium*, which had oversight of the material affairs of the congregation, not only supervising the finances of the community itself but also regulating the various trades and professions.

(4) The *Helfer Conferenz* (Helpers' Conference), which was an advisory body charged with keeping a watchful eye over all matters involving the congregation.*

Physically, the town of Salem in 1772 was little more than a suggestion of the place that the first boarding school girls saw when they arrived thirty-two years later; in the whole town, there were scarcely a dozen houses. Yet the neat ticktacktoe pattern of Salem's streets, centered by a large open square, clearly had been drawn with future growth in mind. And even back then, there was something comfortably substantial about the Old World look of the houses—a feeling of orderliness in the way they were lined up, each hugging the edge of the street.

The main thoroughfare, passing along the west side of the square, ran the length of the town. At the extreme south end of it stood the Salem Tavern, a large two-story building of half-timber construction (heavy framework filled with brick and clay). In later years, when the public Examinations of the boarding school drew crowds of outsiders to Salem, elegant carriages would deposit equally elegant ladies and gentlemen at a brick tavern which stood on this same spot (the old one having been destroyed by fire), and in the course of their stay there, the visitors would mingle convivially with the townspeople. But in 1772, the Brethren were content with the caution of the town's planners, who purposely had placed the tavern the greatest distance from the center of town so that the carousing of strangers stopping there would not interrupt (or corrupt) congregation life.

With similar foresight, the planners had staked out the graveyard, "God's Acre," on a gently rolling hillside in the northeast sector of the town—a quiet spot far away from the noisy tavern and somewhat removed, even, from the hum of community activity. Already in the spring of 1772, three Brethren lay buried there; later, simple stones laid flat against its turf would mark the graves of several little boarding school girls.

Most of the families who had moved from Bethabara were crowded into six houses that stood in a straight row along the main street a

---

*The scope of the Helpers' Conference was later expanded to include all of Wachovia, and eventually (called the "Provincial Helpers' Conference") it became the chief administrative body for the Moravian Church in the South, its members serving, among other functions, as trustees of the Girls' Boarding School.

block or two north of the square. By the time the boarding school opened, there would be other houses scattered all over the town—houses whose walls of logs, bricks, or painted clapboards were much more characteristic of this part of Carolina. But those first houses, with their pitched tile roofs and half-timbered sides, might have been lifted straight out of some old European village. And the same might be said of the two massive, medieval-looking buildings that faced each other across the square itself: the half-timbered Single Brothers' House and the *Gemein Haus*, half-timbered at the upper story with the lower story of heavy stone.

In the 1850s, the *Gemein Haus* would be torn down and replaced by the large brick building known as "Main Hall" on the Salem College campus, but throughout Salem's heyday as a congregation town, it was the center of community life. Until the church was completed in 1800, the congregation gathered in the large *saal* (hall for worship) on the second floor for services. Living quarters for the ministers and their families were in this building. And before they moved into their new choir house in 1786, the Single Sisters of Salem made their home in the south wing of it.

There had been no Single Sisters in Wachovia during the early years of the settlement. All of the women either were married before they came to North Carolina, or else had been dispatched from the Moravian communities in Pennsylvania for the express purpose of providing wives for the Single Brothers at Bethabara—in which cases, the wedding ceremonies had been performed almost immediately upon their arrival. It was not until 1766 that a party of four Single Sisters and twelve Older Girls, having walked most of the way from Bethlehem, arrived in Bethabara to begin the first Single Sisters choir in Wachovia.

Although its ranks changed constantly—what with this Sister or that one leaving to be married, and with girls, after reaching the prescribed age (about fourteen), periodically moving in—the Single Sisters' choir was to be one of the strong supporting arms of Salem throughout its years of operation as a congregation town. And the Single Sisters, individually and collectively, were to be the very backbone of the girls' school in Salem for close to a century.

Among the first group of Single Sisters to arrive in Bethabara was a seventeen-year-old girl, Elisabeth Oesterlein. We know very little of her background up to that time—only that she was born in Bethlehem and that when she was two years old her parents (who then lived at the Moravians' Indian mission at Gnadenhütten, Pennsylvania) brought her back to Bethlehem to be educated. There is no record, either, of what her duties were during the span between her arrival in Bethabara in 1766 and the mass exodus to Salem in 1772. All we know is that she was in the echelon of Single Sisters who made the move on April 9, 1772, and that, along with others of her choir (whose number by then had grown to eighteen), she took up residence in the *Gemein Haus*.

It must have been only days after her arrival when Sister Oesterlein found her niche in the life of Salem being carved out for her. Traugott Bagge, Salem's merchant and leading businessman, had a daughter whom he wanted to get started in school; so did Jacob Meyer, the tavernkeeper. And apparently these two influential Brethren wasted no time in acting on the matter, though exactly how they went about it is not reported in the records. Probably they appealed to the members of the Elders' Conference, who in turn conferred with the leader of the Single Sisters, who in her turn, having considered all likely candidates, recommended Sister Oesterlein for the assignment. Whether Sister Oesterlein herself had anything to say about it, we don't know. But the chances are that she accepted the assignment readily—if for no other reason than that teaching school was preferable to washing, cooking, hoeing, weaving, or any of the other manual labor by which most of the Single Sisters had to earn their keep. In any event, Sister Oesterlein opened a school for little girls in one of the rooms in the Single Sisters' section of the *Gemein Haus*.

The exact day the school began is not recorded; perhaps the Salem diarist considered the opening of a school such a commonplace occurrence among Moravians that he did not bother to make a note of it. In all probability, though, the school opened in the latter part of April, for the financial accounts of the congregation as of April 30, 1772, show that from that date the Single Sisters were to be charged rent for four rooms in the *Gemein Haus* and then were to be given credit for the room used for the school. This seems to indicate that the school already was in operation. In the absence of more precise evidence, however, the founding date of the Little Girls' School in Salem has been designated as April 30, 1772, the date on which payment of rent for the schoolroom actually began. As this Little Girls' School was the forerunner of the boarding school that later evolved into Salem Academy and College, this date also is accepted as the founding date of the present institution.

Although in succeeding years all of the little girls in Salem—some from the outlying Moravian communities as well—were to be pupils in this school, Sister Oesterlein's first class consisted of a grand total of three: Anna Elisabeth Bagge, aged two-and-a-half; Maria Magdalena Meyer, aged four-and-a-half; Maria Magdalena Schmidt (daughter of the town blacksmith), aged eight. Considering the ages of two-thirds of her class, it looks as though the good Sister did a great deal more baby-sitting than teaching. And the rate of her pay seems to bear this out. Bagge and Meyer each paid her a shilling a week for their daughters, while the fee for the Schmidt girl was only six pence. According to the late Dr. Adelaide L. Fries, long-time Moravian archivist, the difference was that "doubtless Sister Oesterlein took care of the little girls all day while the older girl came in only for lessons."[1] She must have felt compelled to try to teach them something, though, for, as she herself had experienced when she was sent to school at the age of two, the Moravians believed in starting their children's education when they were hardly out of diapers.

By the summer of 1774, Sister Oesterlein's school had grown to seven pupils. The Bagge, Meyer, and Schmidt girls were still there, and among the others was Martha Elisabeth Miksch, daughter of the town tobacconist. Martha was to have the distinction of being the first of the long line of Salem girls educated at the school who would later return as teachers.

As it was at the beginning, the ages of Sister Oesterlein's charges varied appreciably, and one marvels at how she managed to keep a three-year-old and a ten-year-old at different lessons at the same time and in the same classroom. To complicate her task further, there was no regularity either in the hours that the children were in her care or in the length of their stays in school; those were matters decided by individual parents. And attendance was especially erratic among the little girls from the outlying communities, whose parents sent them to live with families in Salem and attend school for short periods, bringing them back home when they were needed to help with the work or for other personal reasons. On October 31, 1775, for example,

Moravian Archives, Winston-Salem, North Carolina

Gemein Haus, **home of the Little Girls' School in Salem**

it was reported that "Br. and Sr. Bagge have taken one of Melchior Schneider's daughters from Friedland; she can attend Sister Oesterlein's school for one hour each day."[2] And on August 13, 1776: "Daniel Schmidt and his wife have brought their eight-year-old daughter, Betsey, to Br and Sr. Fritz. For a few weeks she shall attend Sr. Oesterlein's school in the mornings."[3]

With this continual coming and going of pupils, along with the wide range in ages, Sister Oesterlein earned every shilling of the six to eight pounds paid her annually, and, at that, she had trouble making ends meet. The only compensating factor was that there were never many pupils in her school at one time, for the simple reason that the little-girl population in Salem in any one year during her tenure was seldom more than ten. So under the circumstances, she obviously did the best she could to give the little girls at least an education of sorts. And the town's leaders seemed to appreciate both her efforts and her limitations. Late in 1779, the Elders' Conference noted:

Arrangements should be made to give our little girls lessons in arithmetic. Sr. Oesterlein has taught them reading and writing, sewing and knitting, with good success, and that arithmetic has been lacking is only because the Sister knows none.[4]

The fact that the Elders had the time, or the heart, even to notice what was lacking in the Little Girls' School is itself worth noting. For this was 1779, and the Moravians of Salem, along with colonists all up and down the Atlantic seaboard, were caught up in the agonies of the American Revolution. For the Moravians, these times held a peculiar kind of distress. By an act of the British Parliament in 1749, the Moravian Church had been legally recognized as "an antient [sic] Protestant Episcopal Church,"[5] with fully guaranteed freedom of worship and of conscience—including exemption from military service. But the Moravians had not forgotten what happened in Georgia when the Brethren had believed themselves secure in a similar, if less official, guarantee from England. So soon after the news of the Battle of Lexington reached Salem, a committee of the town's governing boards had met to decide what the congregation would do if this growing insurrection should spread to their area. The consensus of the meeting was "that we should do nothing contrary to our consciences, and that what we could not help we would endure."[6]

The Revolution, of course, did reach North Carolina. And the Moravians of Salem, like their Brethren in Pennsylvania, were called upon to endure the suspicion and often the abuse of both sides in the conflict. Generally, the higher ranking officers respected the Moravians' reason for strict neutrality and were as considerate of them as the stresses of war would allow. But these gentlemen were not always present when bands of their men, sometimes entire companies, swarmed into Salem, and the lesser officers ostensibly in charge either would not or could not exercise control. Consequently, time after time, the town was subjected to soldiers' brawling, willful destruction, insults, threats, hostile demands, and out-and-out thievery. As Marshall later wrote in his report to Herrnhut, ". . . each morning we were glad to see each other again, and to know that no one had suffered injury to his person, and that neither the town nor a part of it had been burned."[7]

If Salem's leaders lived with apprehension, one can imagine how terrifying the crowds of boisterous soldiers must have been to a little girl as she walked from her home to the *Gemein Haus* for her lessons—how anxiously her father must have held onto her hand as they crossed the noisy square. And doubtless there were days when it was not safe for the children even to venture outside their own doors. But Sister Oesterlein never closed the school itself; nor, as far as we know, did it ever occur to any of the harried Brothers and Sisters to suggest such a measure, although from the financial standpoint alone, they might have had just cause to do so, for the war had torn Salem's previously sound economy to shreds. Ironically, financial disaster was hastened by the very factors most responsible for the town's economic strength: the skill of the Salem craftsmen and the providence of Moravian ways. With European trade cut off, the wares of Salem's craftsmen now were more than ever sought after by inhabitants of the surrounding area. And with armies desperately needing food, the stores that the thrifty Moravians had laid by were like manna to passing companies of soldiers. In their precarious position, the people of Salem did not dare refuse to sell either their wares or their precious food supplies, though they did so at a tremendous loss, as the paper money which they were forced to take in payment was either counterfeit or else so dwindled in value as to be almost worthless. A further drain on the town's resources was the three-fold tax which the Brethren were forced to pay in exchange for exemption from military service.

During the war years it thus was struggle enough for Salem's fathers to feed and clothe their children; finding money for school fees as well presented an extra burden which men less dedicated to education would undoubtedly have refused to carry.

As the battles moved closer, wounded men were brought to Salem to be cared for. Once a company of soldiers brought smallpox into town, and scarcely a child in Salem escaped its vengeance. But the children, matching the fortitude of their elders, took the epidemic in stride. The records show, in fact, that those who did not contract the disease felt personally slighted—one of Sister Oesterlein's first pupils, for instance: "Little Betsy Bagge, who has often wept because she was the only little girl who did not have small-pox, has now taken it."[8]

Isolated politically from everyone around them, the Moravians also were cut off from any communications with their own Brethren and Sisters in Pennsylvania and Europe to whom they had always looked for encouragement and guidance. So the years of the Revolution were as lonely as they were taxing, and it could have been only the strength of their faith that carried them through the long ordeal: "Prayer is our weapon, with which we have long since armed ourselves; and our strong fortress is our God . . ."[9]

Their institutions, grounded on this faith likewise, also survived. Not once in all of the war's turmoil did either the Little Girls' School or the Little Boys' School (operated in the old "Skin House" on the main street) close its doors. The customary church services were faithfully held except at those times when it clearly was unsafe for the people to leave their homes. The town boards continued to meet and decide matters of civic, spiritual, and material importance. And the institution of marriage, in which the Moravians believed implicitly—despite the fact that they kept the Single Brothers and the Single Sisters carefully separated beforehand—held fast.

In 1780, Elisabeth Oesterlein forsook her teaching duties and the ranks of the Single Sisters to become the wife of Rudolph Christ, the talented Salem potter. But there was another Single Sister, Catharine Sehner, able and willing to take her place. Sister Sehner also had been born and educated in Bethlehem, and had come to Bethabara before the mass move to Salem. Apparently, though, she entered upon her teaching duties somewhat better equipped than had Sister Oesterlein; at any rate, the records show that she could, and would, teach arithmetic. Otherwise, she was expected to cope with much the same problems that had plagued her predecessor—pupils of varying ages, a constantly changing enrollment, erratic attendance, sub-standard income.

Since each Single Sister was expected to pay for her own board, lodging, clothing, and other personal expenses, there were times when the school fees did not nearly meet Sister Sehner's cost of living. It was soon after she began teaching that the congregation leaders, aware of the financial problem, declared that "school matters should be arranged that teachers receive proper salaries so that they may be in good heart for their tedious job."[10] From then on, teachers in both the girls' and the boys' schools in Salem received a subsidy from the congregation treasury—in Sister Sehner's case, four shillings a week.

Even so, when Martha Miksch was asked to help out at the school, it was suggested that she also learn to stitch gloves so that during the times when she was supervising the children but not actually teaching, she could earn a little extra cash for her needs.

The addition of Martha Miksch to the hitherto staff-of-one at the school seemed to acknowledge that some separation of the girls by age was essential to effective teaching, for she was assigned the smaller girls while Sister Sehner taught the more advanced class. At no one time throughout the 1780s, though, were there more than twelve girls enrolled in the school. A few from the outlying communities continued to be admitted provided they were "clean, free of the itch or lice, etc.,"[11] and if promptly every Monday they brought in their school fees for the week. And in 1785, Adam Schumacher, a member of the Salem congregation who lived on a farm a few miles from town, asked that a Negro girl on his place be permitted to attend the school —a request that was granted apparently without question.

In her memoir, Sister Sehner recalled her eleven years as head teacher in the Little Girls' School as filled with "hard experiences," but, she wrote, "it was a satisfaction to me to teach the young."[12] As it turned out, she was to spend the greater part of her life teaching or being associated with the teaching of the young in the girls' school in Salem. Abraham Steiner, to whom she was married in 1791, served many years as inspector of the boarding school that grew out of the Little Girls' School, and their daughter, Maria (Polly), was not only in the boarding school's first class but also, later, one of its brightest and best-loved teachers.

There is little in the records to indicate when the simple curriculum (reading, writing, arithmetic, knitting) began to expand. More than likely something of a spurt came in 1790 with the appointment of Sister Anna Benigna Benzien to the teaching staff. Up to then, contrary to Comenius's maxim, the teachers had taught "all they were able to teach"; the trouble was, their own schooling was so limited that they weren't able to teach very much. Sister Benzien's educational background was considerably broader. Born in London, she had attended a Moravian nursery school there, and after coming with her parents to America, she had spent a number of years in the girls' school at Bethlehem. There she proved to be such a good student that she had been employed as an assistant for the little girls, and in

1785 she had been appointed principal of the congregational girls' school in the Moravian settlement at Hope, New Jersey. It was only natural, then, that when she came to Salem with her brother five years later, she would be recruited immediately for service in the Little Girls' School, first as assistant to Sister Sehner and then, when Sister Sehner left to be married, as head teacher. Thus in the summer of 1791, for the first time since the school had opened nearly twenty years before, it was in the hands of an experienced teacher—and a teacher whose background enabled her to go beyond the simple "three Rs."

That Sister Benzien had administrative ability is evidenced by the fact that she later was appointed choir leader of the Single Sisters. And we can guess that after taking over the Little Girls' School, she proceeded to tighten up a few rules here and there. At any rate, less than a year after she became head teacher, the *Aufseher Collegium* reported: "Complaint is made that little girls are not allowed to attend school without shoes and without flutings on their caps. Parents must be allowed to dress their children in the way they can afford and teachers must insist only on cleanliness."[13] Otherwise, though, the town fathers appeared to be satisfied with the job she was doing, and even after she became choir leader in 1797, she continued, at their request, to exercise general supervision over the school operation.

Undoubtedly it was she, as much as anyone, who made the English language a strong part of the classroom. The traditional language of the Wachovia Moravians was German, and in the early years of the settlement, they had used it exclusively in speaking with one another, in their church services, and in their letters and records. German was to remain both the official and the household language among them until the middle of the nineteenth century. But North Carolina was an English colony, and English was the language of the new nation of which the Moravians were now a part; it was essential that they speak and understand English in order to communicate with others. Some of the university-trained leaders—Marshall, for example—and, of course, the English Moravians in the congregation spoke the language fluently. An effort was made to teach it to others through special classes for the Single Brothers and occasional church services conducted in English. Almost from the beginning, too, the children in the school were taught to read and write in English as well as in German, but, here again, it was not until Anna Benigna Benzien came that the girls' school had a teacher who was really proficient in the subject.

Late in the eighteenth century, the love of music which the Brethren had brought with them from Herrnhut led to the purchase of a clavier for the Little Girls' School, and pupils who showed an aptitude for music were given lessons. Thus, little by little, the limited curriculum of Sister Oesterlein's day was expanding. Early in 1801, members of the Elders' Conference met with the teachers, and "... among other things it was decided that the three hours in the afternoon should no longer be used entirely for sewing, knitting and other feminine work, but that the first of those hours should be taken for the equally necessary subjects of geography, orthography, biblical history and singing."[14]

In the same year, parents and other members of the congregation were invited to be present when the school girls were examined on what they had learned. Both the girls and the school passed this first public test with flying colors, for, reporting the examination in its minutes,[15] the Congregation Council expressed "great pleasure" at the progress noted.

3

'Nursery for Tender Plants'

As FERVENTLY AS ANYONE, THE MORAVIANS OF Salem had greeted the peace following the Revolution with prayerful thanksgiving. Again their little girls could walk to school in safety. Once more they were able to correspond with Brethren in Pennsylvania and Europe. And they had accepted the authority of the new independent nation as Moravians traditionally accepted whatever the authority was under which they lived—with loyalty and respect. Financially, they were no better off than most of their neighbors. But dogged industry was a part of their Germanic nature, and despite the war's drain on their energies and material resources, they had resumed the building of Salem. When fire destroyed the old tavern in 1784, they had the site cleared within a week; in less than three months, they were laying the brick walls of a new tavern. One by one, solid structures of brick and stuccoed stone began to fill the vacant lots ringing the square—a dwelling house for the storekeeper, a handsome two-story building with large attic for the Boys' School, a brick addition doubling the size of the Single Brothers' House and, most important to this story, a house for the Single Sisters.

The Single Sisters had waited a long time for a home of their own. For fourteen years, they had had to share the *Gemein Haus* with ministers' families, sundry widows, congregational meetings of all kinds, and school girls at their daily lessons. Even though Single Sisters were committed to communal living, there must have been times when all that "togetherness" rubbed their patience thin, and it is no wonder that most of them hesitated only briefly when a proposal of marriage came their way. Finally, though, the house planned for the Single Sisters worked its way to the top of Salem's priority list, and in February, 1785, workmen began to dig the cellar. A little over a year later—on the afternoon of April 5, 1786—thirty-three Single Sisters and Older Girls, marching two by two to the accompaniment of a trombone choir, moved out of the old *Gemein Haus* into the peace and privacy of their splendid new home. From that day to this one, the house has served as a residence for "single sisters"—though the Salem College women presently living in dormitory rooms there will hardly approve that description.

The Single Sisters' House stood south of the *Gemein Haus*, facing the southeast corner of the square. Made of brick with a tile roof, it was the largest building in Salem at that time, and it is the oldest building on the Salem Academy and College campus today. Like the other buildings in Salem, its front doors opened directly onto the street, but back of it, towards the east, its grounds stretched "down the hill, across the brook, and up on the other side again."[1] Strategically placed over this expanse was quite a complex of gardens and out-buildings. Just behind the north end of the house itself were a wash-house and ironing room, a small smokehouse, and woodsheds. Where Clewell Dormitory of Salem College now stands were the Sisters' "necessary" (toilet), linen weave house, and pig pen. The site of the present Bitting Dormitory served as their kitchen garden, and their cow stables and cow pen were on the spot now occupied by Strong Dormitory and the college refectory.

More than a hundred years were to pass before the school began to absorb the Single Sisters' land and buildings for its own use. When the Sisters moved to their new house in 1786, the classroom of the Little Girls' School remained in the *Gemein Haus*, and it stayed there until after the turn of the century. But the lifeblood of the school —its corps of teachers—flowed always from the big brick house down the street. And it is safe to say that had there not been such a depend-able source of teachers handy, or had the kitchen in the Single Sisters' House not been adequate for cooking meals in large quantities, the good Brethren of Salem might have listened with less interest to the pleas that they open a boarding school for girls.

As it was, they listened with keen interest. Moravians had long believed that boarding schools, which brought together children at their most impressionable age, offered a fertile opportunity to "plant the good seed of His word."[2] So they needed no persuasion to accept the *idea* of starting a boarding school in Salem. It was just that since coming to North Carolina, they had had their hands full with other and more pressing obligations. Now, with the basic buildings in Salem completed, they had the time and the manpower to go on to something else; in the resources of the Single Sisters' House, they had the tools; and, thanks to the Revolution, the climate in Salem was ripe for considering a boarding school.

The Moravians' closed community and the peculiarities of their mode of living had set them rather apart from the rest of the colony, and the chances are that, had there been no war, Salem would have remained for many years a tight little island, sufficient unto itself and without knowing or being known very well by outsiders. But the Revolution had brought men from many places into Salem, and this association with strangers not only had pried the Moravians out of their own isolationism but also had let others see that these "Germans" were not nearly so odd a lot as they had appeared. Especially the officers of the State Militia—men who later would be prosperous planters, governors, or representatives in Congress—had been impressed by the intelligence of the Moravian leaders, by the innate kindness and honesty of the town's people, by their industriousness and skill, and by the sincerity of their simple faith. After the war, these gentlemen often came back to visit, sometimes bringing their families with them, and they were welcomed warmly.

President Washington himself spent two nights at the Salem Tavern on his Southern tour in 1791, and upon leaving issued a special "address":

From a Society, whose governing principles are industry and the love of order, much may be expected towards the improvement and prosperity of the country in which their Settlements are formed—and experience authorizes the belief that much will be obtained.[3]

One of the aspects of Salem that impressed visitors most favorably was the quality of its schools, particularly the girls' school, when any school for girls was a rarity in the South at that time. There is evidence that as early as 1788 non-Moravians were asking to send their daughters to live in Salem so that they might attend its school. And the *Memorabilia* (year-end report) of Wachovia in 1792 observed:

Many persons living outside our town, some of them people of importance, have often asked whether we could not open a boarding school for girls for the southern part of the United States, similar to one in Bethlehem. This matter did not remain unconsidered by our Conferences, and on one occasion we were disposed to answer the request of a certain friend and take his daughter into our school, which might easily have led to more. But it was difficult to find the proper persons for the school, and by the advice of our Lord we laid aside such plans for the time.[4]

On several occasions during the next few years the question came up again. And each time the Brethren asked "the advice of the Lord" through the "Lot." This method of seeking direct counsel on specific questions, brought by the Moravians from Europe, was simple in its concept. When faced with important decisions that they did not feel qualified to make without higher help—and this included approval of marriages within the congregation—members of the Elders' Conference gathered around a small wooden bowl in which three reeds had been placed. One reed was marked "*Ja*" ("Yes"); another, "*Nein*" ("No"); the third was a blank. Prayerfully the Elders submitted the question and drew a reed out of the bowl. Whether the reed drawn said "*Ja*" or "*Nein*"—or was the blank, which meant that it was not a proper question or that the time was not appropriate for asking it—they accepted the verdict wholly.

Each time the Elders had submitted the question of a girls' boarding school to the Lot, the answer had been "*Nein*." And it would seem that in advising against it, the Lord had had a point. For after Sister Benzien left the Little Girls' School in 1797 to become head of the Single Sisters, there were a few years during which qualified teachers in Salem were in short supply, and the school had to make do with younger Sisters who lacked both maturity and training.

Moreover, one of them, Dorothea Meyer, compounded the problem by sneaking off one night with the Single Brother Isaac Boner. They were married the next day, ultimately were accepted back into the congregation at Salem, and became the grandparents of the well-known Salem poet, John Henry Boner. But at the time, the incident, aside from creating a serious shortage in the teaching ranks, stirred up considerable consternation in the community. And to make sure that no such scandalous goings-on would be repeated, the rule was made that a Brother bringing work (washing, mending, etc.) to the Single Sisters' House would be received only by the choir leader—thus cutting off any opportunity for a Single Sister and a Single Brother even to strike up a speaking acquaintance, much less progress to the point of romance.

The boarding school nevertheless remained uppermost in the Brethren's minds—kept there not only by the pleas of outsiders but, more forcefully, by their own deepening sense of mission. So they had not been discouraged by the *"Nein"* answers; one day the right moment would come.

By the summer of 1802, circumstances had somewhat stabilized the teacher situation at the Little Girls' School. In late May, the Single Sister Sophia Dorothea Reichel had arrived in Salem with her parents and brother—her father, Bishop Carl Gotthold Reichel, having been called as pastor of the congregation. Sister Reichel had attended the Bethlehem Female Seminary, and if a circular issued by that school in 1790[5] can be used to measure her training, she was qualified to teach reading, writing, grammar, history, geography, plain sewing, knitting, music, fine needlework, and drawing. As might be expected, she had barely unpacked her trunk when she was pressed into service at the Little Girls' School. By then, too, several of the younger teachers had been tutored in subjects in which they were weak. So the Brethren were moved to try the question of the boarding school once more. And this time the Lord's answer was *"Ja."*

The exact date on which this long-awaited approval was given is uncertain, but it must have been sometime in the fall of 1802, for the minutes of the Elders' Conference dated November 1, 1802, report that Samuel Gottlieb Kramsch had been called to Salem as "head of a Girls' Boarding School to be set up."[6] The actual call, according to Dr. Adelaide L. Fries,[7] was made the day before, October 31, 1802. And that is considered the founding date of the boarding school.

Kramsch was the pastor at Hope, a community of English-speaking Moravians not far from Salem. And at the time he was chosen, at any rate, he seemed ideally fitted for the position of inspector of the new school. Born in Silesia, the son of a Lutheran minister, he had become acquainted with the Unity of Brethren when he was a student at the

Samuel Gottlieb Kramsch, Inspector 1802–1806

Moravian school at Gnadenberg, and eventually became a Moravian minister. A scholarly young man—with a particular interest in languages, botany, and art—he was soon recruited for work in the Brethren's schools, and in 1783, when he was about twenty-seven, he arrived in Bethlehem to head the boys' school there. For a time, he also taught at Nazareth Hall, the Moravian boarding school for boys in Nazareth, Pennsylvania.

Kramsch first came to Salem in 1788 as *Helfer* (Spiritual leader) of the Single Brothers. Two years later, he was appointed inspector of the Boys' School, and in 1792, he received a call to become the minister at Hope. But Brother Kramsch was a bachelor—in Moravian circles, certainly not a suitable status for a congregation's pastor. So, before assuming his duties at Hope, he went to Pennsylvania and returned with a wife—the former Susanna Langaard, who was the daughter of a professor at the Bethlehem Female Seminary and had herself been one of that school's first teachers. No doubt the Elders in Salem were mindful of Sister Kramsch's educational qualifications as well as her husband's when they called the two back to Salem to work in the new boarding school. Besides, the Elders were well aware that English must be the everyday language of the school, and Kramsch's well-known linguistic bent, honed by his ten years as minister of an English-speaking congregation, must have seemed heaven-sent.

By mid-January, 1803, the Kramsch family was settled in Salem. The two daughters, Louisa Charlotte and Christiana Susanna, entered the Little Girls' School, and Kramsch himself plunged into his new assignment with zest. Preliminary discussions with members of the Helpers' Conference determined in short order that there was no existing space in Salem appropriate for a girls' boarding school and that a new building would have to be constructed. This finding was reported on January 20, 1803. By February 10, the Brethren had asked for and received the approval of the Lord for the project; a site had been selected—between the *Gemein Haus* and the Single Sisters' House; a building committee had decided that the structure would be made of brick and would be large enough to accommodate sixty girls; the Congregation Council had agreed unanimously that the Community Diacony (business organization of Salem) would underwrite the building costs. Two months later, workmen began to break stone for the foundation.

The Moravians' traditional early morning Easter service that year brought visitors to Salem from all over North Carolina, Virginia, and parts of Georgia, a number of whom evidenced keen interest in the planned boarding school. And when they returned home, they must have spread the word. For within weeks, Marmaduke Norfleet, a planter of Halifax County, made a special trip to Salem to inquire about the school and begged that his daughter be allowed to attend the Little Girls' School until the boarding school could be opened. But he was turned down; the methodical Moravians were not to be rushed.

On August 6, 1803, the building was staked out, and excavation for the cellar was begun. By September 1, all of the bricks "except the last 40,000"[8] had been burnt. On October 6, the foundation was ready for the laying of the cornerstone—an occasion which, according to Moravian tradition, called for a full-dress ceremony.

The festivities began at 9 A.M. with the entire congregation, including the children, assembled in the church. According to an eye-witness account,[9] Bishop Reichel spoke fervently of the opportunity God had given the Brethren "to extol His great love for all mankind . . . to so many children, including those whose parents do not belong to the Unity but have entrusted them to our schools for their education . . ." He talked of the boarding school about to be established in which children "may be brought up in the nurture and admonition of the Lord, and may be instructed in useful knowledge and learning and the womanly arts . . ." And he urged both the members of the congregation and the children "to unite their prayers with his that the Lord would bless the house which was to be built for the boarding school for girls as the work of His own hand, and as a training school in which His Holy Spirit might be revealed, and that He would give grace that His praise might ever arise from the hearts of children thankful for His incarnation, sufferings and death."

Then Bishop Reichel read the inscription which, written in both English and German, was to be placed in the cornerstone:[10]

In the Name of God

The Father and the Son and the Holy Ghost

In the Year

after the birth of our Lord & Saviour Jesus Christ

One thousand eight hundred & three

on the sixth day of October

In the twenty seventh year

of the Independence of the United States of America

when Thomas Jefferson was President of them

In the fiftieth Year

after the settling of the first members of the Church of the

United Brethren in North Carolina &

the beginning of building Bethabara

In the thirty eighth Year

since the beginning of building Salem

the foundation stone of this house

was laid in a solemn manner

in the presence of the whole Congregation

with fervent Prayer to our Lord

that by the School, to be established in this House

His Name may be glorified

His Kingdom of Grace be enlarged in this Country

and the Salvation of those, who shall be

educated therein, be promoted.

The inscription was placed in a copper box, along with a list of names of the members of the Unity Elders' Conference, the Helpers' Conference of Wachovia, the Elders' Conference in Salem, the ministers of the country congregations and their wives, the missionaries of Springplace in the Cherokee country, the teachers of the Little Girls' School and "all the little girls who belong to the congregation of Salem numbering forty-two, of whom twenty-three go to school, and twenty-seven live in the town and fifteen outside."[11]

The box was sealed, and then, with Kramsch ceremoniously carrying it, the congregation marched in procession from the church to the building site while two choirs of trombones played hymns. When all had re-assembled, the copper box was laid in a stone at the northwest corner of the house, and, with another stone laid over it, was sealed into place—all to the accompaniment of prayers and singing. "Throughout the proceedings a sweet spirit of peace and of the presence of God pervaded the hearts of members and children and also of the friends present. . . ."[12]

It would be almost two years before the building was ready for occupancy. But once construction of the building actually got under way, the Brethren—never ones to squander time—decided to go ahead and get the school itself started, accepting a limited number of pupils and arranging temporary quarters for them in the *Gemein Haus*. The target date was May, 1804. This meant that a teaching staff had to be lined up, admission requirements and tuition fees established, a curriculum planned, furniture and school materials purchased, boarding arrangements worked out. In all these matters, Kramsch and the Elders' Conference drew heavily on the format of the Bethlehem Female Seminary, departing from it only in such minor details as that the head of the Salem school would be called "inspector" rather than "director."

At about the same time that Kramsch was called to Salem—late October, 1802—Sister Dorothea Reichel had been made head mistress of the Little Girls' School, assisted by Salome Meinung, one of the Older Girls who had been given extra instruction to prepare them for teaching. And in the summer of 1803, Sister Elisabeth Praezel, a talented young musician in Salem, had begun to give clavier lessons in the school. Apparently the three made an effective teaching team, and they must have been such willing workers that Brother and Sister Kramsch had no hesitancy in loading them with additional responsibilities. In the Kramsch opinion, there was no need to bring in other teachers for the boarding school; the Sisters Reichel, Meinung, and Praezel were quite capable of handling the boarding pupils as well as the town girls. And when the subject was broached to them, all three agreed to take the extra burden.

Throughout the month of February, 1804, the matters of ages for admission, fees, and curriculum were thoroughly discussed. By the middle of the month, enough of these decisions had been made that copy for an informational circular was sent to a printer in Salisbury, although blank spaces were left so that both age requirements and costs could be filled in by pen. Either those items had not been fully decided, or else the frugal Moravians, who had ordered three hundred copies, did not want to be left with obsolete circulars in case they made revisions at some later date.

A copy of this first circular, dated May 22, 1804,[13] sets forth the "Terms and Conditions of the Boarding School for Female Education in Salem, N.C." Girls would be admitted between the ages of eight and twelve, and at the age of fifteen they would terminate their stay in school "unless parents choose, to order their return home sooner, or their deportment should be such, as not to admit their continuance in the School." The "branches" taught would be: "Reading, Grammar, Writing, Arithmetic, History, Geography, (German, if desired), plain Needlework &c." Music, fine needlework, and drawing were "extra branches in which instruction is given, if expressly desired."

Parents could calculate that the total yearly cost of keeping a daughter in school in Salem would be "between 160 and 180 Dollars, more or less." This would include an entrance fee of $5.00, $20.00 quarterly for board and tuition (bedding included), and $3.00 quarterly for laundry for pupils under twelve years of age and $4.00 for those twelve and over. Music and fine needlework were $2.00 each per quarter. "Cloathing, medecine [sic], books, paper and other contingent expences" also were to be figured quarterly.

Dress of the pupils should be "decent, avoiding extravagance." And the circular expresses the desire that all applicants "should have had the small or kine pox and measles," although there is no evidence that girls delinquent on that requirement were ever turned down.

The Elders' Conference did not read proof on the circular until February 25. So it was hardly possible that it could have been printed and distributed by March 7, when the minutes of the Elders' Conference report that applications had been received for the entrance of four children from Hillsborough. Perhaps the terms and conditions of the school had been sent to Hillsborough by letter—or it could be

TERMS AND CONDITIONS
OF THE
BOARDING SCHOOL
FOR
FEMALE EDUCATION
IN
SALEM, N. C.

,,,,,,,,,,,,,,,,,,,,,,,,,,

THE age of admittance of pupils is between *8* and *12* years. The age of *15* terminates their stay in the School: unless parents choose, to order their return home sooner, or their deportment should be such, as not to admit their continuance in the School.

Every attention is paid to the health and morals of the pupils.

The branches taught are: Reading, Grammar, Writing, Arithmetic, History, Geography, (German if desired), plain Needlework, &c. Music and fine Needlework, including Drawing are two extra branches, in which instruction is given, if expressly desired.

Entrance money is *5* Dollars

The quarterly expence for board and tuition, bedding included, is at present *20* Dollars, to be advanced every quarter. Washing is a separate charge, viz. *3* Dollars per quarter for pupils under 12 years, and *4* Dollars for those above that age. For instruction in Music and fine Needlework, each *2* Dollars per quarter. Cloathing, medecine, books, paper and other contingent expences are charged quarterly.

Punctual payment of the bills is expected, and a settlement in full at the removal of children.

The amount of the yearly expences collectively may be calculated at the rate of between *160* and *180* Dollars, more or less.

Parents may either, if they have it convenient, furnish the articles of cloathing, or the pupils may be found here.

Every article of cloathing, they bring along, should be marked, so as to stand washing.

The dress to be decent, avoiding extravagance.

Applications are to be made in writing, addressed to *the Revd Samr Kramsh* the present Inspector of the Seminary at Salem, N. C.; informing him of the age, name and character of the child, the name and place of residence of the parents, guardians, &c. and it is requested, that no child may be brought or sent without leave obtained from him in writing, appointing the time of admittance. It is desirable, that such as are applied for, should have had the small or kine pox and measles.

Parents and guardians &c. may rest assured, that the undersigned will endeavour to merit their confidence by paying the most faithful attention to the education of pupils intruded to his care.

Salem, N. C.

May 23. 1804   *Samuel Kramsh* that these parents were so desperate to get their daughters into school that they did not wait for details. At any rate, the minutes report, applications had been received for Mary Exum Phillips, Ann and Elizabeth Kirkland, and Elizabeth Strudwick, and "since these come within the age-range and all come from one locality, it was felt they would fit for the beginning."[14]

It had been agreed that the number of pupils at the outset would be limited to eight. Kramsch suggested that two of that number be carefully selected congregation girls who would serve more or less as ambassadors among the girls from outside Salem, helping to acquaint them with the unusual customs and practices of the Moravian community. The Elders agreed that this was an excellent idea. So, counting the four girls from Hillsborough and the two from Salem, already six of the allotted eight places were taken. Within a week, Marmaduke Norfleet, who had been refused the year before, applied again—this time for his own daughter and the daughter of a relative—and his application was accepted. Two months before the boarding school was scheduled to open, enrollment was complete.

In April, salaries for Sister Reichel and Sister Meinung were set at thirty pounds ($75.00) a year. (Although the school's charges to outsiders were listed in dollars and cents, exchange within Salem remained for a while in North Carolina currency, a pound being worth $2.50.) The teachers' salary figure was "reckoned not only that they may not suffer want, but also that they devote all their time to the Anstalt [school]."[15] The sum was raised shortly afterwards to thirty-three pounds and nine shillings (a little over $83.00). Of this total, the teacher would receive twelve pounds a year in cash, out of which she was expected to pay a church contribution of one pound, thirteen shillings and ten pence. The rest of her salary would be paid in kind: three pounds and five shillings in laundry services, fourteen pounds and six shillings in dinners and suppers, three pounds and eighteen shillings in coffee and sugar for breakfasts and "vespers" (late afternoon meditation and refreshments). Sister Praezel, who would work part-time, would receive half the amount paid each of the other two.

All three of the teachers would live in the *Gemein Haus* with the boarders—at least one of them, and more often two, to be on duty at all times, day and night. And though they had willingly agreed to do it, the prospect of leaving the comforts of the Single Sisters' House must have stirred a few regrets. To be sure, there was ample sleeping space in the old Single Sisters' sleep hall in the *Gemein Haus* attic, but otherwise the temporary quarters of the boarding school would be painfully cramped. There were only the two rooms being used by the Little Girls' School readily available for the boarders' classes and recreation, and those would have to be shared with the town girls, as the admission of boarding students by no means meant that the Little Girls' School in Salem would be discontinued; it would go on, just as before, for the education of the congregation girls. It soon became all too apparent that the twenty or more pupils of the Little Girls' School, plus the eight boarding students, plus teachers and teaching equipment (including a clavier) simply could not be fitted into two rooms. So the Elders agreed to give up the room in the *Gemein Haus* that they had been using for meetings. At that, space was far from ample, or even adequate, but it would have to do until the new boarding school building was finished.

The Single Sisters contracted to handle all of the laundry for the school, bed and table linen as well as the boarders' clothing. The Sisters would also provide meals:

BREAKFAST: milk, bread and butter. The Inspector will attend to coffee, tea, sugar

DINNER: soup occasionally, meat, vegetables, bread

VESPER: bread and butter

EVENING: milk, warmed up items, pancakes, mush, chocolate[16]

For food, they would charge six shillings and six pence a week for each outside girl, and five shillings and six pence weekly for the two congregation girls (who would take the noon meal with their parents).

We can only guess at the criteria used by the Brethren in choosing the two girls who would represent the congregation in the new boarding school. Undoubtedly each girl's age, aptitude, and attitude figured to some extent. But in making the selection, the Brethren surely did not overlook certain pertinent attributes of the girls' parents as well. One of the two chosen, Maria (Polly) Steiner, was the daughter of Abraham Steiner, a minister and a former teacher at Bethlehem, and Catharine Sehner Steiner, who had taught at the Little Girls' School before her marriage. The other, Paulina Schober, was the daughter of one of the most prominent men in Salem, Gottlieb Schober, who was a tinsmith, organist, lawyer, owner of a paper mill, and later a State Senator. Both the Steiners and the Schobers thus were well above the average families in Salem both in educational background and in community influence. And, as the Brethren probably saw it, their daughters would fit in well with the girls who would be coming to Salem from prominent families elsewhere.

Such major decisions relative to the boarding school were handled by Kramsch working with members of the church boards. Smaller matters, those relating to the day-to-day operation of the school, were left in the hands of a "House Conference," which was made up of Brother and Sister Kramsch, the three teachers, and Salem's two ministers and their wives: the Carl Gotthold Reichels and the Christian Lewis Benziens. The House Conference met for the first time on April 26, 1804, agreed to meet thereafter once a month, considered such details as what kind and how many lamps should be placed in the sleep hall, and decided that "should their [the girls'] commode be put in the dormitory, a so-called 'Spanish screen' should be placed in front of it."[17]

The House Conference would not meet again until after the boarding school was nearly under way. For a little over two weeks later—on Tuesday, May 15, 1804—William Kirkland rode in from Hillsborough with three little girls in tow. And that evening, these three—Ann and Elizabeth Kirkland and Elizabeth Jane Strudwick—climbed the stairs to the attic of the *Gemein Haus*, where on narrow wooden beds, fitted with chaff mattresses, they became the first boarding pupils to spend a night in Salem. The next day, the two Salem girls, Polly Steiner (eleven) and Paulina Schober (twelve), moved in. On Friday of the same week, the fourth Hillsborough girl, nine-year-old Mary Exum Phillips, arrived—brought by Duncan Cameron, an attorney, as she was an orphan.

At last the boarding school in Salem—so often prayed over, so long planned for—had become a reality. And at the congregation meeting the following Monday, "special prayer was offered for the Boarding School begun here last week, and the Saviour was asked to bless it and make of it a nursery in which His Holy Spirit might care for the tender plants."[18]

Anna Paulina Schober, teacher in the Girls' Boarding School 1812–1820

4

'A Dwelling of Blessing'

THE POST RIDER PASSED THROUGH SALEM ONLY once a week, and, even then, news in the letters and papers that came out of his saddlebags was often weeks old. So the Moravians had no way of knowing that in the very same week in which they were receiving the first pupils into their boarding school, Napoleon Bonaparte was making himself Emperor of France or that two intrepid explorers, Meriwether Lewis and William Clark, were embarking on an expedition that would lead to the settling of the American West. Word of those historic events would find its way to Salem in due time; meanwhile, there were matters of moment at home needing attention.

Apparently the girls from Hillsborough had been left free for a few days to rest up from their journey. But Salem ranked idleness virtually in the league with sin. And in less than a week after they had come, the school girls were hard at their lessons. Sister Reichel held the classes in history, geography, English grammar, arithmetic, and embroidery. Sister Meinung taught writing (both in German and in English), sewing, and knitting. Sister Praezel, in addition to teaching music, was assigned to "devote herself specially to the younger ones."[1]

If there were any kinks during the first weeks of the school's operation, they were too minor to be mentioned when the House Conference met again on June 13. Things seemed to be going so smoothly, in fact, that some members of the conference (undoubtedly the nonteaching ones) must have suspected that the teachers weren't kept busy enough. At any rate, it was suggested that, as the cleaning was taken care of by another Sister, the teachers ought to be willing to do some sewing for the school from time to time, and that Sister Praezel should "take lessons from Sr. Kramsch in playing the zither, so as to be able to teach it."[2] The absence of major problems at the outset did not mislead the conference members, though. Troubles could spring out of nowhere, they readily realized—the spread of itch, for instance, or the unwelcome presence of "reprehensible books or music."[3] And the teachers were alerted as to what to do should either calamity occur.

Classes had been going on for exactly a month when Marmaduke Norfleet, the Halifax planter who had pestered the Moravians so long about taking his daughter into the school at Salem, finally arrived— bringing his daughter, Anna, and Felicia Norfleet, the orphaned daughter of a relative. These two, with the four girls from Hillsborough and the two congregation girls, brought the number of boarders to the eight that had been set as capacity until the new building was completed. As it turned out, the Brethren were too softhearted to hold to that limit. In July, when Sebastian Staiert, a merchant from Fayetteville, arrived with his daughter, unannounced, and begged that she be allowed to enter the school, they let her stay. And two months later, when Jesse Carter, a Caswell County merchant, did the same thing, they somehow made room for little Rebecca Carter too.

Actually, by the time the new building was ready, there were eighteen students from outside Salem enrolled in the school, plus the two congregation girls. But in late June, 1804, the members of the Elders' Conference innocently believed that with the arrival of the Norfleet girls, the school's capacity had been reached. And to celebrate the occasion, the Brethren and Sisters of the conference joined the teachers and pupils in a "lovefeast."

To twelve-year-old Felicia Norfleet, in Salem barely a week, this lovefeast, her first, must have been a puzzling experience. Refreshments (probably tea or coffee and cakes) were served, and that made the occasion seem like a party. But, at the same time, everyone sang hymns, as people did in church; there were prayers; and, at one point, the Bishop stood up and spoke quite seriously to the little girls:

Br. Reichel, who held the service, expressed our hearty joy and thankfulness that under the good guidance of our Lord a Boarding School for girls had been begun here, gave in the name of the Aeltesten Conferenz a warm welcome into the midst of our congregation to the six pupils from elsewhere, and wished for them that they might live contentedly in Salem, that through love and obedience they might make pleasant and agreeable the duties of Br. and Sr. Kramsch and the Sisters who are to instruct them; and most especially he hoped for them that they might learn to know and love the Saviour Who purchased them with His own blood, and might be guided and led by His Holy Spirit. . . . [4]

In time, Felicia and the other boarders would come to look forward to these lovefeasts, which were held in Salem on any occasion of special significance—Christmas, Easter, the dedication of a new building, the festival days of the various choirs, or even the arrival or departure of a beloved teacher. Like so many of the Moravian traditions, the lovefeast had had its beginning in Herrnhut, this one dating from August 13, 1727, when a spirit of brotherly love seemed to be extraordinarily present during a celebration of the Holy Communion. Following the service, a group of the Brethren, reluctant to break the spell, lingered at the church. Count Zinzendorf sent food to them there, and they ate it together, much as the early Christians had broken bread together to signify unity. Thus, from that day, the lovefeast—the partaking of a simple meal together—has been the Moravians' way of expressing Christian unity and good will.

From the first, the boarding school girls were brought into almost all of Salem's religious activities, and as Salem was a church-oriented town, there were a great many of them. But there was never any attempt then—nor has there been throughout the long history of the school—to proselytize the girls. On the contrary, the Moravians looked with something akin to disgust on the Methodists and Baptists who "were always insisting that one should find church membership exclusively in their respective denominations." [5] The Moravians considered that their mission among the boarding school girls, as among all outsiders, was simply to lead them along the path to Christianity, and that they did with zeal. But whether the led chose to live the Christian life under the label of "Moravian," "Episcopalian," "Presbyterian" or even "Methodist" did not concern them.

So that the school girls could participate more fully in the religious life of the community, stanzas of hymns were copied into English, and the students were encouraged to memorize them. Church services conducted in English also became more frequent, and when special services were held in German, the teachers often read and explained the liturgy beforehand. Apparently the girls took all this religiosity in their stride, even though few, if any, of them had been accustomed to such heavy doses. Once the strangeness wore off, they probably enjoyed it, for the Moravians seldom cloaked their religion in somber hues; much of it was expressed in colorful ways—the lovefeast, for instance—that would be quite appealing to a little girl. Always, too, the church services were laced with good music: band, organ, choir, congregational singing, sometimes chamber orchestra. And often there was an element of pageantry, such as that on the festival day for the Little Girls' choir on August 17, 1804, when "all the little girls, including the out-of-town pupils, all clad in white, went in procession through the streets of the town."[6]

All this exposure to religion by no means transformed the school girls into paragons of piety, of course; little girls were little girls then as always. They pilfered goodies from the cupboard with such regularity that the inspector put a lock on it. More than one window in the old *Gemein Haus* was shattered during rowdy romps. They were careless about keeping up with their pencils and making up their beds. And it was called to the attention of the House Conference on one occasion that "it is naughty for the children to bore holes in the congregation's furniture, and they should be admonished about this."[7]

Because there were so few boarders and because their quarters in the *Gemein Haus* were temporary, the inspector and the teachers seemed to run the little school more or less by ear. Classes were obviously held with regularity, but otherwise the House Conference dealt with operational matters as they came up: the school subscribed to a newspaper; it was ruled that girls should wear gloves when they took walks, and that when they crossed the street into the center of town, it was only proper that they wear bonnets; painting was added to the curriculum and a piano to the school's equipment; after much deliberation, it was agreed that grease was more practical for the girls' shoes than blacking. On May 16, 1805, a lovefeast was held to commemorate both the anniversary of the boarding school and the occasion of the departure of Paulina Schober from its ranks, the first pupil to leave.

Generally, though, the school seemed to be simply marking time until the new building could be completed. And by the spring of 1805, that happy event, at last, was in sight. Work had progressed rapidly since the cornerstone was laid on October 6, 1803. The masons especially had proceeded with dispatch—helped along, no doubt, by such considerations as the "6 gallons of whiskey to bricklayers & tenders"[8] which the building accounts itemize along with nails and sundry other essential materials. As the completion date approached, the Elders began to accept applications for additional boarding students, and parents wasted no time in getting their daughters to Salem. In early April, Malvina Smythe, the first pupil from Virginia (Wythe County), arrived, followed later that month by Mary Adelaide Stokes of near Salisbury and Mary Williams Smith of near Morganton. During June and the early part of July, Sarah Dry Brice came from Moore County, Eliza Ruth Sanderson from Fayetteville, and three girls from Lincoln County: Mary Greaves and Mary and Elizabeth Fullenwider. As there wasn't nearly enough room for all of the newcomers in the *Gemein Haus*, some had to be lodged in the Kramsch home.

Finally, though, came the day set for the consecration of the new Girls' Boarding School: Tuesday, July 16, 1805. And, in true Moravian style, it was a ceremonious affair, with all of Salem's three hundred or so residents participating at one time or another during the day-long festivities:

. . . in the morning at seven o'clock, two choirs of trombones announced to the congregation the solemn service of the day, playing appropriate tunes from the new house. In the afternoon at one o'clock there assembled in the Saal of the Gemein Haus the members of the Aeltesten Conferenz, the other ministers of the Wachovia congregations and their wives, the girls who live in the Boarding School, the school-girls, and the teaching Sisters. About half past one they marched out in procession, two by two, and proceeded to the new house, in the following order: 1) the Brethren of the Aeltesten Conferenz and other ministers; 2) the Sisters of the Aeltesten Conferenz and other ministers' wives; 3) the daughters living in the Boarding School; 4) the school-girls; 5) the Boarding School Sisters. As the first Brethren left the door of the Gemein Haus one choir of trombones played from the windows of the conference room:

May God bless your going out, etc.

Another choir of trombones played from the new house as the procession entered it:

Now thank we all our God, etc.

The parents present, the other invited guests, and the musicians, assembled in the sleeping hall of the new house. When place had been taken by the ministers and their wives, and the boarding and day pupils and their Sisters, all clad in white, had arranged themselves in a double semi-circle, the choir sang, accompanied by a pianoforte and other instruments:

> Peace be to this habitation,
>> Peace to every soul therein,
> Peace which flows from Christ's salvation,
>> Peace the seal of cancelled sin;
> Peace that speaks its heavenly Giver,
>> Peace to earthly minds unknown,
> Peace divine that lasts forever,
>> Here erect its glorious throne.

The congregation sang:

> This habitation
>> And all who dwell therein
> Fill with salvation;
> O may in each be seen true grace
> And lovely childlikeness.

Then in a fervent prayer by Br. Reichel, in which all hearts joined, this house was solemnly dedicated to the Lord as a place of peace and a dwelling of blessing. Heartfelt thanks were given that the erection had been successfully accomplished and without serious injury to any workman; and a petition was offered that the entire house, and every room and every spot in it might be filled with His presence, His grace, and godly peace; that His eyes might be open day and night upon all who go out or in; that all those who now or in the future would be entrusted with the parental care, nurture, training, and education of youth might be blessed with wisdom, patience and a tender love for children and might be supported daily by His grace and strength; and that all daughters who live in this house and attend the school might be obedient, industrious, and willing to learn all that they should, and all that adorns and honors His teachings. Especially he asked that all hearts might be filled with His love; that He would care for them as His lambs, as the children of His father, and through His Spirit prepare them for the joy and salvation of heaven; and that He would approve the praise which in this house should arise from the lips of children for His incarnation, sufferings and death.

After singing the verse:

> The grace of our Lord Jesus Christ,
> The love of God, so highly prized,
> The Holy Ghost's communion be
> With us in this house sensibly,

the lovefeast began, during which there was sung an ode of praise and thanksgiving which had been especially prepared for this solemn occasion, in which the singing of the children and of the boarding pupils was pretty and dear.

Including Br. and Sr. Kramsch and their two daughters and a serving Sister, about thirty persons became the first residents in the house, that is eighteen boarding pupils from elsewhere, two from the congregation, four School Sisters, and one more Single Sister to supervise the housekeeping. After the lovefeast the members of the Aeltesten Conferenz and other guests visited them in their living rooms, greeted them, and wished them grace, blessing, good health, and all good things. Among the boarding pupils from elsewhere were two from Camden, South Carolina, the first from that state, who arrived yesterday with their parents. The latter attended the service of dedication, and the other services of the day, with approval and with touched hearts, and were especially glad that they came just in time for the opening exercises.

The evening meeting at half past seven o'clock was attended by the congregation, the children and many visitors, so that the church was entirely filled. Br. Benzien gave a description of the noteworthy and joyful events of the day . . . then a hymn of praise was sung, the two choirs rendered an anthem expressing the happy experience, the thankful joy, the prayers for grace, blessing, salvation, and happiness, and English hymns were sung to God our Saviour by the presiding minister and the congregation with moved hearts and happy mouths.

The close of this day of grace, blessing and joy, was made in a solemn evening service, held by the congregation and children on the Square in front of the new Boarding School house. The boarding and day school girls stood in a semi-circle opposite the front or west side of the house. That side, and the north gable side toward the Gemein Haus, were lighted up. In the beautiful weather this evening blessing together with all the other services of the day made a deep impression upon all present. . . .[9]

The Girls' Boarding School building faced the center of the square. Constructed of brick laid in a Flemish bond pattern, it measured sixty-two by forty feet and was two stories high, with a cellar underneath and an attic area, the length and width of the house, under a red shingled roof. Like most Moravian architecture, the building reflected an eye for the aesthetic as well as for the practical. The moldings over its shuttered windows were arched, and there was an arched overlight above the double front door. A rounded hood protected the entrance, which was reached by steps flanked by forged iron railings. The economy-minded Brethren had achieved the effect of expensive rubbed brick by painting the brick quoins at the corners of the building and at the jambs of the window and door openings. But they had spared no expense in building a house that would withstand the buffeting of time and the elements. The outside walls in the lower story were eighteen inches thick; those of the second story, fourteen inches; all dividing walls, nine inches.

Behind the main building was a large one-story washhouse measuring sixty-two by twenty-five feet, with ample storage space under the roof.

The total cost of the school building was $5,887.50. The school borrowed this amount from the Congregation Diacony, and paid off the debt, at five per cent interest, out of its income, the final payment being made in 1825.

Through the years, the exterior of the building would be spruced up, altered, added-onto, and eventually (in 1966) restored to its 1837 appearance. Except in restoration terms, it has long since ceased to be referred to as the "Girls' Boarding School"; its popular name now is "South Hall." But never once since the boarding school girls marched into it on July 16, 1805, has its primary use been other than to house students in the girls' school at Salem, its present occupants being Salem College women.

1805 Girls' Boarding School building

The interior, too, would bow from time to time to modern conveniences and the changing patterns of student life. But Salome Meinung's brother, Frederic, who designed the building, had drawn the original inside partitions with a full understanding of the Brethren's intent to create as much of a family-circle atmosphere as possible for those who would first live in the house.

The front doors opened into a twelve-feet-wide hallway that ran the width of the building, ending at a staircase which wound to the second floor via two landings. The rooms opening off this hallway on the north side were the living quarters of Brother and Sister Kramsch and their two daughters. A drawing of Meinung's plan shows that this apartment consisted of only two large rooms, each measuring approximately twenty-two by eighteen feet, but other records indicate that the back room, which had a fireplace where Sister Kramsch cooked the family meals, was partitioned. And there is some evidence that the front room also may have had a partition separating

Brother Kramsch's office from his bedroom. Two large rooms, the same size as those on the north side, opened off the hallway on the south side, the front one being used at first as a storeroom and the back one as the town girls' schoolroom.

The boarders' bailiwick was the second floor and the attic. The attic had been finished into one large room, twelve feet high, with a coved ceiling and with storage cubbyholes running the length of the building under the eaves on each side. At either end of the long room were two small windows curtained with blue muslin, and that was the extent of light and ventilation. The room was called "the sleep hall," which is precisely what it was. All of the girls and the teachers slept up there, their narrow bedsteads of walnut or poplar standing close together in straight rows. Mattresses in summer were filled with chaff; in winter, with feathers. Pillows followed the same seasonal pattern, and the sheets and pillowcases were made of cotton or linen. There was no heat in the sleep hall in winter, but in summer, with only the four small windows, there must have been heat to spare—and then some.

Fortunately for comfort's sake, the girls and teaching Sisters spent only their sleeping hours in the attic. The rest of the time they were on the floor below, where the windows, curtained with white muslin, were much larger and more numerous and where, in winter, warmth poured cozily out of tile or iron stoves. The "sick room" was at the southwest corner on the second floor. Behind it was the room where the girls had their sewing and music lessons.

As the student body grew, uses of the various rooms would be changed to accommodate the increased numbers. But in those first months after the building opened, the bulk of the school's activity was confined to the two rooms on the north side of the second floor. And as those rooms were directly over the Kramsch living quarters, it isn't likely that either the inspector or his wife found many moments for quiet meditation.

The girls were divided into two "room companies" according to age. The older girls, supervised by Sisters Reichel and Praezel, were assigned the front room as their headquarters, and the younger room company occupied the back room under the watchful eyes of Sister Meinung and a new teacher, Johanna Sophia (Hannah) Schober.

The room company was to remain the core of student life at the

boarding school for over a century. A workable system psychologi-
cally as well as practically, it had stemmed from the Moravians' genuine concern that the girls who came to Salem from elsewhere not
only be well cared for in every respect but also be happy and contented.
Under the circumstances, this was quite an ambitious undertaking,
and it placed an enormous burden on the school's teachers, none of
whom in those first years was past her mid-twenties.

The girls in their care were children, actually; few were older than
twelve. And traveling conditions of that time were such that when
the girls came to Salem, they stayed—sometimes as long as two or
three years—without going home and often without seeing any of
their old friends or kinfolk. This meant that the teachers had to be
mothers even more than teachers, seeing that the girls ate properly
and took sufficient exercise, that their clothes were in order, that they
were put to bed when they were sick, that their manners and morals
conformed to the highest standards, that they were punished when
they misbehaved, and—perhaps the most demanding of all—that, far
away from home, they did not lack for the security of love and kindness.

Without some sort of system, it would have been impossible for
the Sisters to give the girls such constant, personal attention. So the
pupils were divided into room companies of twelve to fifteen, with
two teachers assigned to each—one of them, usually both, overseeing
the company at all times. Although in their school classes the girls
were assigned according to their ability, in all else they lived with
their two teachers and the other members of their room company as
a large family—eating together, sitting in church together, playing
and doing their chores together, having their own little parties and
outings. And as most of what they did was done within the confines
of the room to which their company was assigned, the plain-speaking
Moravians had given it the right name: a "living room."

The floors of the living rooms were sprinkled with white sand,
which regularly was taken up, carried outdoors, sifted, washed and
stored in barrels to be ready for spreading again. As one of the teachers recalled:

We could not sweep the sanded floors, of course. Going over it lightly
with a broom, we would collect what lint had fallen from the sewing and

at the same time brush it [the sand] into the most wonderful design. We put fresh sand down on Wednesdays and Saturdays, and it kept the floors so clean that when in the weekly cleaning we had swept all the sand out, the floor needed no scouring—only to be wiped up with a wet cloth.[10]

At first, the pupils themselves were given the task of washing the sand, but it soon became apparent that little girls from elsewhere were not as robust as Moravian children; they caught cold easily. Nor did most of them, unaccustomed as they were to menial labor, do the work either cheerfully or well. So it was not long before the House Conference was forced to make other arrangements for getting the sand washed.

Meals for the school were cooked in the kitchen of the Single Sisters' House next door and brought to the cellar of the school building, where pupils and teachers ate at tables made of boards laid across sawbucks and covered with cloths of coarse tow linen. When the weather turned cold, the tables were set up in the town girls' schoolroom on the first floor. Plates and tableware were of pewter, as were most of the serving dishes. Mugs, which were soon substituted for teacups "because the latter make too much noise,"[11] were probably Queensware, as one inventory lists a number of Queensware items, including mugs. And it is known that the Salem potter was making Queensware at that time.

At one point before the new building opened, complaint had been made that the meals provided by the Single Sisters were at times skimpy, but the Sisters promised to improve the menus and apparently did. In addition to the three meals served daily, thick slices of crusty bread were passed out to the room companies at mid-morning, and there was another snack at vespers in the afternoon. So if any of the girls went to bed hungry, it wasn't because the school failed to provide enough food. To be sure, many were accustomed to fancier fare than the Sisters ladled out of the big iron pots hanging in their kitchen fireplace. But the rigid discipline of the Girls' Boarding School in Salem probably made no more allowance for finicky eating habits than for other brands of non-conformance. And it did not take long, one suspects, for a wayward appetite to fall into line.

5

The Kramsch Affair

ALMOST EVERY WEEK DURING THE SUMMER AND
fall of 1805 one or more girls rode into Salem to enter the
boarding school. Amelia Adamson and Charlotte Mortimer, who
had come the day the school building was dedicated, were the first
from South Carolina. The following week, "A gentleman, James
Sanders by name, who lives near Nashville in the state of Tennessee,
brought his daughter, Laetitia, to the Boarding School, the first from
that state."[1] In late July, a member of Congress, Richard Stanford of
Hawfields, brought his two daughters, Ariana and Mary. And about
the same time, General William Richardson Davie of Halifax arrived
with his daughter, Sarah, and three other little girls from his area
of the state. This was the same William Davie who during the
Revolution had helped harass Cornwallis near Charlotte, who later
was instrumental in the founding of the University of North Carolina and in the adoption of the state constitution, and who had served
a term as Governor.

Taking advantage of passable roads during the warm weather, a
Presbyterian minister came from Lincoln County with his daughter.
And so did the postmaster of Camden, South Carolina, the clerk of
court of Rutherford County, a merchant from Salisbury, and an attorney from Iredell County named Adlai Osborne, who was an an-
cestor of Adlai E. Stevenson, Democratic candidate for President in
1952 and 1956. In early September, ". . . a gentleman from Jackson
County, Georgia, named Samuel Gardner [Gardener], merchant

and postmaster there, stopped on his way to Virginia to take his daughter Louisa Ann to relatives there. He had not known of our Boarding School but liked its arrangements, and asked permission to leave his daughter here, which was granted. She is the first pupil from Georgia."[2]

By this time, there were more than thirty pupils in the boarding school, and the storeroom on the first floor was converted into a living room for a third room company. This meant that the school had to dip into the ranks of Single Sisters for two additional "tutoresses." So Anna Susanna (Susel) Praezel, the eighteen-year-old sister of Johanna Elisabeth (Betsey) Praezel, the music teacher, joined Sister Reichel in supervising the room company of girls thirteen and fourteen years old. And Johanna Elisabeth (Hannah) Reuz moved from the Single Sisters' House to assist Sister Meinung with the eleven- and twelve-year-olds. The youngest girls (eight, nine, and ten) were under the care of Sisters Betsey Praezel and Hannah Schober. Also at that time, the Praezel sisters' widowed mother, Maria Elisabeth Praezel, who many years before had taught the children at Bethania, was employed to work with the younger children of the congregation.

In mid-September, before cold weather set in, several of the school girls were taken on an overnight excursion to Bethabara, Bethania, and Pilot Mountain. And the tales they must have told their envious schoolmates when they returned! For they had climbed all the way to the Pilot's rocky knob, from which height "the Yadkin and Dan rivers show beautifully in the unmeasured forests . . . [and] the farms and other clearings look like tiny specks."[3] Generally, though, the girls did not venture far, their sphere ranging little beyond the church up the street or the "necessary" in back of the school building. With the formation of the third room company, the school had settled into a tight little routine of academic and domestic life that seldom broke out of its narrow bounds.

There had been a few minor incidents since the new building opened. Two girls from near Salisbury had "arrived with a rash that causes apprehension,"[4] and there was a little unpleasantness four weeks later when their father took them out of school, claiming that "they felt hurt because the other children did not have anything to do with them."[5] But the House Conference was not especially perturbed, taking the position that indeed the other girls had not been encouraged to fraternize too closely with these two "in view of their rash."[6] At one point, too, eleven-year-old Mary Trotter had such a bad case of homesickness that the Sisters notified her parents. Within a week, though, the pains seem to have miraculously disappeared, and, as it turned out, Mary stayed on in Salem for more than a year— presumably quite content.

But the little girl from Georgia, Louisa Gardener, stayed less than a month. Apparently her father, who had left her in Salem instead of taking her on to relatives in Virginia as he had set out to do, would have done well to consult his wife before changing the plans. At any rate, he was soon back in Salem to take Louisa home "because, she being an only child, she is too far away from her mother."[7] According to the House Conference,[8] "she [Louisa] and we were sorry for this" as the child "had fit in well in every respect."

The Elders' Conference continued to keep a guarding eye on the overall operation of both the boarding school and the town girls' school, but the small internal crises were left in the hands of Inspector Kramsch and his staff of Single Sisters. And once the new school building had been completed and duly dedicated, most of the rest of Salem's residents turned to other obligations.

It was not a particularly good year for them. The price of tobacco had dropped; work for the craftsmen had fallen off; bills had been hard to collect; there had been epidemics of smallpox and influenza; wolves had done considerable damage to outlying farms. Even so, the Moravians were looking ahead. Despite their reluctance to get involved in politics, they saw the wisdom of having someone in the state capital who would look after their interests. So Gottlieb Schober ran for the State Senate and was elected. And when word came that the federal government was planning a mail coach road in the vicinity, strong effort was made to get it to pass directly through Salem, as "this would be of service not only to us but to the parents from this and other states who have daughters in our Boarding School."[9]

As the warm days of October passed, Salem began to settle in for the long winter. In the boarding school and in houses all over town, wood fires burned in the big tile stoves. And the bell for stopping work (which the tailor rang when it became too dark to thread a needle) was sounding a little earlier each day. Within a few weeks, the roads would be either frozen so hard or so axle-deep in mud that travel would slack off—at times, stop altogether. Winter was ordinarily a quiet time in Salem, and this winter of 1805 started off no differently from usual.

Then in mid-November, it happened: Out of the blue came the devastating discovery that "Br. Kramsch in his associations with the sisters and the children of the Girls Boarding School has behaved in a most improper and objectionable manner".[10]

Exactly what he did, we aren't likely ever to know. For the minutes of the emergency board sessions that followed scrupulously skirt around any revealing details. And not a tattered corner can be found from the few highly confidential letters in which certain Brethren in high places were apprised of "the whole nexus of the matter."[11] Because the Moravians customarily were so meticulous about keeping complete records, we can only conclude that, in this case, they deliberately left posterity in the dark, carrying the secret with them to their graves, where it now lies buried under the flat stones at Salem, Bethlehem, and Herrnhut.

It might have been kinder to Samuel Kramsch's memory if the well-meaning Brethren had not been so close-lipped. Mores change, and the chances are that what Kramsch did then would barely raise an eyebrow now. But the point is, he did it, and whatever it was that he did shook the ruling Brethren of Salem to the core. The Helpers' Conference met in special session on November 14 and sorrowfully (1) excluded Kramsch from Communion, (2) removed him from the Board of Elders, (3) relieved him of his post as inspector, and (4) agreed that he not only should vacate the school building but also, as soon as possible, should be dispatched to Pennsylvania.

Members of the conference made these drastic decisions in neither heat nor haste. Clearly, the whole matter was extremely painful for them, and on the question of whether Kramsch should be sent to Pennsylvania, they were not willing to act without first asking guidance from the Lord through the Lot. But they were realistic men, and they knew full well that if word of the scandal ever leaked out, the moral pillars on which so much of the school's reputation had been built would be seriously undermined, possibly leaving the future of the school itself in doubt. Also, for all his fall from grace, they were not insensitive to Kramsch's own feelings. So they worked out

an arrangement whereby Bishop Reichel would take over management of the school temporarily "except for correspondence with the
parents of the children; this is to continue to be entrusted to Br.
Kramsch, mainly to shield him in so far as possible in his non-Church
relations."[12] This was a shrewd way, too, of course—and the Brethren were smart enough to see it—of keeping parents from knowing
that there had been an abrupt change in the school's administration.

Just how much the school girls or the rank and file of Salem residents knew of what was going on behind the closed doors of conference rooms can only be conjectured. At their age, the girls probably
accepted whatever explanation their tutoresses offered for the sudden
move of the Kramsch family, which must have been simply that more
room was needed for the growing number of pupils. But the Moravians, for all their piety, were no less endowed with human nature
than most, and we can imagine that there was buzzing aplenty elsewhere in town.

For their part, Salem's leaders maintained strict silence except
among themselves. The Helpers' Conference reported its action to
the Elders' Conference the next day. The Elders' Conference in turn
asked the *Aufseher Collegium* to "participate in the great regret,"[13]
and the *Aufseher Collegium* in its turn "strongly recommended to
keep these things secret."[14] Even in reporting the case officially to
Bethlehem and Herrnhut, the Brethren carefully avoided spelling
out the details, leaving that to confidential personal letters which Bishop Reichel wrote to his counterparts in both places. The Helpers'
Conference nevertheless was worried:

It is to be feared that the distressing occurrence which took place in our
Boarding School could become known in non-Church circles and false
or exaggerated reports concerning it spread about, with this institution's
being given a bad reputation without cause and the real confidence that
it enjoyed be lessened. Therefore it appeared necessary to take, as promptly as possible, such measures as could counteract false and exaggerated
rumors about the matter. It was thought that for the present the best
means to that end would be to set forth the whole nexus of the matter in
a confidential letter to Br. Schober, who is attending the Assembly in
Raleigh as a Senator and therefore could likely be approached about it.
He could be instructed in it to make no other use of it except in case of

being led to do so by questioning or other circumstances which would indicate that untruths had been circulated.[15]

Kramsch and his family moved out of the school building on November 23, 1805. He was forty-nine years old, and from that time until his death in 1824, he seemed to be plagued with one trouble after another. He continued to handle the correspondence for the boarding school until the fall of 1806 when, with the appointment of a new inspector, he was severed of all connections with the school. As it turned out, Bethlehem never found a place for him, and he stayed on in Wachovia. The forgiving Brethren eventually readmitted him to Communion and, in his later years especially, cared for him with loving-kindness, although there were times when he must have been a trial for them. Soon after he left the school, he was given the job of running the town's odds-and-ends store, but was somewhat less than successful. He kept a dog that apparently was a nuisance for the neighbors. And at one point, to the consternation of the Elders' Conference, he was found to be distributing the writings of the German mystic, Johann Heinrich Jung, which, in the Elders' view, had "a bad effect on weak minds."[16]

In 1813, however, Kramsch was allowed to return to the ministry. He and his wife went back to Hope as assistant ministers of the congregation there, Salem bidding them farewell "with grateful recognition of their services rendered to the community."[17] Within a year, though, his eyesight began to fail, and in 1819, the various treasuries of Salem, including that of the Girls' Boarding School, contributed the necessary funds to send him to Raleigh for an operation. The surgery was not successful, and as he could no longer carry on his ministerial duties, arrangements were made to bring him back to Salem. Bishop Jacob Van Vleck and his wife gave up one of their rooms in the *Gemein Haus*, and the school moved the town girls out of their classroom in the same building in order that the Kramsches might have a comfortable apartment.

In 1823, Kramsch submitted to another operation, this one by a Salisbury surgeon, and, as a result, he "had the joy of again being able to see his family and friends."[18] But time was running out for him; on February 2, 1824, he died at the age of sixty-seven and was buried in God's Acre in Salem. His wife lived on in Salem until her death in

1831. And their daughter, Louisa, who had come back to the school in 1814 as a teacher, served it faithfully for more than twenty years.

Kramsch's indiscretion had scandalized the Brethren and, had it not been wisely handled, could indeed have jeopardized the future of the school. But in the end, all it really amounted to was a pathetic personal tragedy. The school itself survived without a visible scar, continuing to operate on the solid groundwork that the Kramsches had laid. On balance, then, the contribution that these two able people made to education in Salem far outweighs the temporary distress that they caused, and their place in history is, as the good Brethren meant it to be, an honorable one.

The Kramsch family had moved out of the boarding school building on a Saturday. On the following Monday, the House Conference, shaken by the events of the preceding ten days, met to carry on the business of running a boarding school. Members solemnly pledged their support to Bishop Reichel as he assumed the responsibilities of inspector and pledged themselves anew to the principles of the school, "particularly to see to it that the children who are entrusted to us are exhorted to cherish true fear of God and to know their Saviour."[19]

For his work with the school accounts and in the correspondence with parents, Kramsch was permitted to use his former living room and bedroom as an office. Sister Kramsch's room at the back of the building was made into a classroom for the town girls, and the adjoining kitchen was taken over by the school for use in the preparation of breakfasts and refreshments for vespers.

Apparently the Brethren had succeeded well in suppressing the Kramsch affair—at least outside Moravian circles. For the flow of new pupils continued without noticeable interruption throughout that winter and the following spring. Among the arrivals were Clementina Brown, daughter of a Presbyterian minister of Anson County; Anna Newman, Christine Beard, Eliza and Rebecca Nisbet, all of Salisbury; Ann White, daughter of the secretary of state at Raleigh, and Altona Gales, daughter of the state printer; Mary Lowrie of Mecklenburg County, whose father was a member of the state Assembly; Lucy Ann Brown of Wilmington; twins, Elizabeth and Sarah McLinn, of New Bern; Rachel Clark of Rockingham; Nancy Leak of Anson; Sarah Guyther of Plymouth; and Sarah Harris of

Cabarrus County. From South Carolina came Maria Rees, Sarah James, Mary Reed, Elizabeth Taylor, Eleanor and Hannah Earle, Harriet English, and Dorothy DeWitt. Nancy Carleton and Sarah Carleton, who must have been cousins, came from Wilkes County, Georgia, and Mourning Micajah Watkins and Sarah Lenoir Chalmers from Halifax, Virginia.

Joseph Graham of Lincoln County brought his daughter, Sophia. And if he was welcomed with extraordinary warmth, there was reason: "During the Revolutionary War, when a party of militia from Wilkes County threatened to destroy Salem, this Mr. Graham, then an officer of the American militia, acted in a most friendly manner, and by urgent representation to his general and to the leaders of Wilkes militia averted the threatened calamity."[20]

General Davie, who already had one daughter at Salem, arrived in early May with a younger daughter, Rebecca. By that time, there were fifty-five boarding pupils, and the House Conference was forced to arrange for a fourth room company even though there was a shortage of qualified teachers among the Single Sisters. Moreover, the school had lost one of its experienced teachers when Sister Reuz was dismissed for accepting a present from a Single Brother whose standing in the community was somewhat questionable. (The Sister later repented and was reinstated.) Barbara Leinbach and Philippina Christman were brought from the Sisters' House to help with the teaching and care of the school girls. But both were novices, and, without the help of Sister Reuz, the older teachers worked harder than ever.

Immediately after the Kramsch case erupted, an appeal was dispatched to the Brethren in Pennsylvania asking for someone among their number to come to Salem and take over the inspector's position. But the months wore on, and for one reason or another, Pennsylvania never seemed able to fill the order. This placed an enormous burden on Bishop Reichel. As he wrote to Bishop George Heinrich Loskiel in Bethlehem: "The circumstances of our poor Br. Kr. [Kramsch] has for some time engaged my feeling outside the deed. It has given me many sleepless hours in the night. Also I have had somewhat more work through this, since the H. C. f. G. [Helpers' Conference] has actually laid on me the running of the Anstalt . . ."[21]

Moreover, in August, 1806, Bishop Reichel's wife died. In the tradition of Moravian wives, she had worked alongside her husband in all of his duties. The loss of her assistance in bearing the responsibilities of the school not only made it impossible for him to carry the extra load but also necessitated the release of his daughter, Sophia Dorothea, from her duties as head teacher in order to manage the housekeeping for her father. So it was a relief to everyone when the Elders, having despaired of getting an inspector from Pennsylvania, asked for and received the approval of the Lord in the selection of one of Wachovia's own, the Reverend Abraham Steiner, for the post.

As Samuel Kramsch had been, Steiner was the minister of the English-speaking congregation at Hope when he received the school's call. This indicates that he had the command of English necessary for dealing with the boarding pupils and their parents. Also like Kramsch, he was in his late forties when he took over the reins of the school. But in background and personality, the two were altogether different.

Born in Bethlehem on April 27, 1758, Steiner had known only the rugged life of early America. While still an infant, he had been sent to school at Nazareth and eventually had advanced to the Boys' School there, where he evidenced an aptitude for mathematics and the sciences. But Steiner was a maverick and, in time, became impatient with his studies; as far as he could see, he had learned all the science that the school was prepared to teach him. So in his midteens, he quit school and returned to his home, where he was apprenticed to his father, a smithy in the small settlement of Schoeneck, near Bethlehem. Totally uninterested in becoming a blacksmith, Steiner soon enough came to regret his haste in leaving school. It was then that he began to read avidly. Available books were few, but he read and reread every one he could find, especially the Bible, which stirred him to a fervent desire to serve the Lord.

The young Steiner was too much of an individualist, though, to slip docilely under the yoke of anyone's will, including the Lord's. And in his memoir,[22] he describes vividly the years of inner struggle during which time and again he broke the traces before finally coming to terms with himself and his God.

His restlessness at the smithy prompted him to apply for permission to join the Single Brothers at Bethlehem, but the Brethren must not have considered him a good risk; they turned him down. Later, the Single Brothers at Lititz accepted him, and he was received into the

Moravian congregation there in 1780. In Lititz, he had been appointed master blacksmith, but as he had never finished his own training, he was not very good at the job. So in 1781, he was allowed to move to the Single Brothers' House in Bethlehem and to work as an assistant to the instructor of the Boys' School, studying on his own in his spare time. The Brethren did not seem impressed with his potential as a teacher, though, for five years later, he was asked to go to Hope, New Jersey, as helper in the congregation store. Although he went reluctantly, this time apparently he carried out his assignment well— so well that in August, 1789, he received an offer to take over the operation of the store at Bethabara in Wachovia.

He arrived in Salem on October 16, 1789, and on December 2, was married to the Single Sister Christine Fischer. They moved to Bethabara later that month. Only sixteen months after their marriage, Steiner's wife died giving birth to twin daughters, who also did not survive. However, the Moravians of that time did not believe in long mourning periods any more than in long engagements. "Hardly four months had passed," Steiner wrote, "when the Wachauvian Directorate proposed that I marry again."[23] Consequently, on July 31, 1791, with the Lord's approval, he was married to Catharine Sehner, then a teacher in the Little Girls' School at Salem.

From boyhood Steiner had been fascinated by the Indians; at one point while he lived in Pennsylvania, he had accompanied a party of Brethren into Indian country. Upon arriving in Wachovia, he was disturbed to find that nothing had been done to establish missions among the Cherokees, and he mounted something of a campaign toward that end, badgering the conferences until finally they agreed to send him into the Indian settlements to determine whether indeed a mission there was feasible. From 1799, when he made the first journey, until 1806, when he received the call to the boarding school, work among the Cherokees absorbed much of his time and interest. He made numerous trips into the rugged mountains of North Carolina, Tennessee, and Georgia, often spending months at a time among the Indians, and was largely instrumental in establishing the mission at Springplace in Georgia, where the Moravians were to labor until the Cherokee Nation was forced to leave its home and follow the "Trail of Tears" west.

In the late fall of 1802, Steiner was ordained a deacon in the Unity

Abraham Gottlieb Steiner, Inspector 1806–1816

of Brethren and became minister of the Hope congregation, replacing Samuel Kramsch, who had been called to Salem to open the new boarding school for girls. While still in the ministry at Hope, he made one more trip to the Indian lands, this time to try to begin a mission among the Creeks. And much of his heart must have remained there forever afterwards. For in his memoir written in his declining years, he describes his experiences among the Indians warmly and at length, disposing of his work at the boarding school in one short, matter-of-fact paragraph. Yet, being a dutiful man, he accepted the call to become inspector of the boarding school willingly, although, he admitted, it was "an entirely new field of endeavor"[24] for him.

As it turned out, the Elders could hardly have chosen a better man for the job at that particular time. Steiner was not nearly the scholar or the teacher that Kramsch had been. But he was a forceful man whose lessons had been learned through rugged experience and whose feet were firmly planted in the soil of common sense. He spoke his mind at all times and did so with a directness that often bordered on the brusque. But the curtness of his manner was tempered by the warmth of humor, and people were drawn to him in genuine affection and respect—especially the school girls, who soon came to call him "Daddy Steiner." Moreover, as the business side of the school grew more complex, his mathematical bent and storekeeping experience proved to be of inestimable value.

What Abraham Steiner lacked in cultural background, then, he more than compensated for in bringing to the school the stability and forthright leadership that it so urgently needed in the uneasy aftermath of the Kramsch affair.

6

The

Inspector's Lot

THE STEINERS MOVED TO SALEM ON OCTOBER 16, 1806—to a house that stood just north of the Single Brothers' House and diagonally across the square from the school. It was not an especially convenient location; the new inspector was expected to maintain an office in his home, and from that distance, it was hard for him to keep as close a watch over the teachers and pupils as he thought he should. But at that particular time, the Brethren were concerned more with propriety than with proximity; as Bishop Reichel had written to Bishop Loskiel in Bethlehem, "We shall never again let an inspector live in the school house."[1]

The location proved to be additionally awkward in that Steiner also dispensed supplies for the students, which meant that girls were constantly running out of the school building and across the square to his house for a toothbrush or an embroidery needle or a package of "letterpaper." This being a good excuse to skip out of school for a few minutes, the girls no doubt highly approved of the arrangement. But the frequent interruptions came to be a nuisance to Steiner, and he soon ruled that "only on Saturdays shall the children fetch what they need from the Inspector."[2]

At that, keeping track of every purchase made by every little girl was a tedious chore for him. With the inadequacy of transportation at that time, parents were hard pressed to find a way to send even clothing and other personal necessities to their daughters. When a wagon from Salem was scheduled to make a business trip to some distant point, Steiner thoughtfully notified parents who lived along its route so that if they wished, they could use that means of getting packages delivered to the school. More often than not, though, the inspector had to supply what the children needed, charging the cost to their parents' accounts. When requested to do so, he also doled out a girl's "pocket money" (allowance) in the amount specified by her parents (usually fifty cents or a dollar a month).

There was a rule that if a girl broke any school property, she must replace it out of her pocket money "unless it had been an unpreventable accident."[3] Otherwise, with a bit of subtle guidance by the Sisters, she could spend her allowance for anything that caught her fancy—sweets from the bakery, fruit from passing vendors, birthday gifts and other trinkets from the Community Store. But it was a hard and fast rule that no book could be purchased at any place by any pupil until first the inspector had examined it personally and deemed its contents fit for innocent eyes.

Steiner maintained what he called a "private book," in which he listed every item charged to each girl. Sarah Murfree's account for the month of May, 1808, for example, was recorded as follows:

To Pocket money, Medicine, to postage	$1.27
To 1 blank book, 1 cyphering book,	
Drawing pencil	.81
1 Umbrella, 1 shell comb, 1 pr.	
Cotton Mitts	6.62
1 Sliding pencil, Tambour needles & case,	
letterbook	1.13
tape, 1 doz. Needles, thread	.26
Painting paper & other stationery,	
colours p^r month	.22[4]

The following month, Sarah's purchases included:

Pocket money $1.00, hymnbook, writing	
book	$2.58
cambric, cotton Stocking	4.08
Muslin, toothbrush, postage	.70
Expences at the Examination & pleasure ride	.62

Muslin, pr. of shoes, cap ribbon	2.19
towelling Diaper, shell comb	1.37
Letterpaper, colours pr month	.72[5]

At the end of the quarter, Steiner totaled the expenditures for each girl, and billed her father or guardian for such "contingencies," along with her tuition fees, board, and washing. But unfortunately—for him, at any rate—his fiscal responsibility did not end there; parents expected him not only to account for what their daughters spent but also to see that their spending was not extravagant. And if the bills received were considered too high, complaints were quick to come:

On perusing contingent acct am sorry to find it so high particularly these hard times. Presume you're acquainted with disposition of young persons, and, if so, must know they don't consider means parents have to meet Expences. Would therefore request to curtail expences in future to what is absolutely necessary.[6]

Even General Davie, whose attitude toward the school was always sympathetic, once wrote that, although he wanted his daughters to have what they needed, he wished Steiner to use "as much decent economy as you can."[7] Steiner apparently did his best to comply with parents' wishes in the matter. In association with the other members of the House Conference, he ruled that "no child shall be permitted to get more than one pair of shoes in a two month period; similarly 2 haubes [caps] ought to be sufficient each year."[8] But if he felt parents' protests were unreasonable, he could, and did, stand his ground. As he wrote to one father who had taken him to task for the sizable amount charged to his daughters: "In Expence have restrained them to necessaries, but many Items swell at last to a large Sum.[9]

Collecting money due the school was not easy under the friendliest of circumstances. The mails were unreliable, and parents usually waited to pay their accounts until they could send the money via someone whom they could trust to deliver it safely. Thus payment often was delayed for months. Occasionally a father would thwart would-be mail robbers by tearing a bank note into halves and sending only one half by mail. When the school notified him that the first half had arrived, he would then mail the matching half.

161.

Mary Cash. — Dr.

1807

Date			Description		$	C
October 31	117		To Boarding school, for Entrance this day		5	00
December 31	"		To Contingencies to this day as per Journal		23	13½
1808						
January 31	117		To Boarding school, for Board and Tuition		24	00
	127		To Washing, for one Quarter to this day		4	00
April 30	"		To Sundry Accounts, as pr Journal		28	00
	"		To Ditto, Contingencies, pr Ditto	99.11½	14	98	99	11½
July 31	"		To Sundry Accounts, as per Journal		23	00
August 31	"		To Ditto, Contingencies, Ditto		20	11
October 31	"		To Ditto Ditto		28	00
Novem. 29	"		To Ditto		8	50
Decem. 31	"		To Ditto Contingencies Ditto	195.00	5	27½	95	88½
					$ 195	00

Mourning M. Watkins — Dr.

1810

Date			Description	$	C
July 30	185	To Boarding school, for Board & Tuition	24	00
	156	To Washing, for one Quarter	4	00
October 30	135	To Boarding school, for Board & Tuition	24	00
	156	To Washing, for one Quarter	4	00
November 16	186	To Boarding school, for Board & Tuition	3	56
	156	To Washing, for one Quarter a Balance	—	59
Decem. 31	"	To Sundry Accounts, as pr Journal, Contingencies	25	30
			$ 85	45

Elizabeth Eveline Ross. — Dr.

1811

Date			Description	$	C
April 12	187	To Boarding school, for Entrance	5	00
May 31	"	To Sundry Accounts, Contingencies, pr Journal	9	49
			$ 14	49

Student accounts in Girls' Boarding School ledger

In many instances, the past-due accounts were simply a matter of parents' not being willing or not being financially able to pay. Steiner kept a "Letter Book" in which he recorded a digest of every letter either written or received. The book abounds in such patient pleas for payment as that to Captain Richard Jones of Pittsylvania, Virginia:

Having written you repeatedly concerning the debt which you owe for Salem Board^g School, as have made the offer that if you sent me some written acknowledgment, I should wait with you y^r own time, but never had the pleasure to receive an answer from you. It must be obvious to you, that an Establishment like ours, without any other fund than that which arises from regular payments for actual services rendered, is not able to make many and long continued advances, without making sacrifices beyond its ability to bear. Hence I have hitherto always thrown myself on the generosity of Gentlemen, without having any thought of resorting to coercive measures, and I now with confidence expect an answer from you, for I am certain, that you would not give me occasion to resort to measures for the recovery of the debt, which I should adopt with the greatest reluctance.[10]

Some of the responses from parents who received these reminders reflected genuine concern over their delinquency. Thomas H. Blount of Beaufort wrote: "Don't know what apology to make for not sending balance due you for Louise Blount. Thought Guardian had p^d it."[11] Colonel Hardy Murfree, who had moved recently from Murfreesborough to Franklin, Tennessee, was equally embarrassed, but had suffered temporary reverses: "Expected to have made you Remittance ere now, but disappointments prevented me, but can make you Payment beginning of January next. Money is scarce in this state."[12] Others were more caustic. One mother, obviously a little irritated by Steiner's reminders, let him know that she would be "as fond of paying as you are of receiving."[13] The debts hardest to collect were those left by parents who had taken their daughters out of school—and this occurred often with little or no prior notice: "Have sent Benjamin for Caroline, times are so bad that I can't let her stay longer."[14] Once a girl had left Salem, the lines of communication between the school and her parents sagged even worse, and Steiner frequently was unable to rouse any response at all.

When your Daughter Louise 14 months ago, left this school, you remained in my debt $34.50 which is not yet p^d. Have repeatedly written to you on subject, but never rec^d answer. Most earnestly solicit payment shortly.[15]

If parents such as this had ever suffered any pangs of moral obligation, apparently many soon managed to overcome the affliction, or else learned to live with it. And Steiner eventually was forced to write off their debts as uncollectible.

Somehow, though, despite the bad debts, he was able to purchase classroom supplies (often ordering them from Philadelphia or Bethlehem), pay the teachers' salaries, regularly meet installments on the loan for the school building, remunerate the Single Sisters' Diacony for the children's board, keep wood in the stoves and linen on the beds, and still have enough money left over to contribute to worthy community causes such as a house for the doctor, the subsidy for the financially ailing Boys' School, and the "fund for aged tutoresses." Not for naught had the Elders selected an inspector with a head for figures and the practical experience of running a store!

Balancing the school's books was only one part of the inspector's duties, however. Every Monday, Wednesday, Thursday, and Friday morning, Steiner taught the advanced class in "cyphering." And in the evenings (sometimes as often as four times a week), he taught English grammar, geography, and history to teachers who needed further training "and such older girls as give promise of being competent to teach in the future."[16]

As it had been from the early years of the Little Girls' School, acquiring and keeping qualified teachers was an area of constant concern for the inspector. It was a problem generated in no small measure by the Moravians' own structured way of living—and way of thinking. Because teaching positions in their schools were limited to members of the Moravian church, the inspector could look only to Moravian congregations to supply his teachers, and not all of these few sources were readily productive. Single Sisters in Pennsylvania, for instance, seldom were willing to leave that comparatively populous area and come to the North Carolina backcountry. So, for the most part, Steiner was forced to recruit teachers from among the Single Sisters of Wachovia, many of whom had had little more schooling than their pupils.

Even so, there was a continual turnover in the teaching ranks. For in the Moravian view, marriage took precedence over any other occupation for a woman, regardless of her talents or of how badly she was needed in the job that she was then doing. If the Elders felt that a certain Brother needed a wife and that a Sister in the boarding school was the most suitable candidate, they did not hesitate to propose. In fact, teachers, being more accomplished than the general run of Single Sisters and widows, were considered choice matrimonial material—especially for ministers. Faithful disciple of the Brethren that he was, Steiner accepted this riddling of his staff without protest, although, on one occasion in particular, he must have been sorely tempted to question the fairness of it.

It was about a year after he had become inspector, and by a rare stroke of good luck, he had obtained the services of Sister Elisabeth Danz, a former teacher in the Bethlehem Seminary. Sister Danz arrived in Salem on October 28, 1807, and on November 2 was installed in the boarding school as teacher and supervisor. Nine days later, Christian Winkler, a Swiss-born Single Brother, arrived from Lititz to take over Salem's bakery operation. A baker, of course, needed a wife to help with the work. Whether he picked Sister Danz or the Elders chose her for him is not clear. All we know is, her name was submitted to the Lot; the Lord's answer was "*Ja*"—and that was that. Two months and four days after the new teacher began work at the school, she moved to the bakery as Winkler's wife and chief helper, leaving Steiner to fill the teaching vacancy as best he could.

A few months earlier, he had suffered another serious loss when Salome Meinung accepted a call to become a teacher at the school in Bethlehem. Sister Meinung had been at the Salem school longer than any other teacher, having first come in 1787 to help out in the emergency caused by the elopement of Dorothea Meyer and Isaac Boner. At the time, she had had no teaching experience, but she had learned quickly, and Inspector Kramsch had thought highly enough of her ability to ask her to be one of the first teachers in the boarding school. In 1807, when there was a scarcity even of Sisters who could be trained to teach, the school could ill afford to lose a pillar like Salome Meinung. But, again, this was a call to service which the Moravians of Salem would not dream of opposing, and they bade her farewell with a lovefeast and wishes for "every blessing from the Saviour's rich store."[17]

Steiner was forced to fill the vacancy with an inexperienced teacher, Susanna Peter, the twenty-year-old daughter of the Reverend Simon Peter of Bethabara. Little is known of her educational background other than that when she was nearly seven, her parents, who then lived in Bethania, brought her to Salem "to our widowed Sr. Praezel to be cared for and educated."[18] But we do know that she came of an educated and talented family. Her father, an accomplished musician, had taught at Nazareth Hall at one time. And her uncle, John Frederik Peter, was one of the best-known of the early Moravian composers in this country; his six string quintets, composed in Salem in 1789, are believed to be the first chamber music written in America. Susanna herself must have inherited some of this musical talent, as her first assignment at the school was to teach music, along with German reading and writing, to the town girls.

The town girls' school had continued to operate through all of the boarding school's growing pains, although from time to time some of the Brethren and Sisters in Salem had expressed dissatisfaction, feeling that "since the Boarding School was established, their own children seemed to receive less attention."[19] And they may have had some basis for the complaint. Certainly, in the matter of classroom space, it does appear that the town girls frequently were shifted around, taking the leavings after the boarding school's needs were accommodated. Whether or not this was also true of instruction, the Helpers' Conference considered the parents' complaints serious enough to admonish Inspector Steiner that "all care must be taken that our own children receive the necessary instruction."[20] And a few months later, when the fourth room company was discontinued because of a drop in enrollment, the conference itself ruled that "as our own little school girls have had too little place for their classes, the room on the right of the front door [formerly occupied by the now-disbanded room company] can now be cleared out for them."[21]

In the same session, the conference, acknowledging Steiner's difficulties in trying to run the school from his house, suggested that he move his office to a room in the southeast corner of the *Gemein*

Haus, from which, the conference noted, "he can see all that goes on in the yard of the Boarding School."[22]

Being headquartered within watching distance of the school yard undoubtedly made the inspector's working arrangement somewhat more convenient, but it hardly eased his work load. It was not enough that he manage the school's finances, purchase and dispense supplies, personally collect the bills, account for each girl's spending habits, teach classes and tutor teachers, plan the curriculum, direct admissions, make and administer rules of conduct, recruit staff, negotiate with the Single Sisters about board and washing, be ready to preach a sermon when called upon, and operate the school for town girls to the satisfaction of his fellow Moravians. He was also expected to make personal reports to the boarding pupils' parents as to the girls' health, morale, and progress in school work.

Steiner wrote each of these regular reports by hand, and then carefully recorded a synopsis of it in his Letter Book:

Burroughs was sorrowfull when you went away but next morning & ever since cheerful. Her tooth we tried twice but she will not suffer it to be pulled.[23]

Rebecca has had the mumps but is recovered.[24]

Ann has commenced Embroidery already in winter & Fanny lately. At Examination acquitted themselves handsomely, only somewhat defective in Reading.[25]

Sally improves some, is rather proud in dress.
Becky rather careless & will not wash & brush teeth.[26]

[Julia] is well only that she has the Itch which she has probably caught on the way up to this place.[27]

Caroline sedate & very fine & well behaved Lady.
Mary Ann more volatile. She comprehends quicker & Carol retains better.[28]

Ann was first plagued with ringworms, then with Boils, but are now removed & is well.[29]

[Betsy] can play 6 tunes tolerably easy & several others with hesitation.[30]

Polly had measles last month, had cough before which is worse now, with feavers, great perspiration & weakness. Doctor declares it beginning of consumption, advised radical cure, but I wished only Palliatives that I might communicate with you concerning her & obtain y^r advice, for you know her condition better than we. Our opinion is better take her home for a while.[31]

Particularly in situations relative to the girls' health, the terrible responsibility resting on Steiner must have caused him, in Bishop Reichel's words, "many sleepless hours in the night." In the later years of his administration, an epidemic of measles swept through the school, striking seventy-two pupils before it subsided. Once, too, a traveler brought smallpox into Salem, and Steiner wrestled with the dilemma of whether the school girls should be vaccinated. (On the advice of the Elders, he decided against it except with the consent of their parents.) And when the danger had passed, he felt it necessary to insert an advertisement in various newspapers to reassure parents that there was "no longer any fear of infection."[32]

We can imagine the relief with which parents read the notice, and also the apprehension they must have felt when they received a report from Steiner saying that all was not well with their daughters. In the weeks that it took for the report to reach them, they knew, the bad news might have grown even worse. Yet, with travel at the time so arduous and the mails so slow, there was no immediate means of setting their minds to rest. They could only worry and wait helplessly for Steiner's next letter to plod its uncertain way from Salem to wherever they lived—in the Coastal Plain of North Carolina, in Virginia, in Georgia, or across the mountains in Tennessee.

Even in the best of circumstances, parents are given to anxiety about their children, and these were no different. Most seemed to have full confidence in the school, but it had not been easy for doting fathers and mothers to send their little girls so far from home. And often between the lines of their letters to the inspector, their loneliness at the separation is all too apparent:

Tell her to be a good girl.[33]

Catharine was never fond of Pastry nor of Coffee, hope she will find no inconvenience in it, request she may have plenty good milk at every meal if possible.[34]

[Betsy] is only child, we are the more anxious.[35]

Have their Bonnets particularly attended to, family is remarkably easy to freckle & wish the girls to be kept from it if possible.[36]

My dear Mrs Morton makes her respects to you. No stranger ever had a greater confidence in y^r self. However, often the sighs, Oh! that I could once more see my child.[37]

Wish Becky to wear flannel next to skin. Am informed she labors under severe effects of influenza & that cough recurs upon slightest cold. You know her arm was formerly broken & most unfortunately set, ends of bones pass each other, lifting and labor of any kind occasions her pain & swellings. Request therefore exempt her from duties.[38]

If parents were unhappy about being separated from their daughters, there were times also when events at home made the separation extraordinarily hard on the little girls. Early in December, 1808, for instance, Steiner received a letter from William H. Hill of near Wilmington: "My health is still unrestored, but let what will happen, as to the result of that, take care of my little girls."[39] In less than two weeks, Hill was dead, and his brother notified the school: "You'll communicate it to his little daughters Polly & Julia in such a way as will least shock their feelings. Their situation, poor little girls, is surely distressing, to be bereav'd of both their parents in their tender years."[40]

It was in times like these that the inspector was called upon to exert all of the fatherly comfort and counsel that he could muster. Perhaps never in his entire tenure, though, were Inspector Steiner's resources more severely taxed than in mid-May, 1807, when a playful romp turned into a touching tragedy.

It occurred on one of those days in spring when suddenly winter comes bounding back for one final bleak, chilly fling. As the weather was too inclement for the little girls to have their usual play period outdoors, the teachers had allowed them to vent their pent-up energy in the large entrance hall of the school building. Among the pupils at that time were Samuel Kramsch's daughter, Louisa, and an eleven-year-old girl named Sarah Guyther of Plymouth, North Carolina. In an eye-witness account of the incident, written more than seventy years later,[41] Louisa Kramsch (then Mrs. Blickensderfer) recalled that Sarah was "rather a wild little one," and in the romp on that rainy day "somehow in her recklessness precipitated herself with such force against the front door as to become insensible."

Never can I forget that scene, though I was then only 12 years of age. It solemnized us all in a moment! Sarah was tenderly lifted up and carried to the sick-room, where all that medical skill and kindness could accomplish, was done in behalf of the little sufferer. . . . Meanwhile, we frightened children, after the first shock of the accident we had just witnessed was over, seated ourselves on the broad steps inside the door leading to the yard and began talking over the sad event—some of us wondering whether she would recover and others whether she would go to Heaven, as Sarah had been a very naughty child. This worried and distressed me so much, that I remember leaving my companions and going in search of my father, with whom I always sought comfort and explanation in any difficulty.

When, at length, my father . . . could give me a hearing, he spoke very sympathetically of her, saying she had no kind mother as I had, to train her how to act, and we must leave her case to God. Although Sarah's father was living, yet, being a sailor, he was comparatively little at home and, as captain of a vessel, he was sometimes absent on voyages of three years' duration; and the grandmother, with whom she had a home, was probably in too feeble health to do much for the child. . . .

Several days later, Inspector Steiner would describe the episode and its aftermath in sorrowful detail in a letter[42] to a "Mr. Daniel Clark" in Plymouth, who probably was serving as Sarah's guardian in the long absences of her father. At the time of the accident, Steiner wrote, Sarah's injuries were believed to be nothing more serious than a few painful cuts and bruises. And thinking it would cheer her up, he personally delivered to her in the sickroom a letter from her grandmother that had arrived that day. But to his dismay, the letter contained news not only of the death of Sarah's aunt but also of the drowning of a Negro of whom the little girl apparently had been very fond, and so had the opposite effect: "She cried, lamented & wept, and would receive no comfort." By nightfall, she had lapsed into a state of exhaustion and subsequently suffered an attack of nausea that lasted all that night and a part of the next day.

Toward evening of the second day (a Monday), "she declared . . . that she felt much better." But after midnight her condition worsened, and by Tuesday afternoon Steiner realized that, despite all the ministrations of the Salem physician, Sarah was dangerously ill.

I resolved upon two things: first to send for another Physician to consult with ours on the spot, and 2^{d}ly, to send a messenger to you [Daniel Clark] with the acc't of her dangerous sickness. For another Doctor I dispatched a messenger immediately, and succeeded to get him here the next morning. I then dispatched persons into the county to hire a horse, for a messenger to you . . . but did not succeed.

On Wednesday, following the visit of the consulting physician, Sarah appeared to be more alert and "we fondly cherished the hope of seeing her soon restored." But just after midnight, Steiner was summoned by the Sisters who were attending her, and recognizing at once the gravity of her condition, he

went immediately to the Doctor, who had the goodness to come down instantly. He administered somewhat to her relief, but declared that a choking Rheum was approaching, which would take her off in a short time. Upon this I commended her precious soul in a prayer to God our Saviour & Deliverer, till my voice failed me and weeping prevented me uttering a word. In a short time after, that is ¼ past 3 in the morning of the 14th [May] she expired in such an easy and gentle manner as ever I had seen before, in the presence of all the Tutoresses and some of the pupils of the Boarding School.

It was the first death within the ranks of the boarding school girls. And especially because of the sudden, dramatic way in which it happened, the impact on the rest of the pupils must have been altogether shattering. Steiner and his teachers, themselves stunned and grieved by the tragedy, thus bore the added strain of trying to comfort and calm forty frightened, probably hysterical, little girls. Among devout Moravians, though, there is triumph in death. And they made no effort to shield the school girls from its presence. "Carefully and tenderly was our little school-mate robed for the tomb," Mrs. Blick-

Gravestone of Sarah Guyther in the Moravian Graveyard in Salem

enderfer wrote, "and tears were shed when we were taken to the room where she was laid, to give a parting look . . ."[43]

At the funeral service on May 16, the minister addressed his sermon particularly to the boarding school students, she recalled, "urging us most affectionately and earnestly to prepare ourselves in the days of our youth for the important event of our departure to the heavenly home, since, as we had seen in our companion's early death, death came to young as well as to old."[44] Then, in the Moravian custom, those assembled went in procession to the graveyard: ". . . the pupils from the Boarding School, clad in white, walked two by two, with their teachers."[45]

Although Sarah was not a Moravian, all of the girls in the boarding school were considered a part of the congregation during their stay in Salem. So there was no question that her burial would be in God's

Acre. And there today among the rows of flat gravestones is the square of weathered gray rock which was the Brethren's memorial to the little girl who was so briefly in their midst. The letters chiseled out of its coarse surface are crudely shaped but still quite legible:

SARAH A. GUYTHER

PLYMOUTH, N. C.

DIED MAY 1807 A 11Y 3M

It was on the day after the funeral that Steiner undertook the painful task of describing the tragedy in the letter to Daniel Clark. "I ought to console you for the loss," he wrote, "but I stand in need of comfort myself."[46] But according to Mrs. Blickensderfer, no answer to Steiner's letter was ever received, and "several years elapsed before her [Sarah's] books and clothing were sent for."[47] Perhaps it was not until then that Sarah's seafaring father returned home and learned the tragic news.

7

A Code of Conduct

THE MORAVIANS TRADITIONALLY WERE FIRM advocates of physical fitness; it was their conviction that if man were truly to work to the glory of God, he must strengthen his body as well as purify his soul and sharpen his mind. Exercise thus was a natural part of the routine in their schools. And even though Sarah Guyther's accident had occurred during one of the exercise periods, the tragedy altered in no way the boarding school's insistence that pupils engage in some form of physical activity every day, preferably outdoors.

Sometimes the girls romped in the school yard, but usually the prescribed exercise was a walk, which was taken in groups and always under the watchful eye of one or more teachers. The truth is, there were precious few moments in the girls' day—or night—that weren't strictly programmed and closely supervised.

Months before the new school building opened, Inspector Kramsch had begun to formulate a code of conduct, first writing it in German so that the Salem teachers would understand fully every nuance of the rules to be enforced and then in English to be read and explained to the pupils. As time went on, the list was amended and appended until, by 1807, there were almost as many rules as there were pupils in the school:

Rules of the Boarding School at Salem
1807

1. In the morning when the housebell rings first you have to rise and to walk down without noise and confusion. Should any awake before she ought to keep quiet in bed till the ringing of the bell. After having come down you will wash yourselves.

2. After morning prayer which you will attend regularly and breakfast, you will all go upon the sleephall and make up your beds regularly & orderly.

3. You are not to take away any article of bedding from any other and appropriate it to your or other uses, neither will you take away any article from any spare bed that may happen to be in the sleephall. Should you be in want of bedding or any other article thereof, you will mention it to your Tutoresses, in order that you may get supplied in a regular manner.

4. No change of places with your beds and bedstead is to be made in the sleephall without the advice of your Tutoresses, and the little space between the bedsteads allotted for the more convenient going in and out of the beds and the making up the same is to be kept open.

5. Between the hours of 8 and 11 o'clock in the forenoon and after one o'clock the sleephall is locked. The time to go to your trunks is when the sleephall is open under the Inspection of your Tutoresses.

6. After your beds are made up till 8 o'clock you will prepare yourselves for your classes and have your books, slates &c in readiness and in good order.

7. When you meet in your different classes, do it quietly and in good order, avoiding noise and disputes about places.

8. In school remember to sit straight, avoid eating, play, needless talk &c and pay attention to what you are taught with due decorum.

9. At the close of the hours of your several classes, you will not arise from your places till after the clock has struck, or your Tutoresses have told you to do so and you will not leave the room before you have again placed in order your books, paper, inkstands, slates &c and then you will leave the room, and enter another in silence and due order, avoiding hurry and needless noise and running here and there. No class will enter a room before the former has left it, and then not rush in, but go quietly, bringing every thing wanted along with them.

10. In bringing your embroidery frames and things thereto belonging into the room allotted for their reception, you are not to throw them down at random, but to place them upright against the wall and against each other, and in fetching them away, not throw others down.

11. In going to meetings, you will go decently according to your room divisions, and in every meeting you attend you will show that decorum and attention which is suitable in a place of worship.

12. When the bell rings for dinner or supper you will all go silently into the dining room, join in singing a verse for prayer, during your meals avoid noise and strife. Conduct yourselves mannerly, and use the gifts of God with respect.

   It is a very bad habit to scratch or make holes in the plates, and is forbidden. Every one will find by her plate a knife, fork or spoon. These and every other thing belonging to the dining room is to be left there and none to be taken away. Should any thing be wanting at table, you will ask for it with becoming manners.

13. The time between dinner and the schools in the afternoon you will apply in preparing your sewing work, and to fetch from your trunks what may be necessary before the sleephall is locked at one o'clock.

14. The hours appointed for sewing, knitting &c you will attend as diligently as your other schools. All unnecessary talk is then also to be avoided, as likewise the running in and out of the rooms at random, the more so as this would greatly disturb those that have their school in music or any other school.

15. When at any time between or after schools you are allowed to have a little recreation or to take fresh air in the yard, you will avoid noise & rudeness, and also any play whereby you may hurt one another.

16. In your walks, when you go out of the house, keep together, without running too fast, and never walk at such a distance from your Tutoresses as to be out of sight or hearing.

17. When the townbell rings first in the evening, all who are in the yard or entry are to go into their rooms, and during the meetings of the congregation not to be too loud.

18. At bed time, you will all attend in silence to the evening prayers and then go to bed still and orderly. In the sleephall no talk or other disturbance is allowed, but each recommends herself to the protection of God our Saviour.

If those of the first room should perhaps go a little later to bed than the rest, they have to avoid being noisy, as those that are gone to bed before, ought not to be disturbed.

19. The sickroom will always be ready for the sick and indisposed. When you feel sick, you will mention it to one of your Tutoresses, who will procure a place for you in the sickroom. It is to be noticed that too large a company in the sickroom may be hurtful, and surely is irksome to the sick. You will therefore avoid to be in the sickroom in large companies, and without having obtained leave. Neither will you be noisy there, nor go in and out too frequently.

Should any of you in a slight indisposition be indulged with a little repose on her bed in the sleephall, the rest will not disturb her by going in numbers into the sleephall, and remaining there without attendance or inspection.

20. You will in no case absent yourselves from the environs of your house without having first obtained leave of one of your Tutoresses living in the room with you, and not go any where abroad without the company of one of your Tutoresses.

21. Scratching or writing or cutting with knives on windows, walls, doors, tables &c being a very bad custom, is absolutely and strictly forbidden.

22. Carefulness with fire and candles is most earnestly recommended to all our pupils. You are not allowed to go with fiery coals or firebrands in any open vessel.

23. You have to put your clothes, books, stationary [sic] and all other things at their respective places and keep the closet doors always shut, in order not only that when visitors enter the rooms, they may at all times find the house in good order, but also and principally that you may habituate yourselves to regularity and order.

24. The Inspector, his wife and your Tutoresses having upon them a parental charge in educating and instructing you, have a right to expect from their pupils such conduct, as becomes children towards their parents, or those that are in their place by showing towards them a true respect, love, obedience and attention to their admonitions. But not only in their presence, but also when you are alone, act and speak as in the presence of God.

25. Among yourselves you have to behave towards each other with love, kindness, politeness and forbearance, avoiding every thing that may

cause dispute and quarrels, not allowing yourselves to call bad names, to use mean, lowlife and rude language, or to use any one in a contemptible, slighting or overbearing manner either by words, gestures or other behaviour, but endeavour to show an amiable and sweet temper, even when you have been offended, and a readiness to forgive others and acknowledge your own faults.

26. Such as newly entered the school you will in practice & in endeavour to treat with kindness and civility, giving them all aid and assistance in your power, and striving to remove any thing that may cause them to feel unhappy in a situation entirely new & strange always remembering how you felt when you first entered the school, and you will show them good examples.

27. As evil communication corrupts good manners, every one will be careful in her conversation, not to say any thing indecent, nor to communicate bad things or vices she may have been so unlucky as to have seen or heard at other places.

28. As you have to show civility to every one, so you will do it in a particular manner to strangers or company that visit the school, in making your compliments, offering seats &c and avoiding whispering or laughing among yourselves, as being rudeness, when strangers enter the house, you will avoid running to and rushing upon them, and standing around gazing on them, being ill-mannered in the highest degree.

29. The questions put to you by visitors will be answered by you with civility and with an audible voice, and when you are desired to exhibit before them any specimen of your learning, or give a piece on the instrument, you will not show a reluctance but do it with courtesy and affability.

30. Modesty, courtesy, civility, a mild temper and sweet disposition being an indispensible requisite in your sex, you will be attentive to the instructions given you in this respect, so that your behaviour have no tincture of ill manners.

31. You will carry yourselves erect, whether walking, standing or sitting. In writing, drawing, sewing &c you will endeavour to obtain a habit of sitting erect. You will also endeavour to accustom yourselves to a light and easy gate [sic], treading nicely and not in a clumsy manner with all your weight on the floor.

32. Cleanliness in your persons, your dress, books, rooms in the house

and in all things is seriously recommended, not only for ornaments, but for health's sake also, and decency in the same wise, without which you can not gain esteem. This you will also show in your dress, not allowing yourselves indecencies therein, and not appear too uncovered. A neat and orderly dress, covering every part not to be exposed will also be conducive to health.

When you come out of your rooms, do not stand too long in the passage under an open window or door where the air has a strong current, as this will cause the perspiration to cease, and bring on the concomitant evils of colds so much the more when your dress is too loose and imperfect.

33. It is contrary to good manners to run in great hurry into a room, or in going in or out to slam the door after you, neither should you leave the door open when you find it shut. To become troublesome by going too often and too many at once into other rooms, shows bad manners.

34. When you go into another room or any where else, or have a message or errand to make, you will not forget to make a courtesy, and then deliver your message politely.

35. In your correspondence the rule obtains, that all the letters you send and receive are subject to the inspection of the Inspector and your Tutoresses.

36. The rules to be observed by those, whose parents or relations pay them a visit are:

To return to the school in the evening before 8 o'clock. It is not allowed, to stay over night and sleep in the tavern, except leave is granted in particular cases. In the morning not to go to the tavern too early. During the stay of the parents to behave themselves well at the tavern, and to remain with the parents or relations.

If parents give them a ride, and request some of their companions to be of the party, to inform the parents, that it is not to be permitted unless one of the Tutoresses can be spared to go along.

When parents make but a short visit, the children will be indulged to spend as much time with them as possible, but if they stay some days, it is advisable to frequent the schools, and spend the rest of the time with the parents, which they will certainly approve of knowing that your present time is very precious.

37. When any thing is offered for sale at your house, you will avoid rush-

ing upon it and showing too much eagerness. By being modest and first taking the advice of the Inspector or your Tutoresses, you will stand a chance of obtaining the same things for more moderate prices.

38. Your clothes and other things you can not be allowed to give or barter away on exchange, or to alienate them in any manner whatever.

39. The monthly allowance of pocketmoney from your parents for your own little expence is to be under the control of the Inspector and your Tutoresses, and you have to make use of it with prudence & economy. You will not suffer any thing to be wasted, and habituate yourselves to putting your clothes and every thing in its proper place and in proper order and keep them so. This will teach you also to husband your time and will be the means of your coming into the very important habit of economy and frugality, which is such an essential requisite in your sex for housekeeping.[1]

Although the point seems to have been made rather forcefully already, someone later felt obliged to add this postscript: "If you go out of the school with bad manners, we have not done our duty. We are constrained by a sense of duty."[2]

Yet with all the exacting discipline, there is no indication that either the inspector or his teachers were ever harsh in their treatment of the girls. On the contrary, the Moravians were genuinely fond of children, and their attitude toward the school girls in their care was one of parental affection. Using the room company system, the school made an honest effort to create a family-like atmosphere in which the stern mixture of rules and religion would be tempered by close personal relationships and simple pleasures.

The girls were encouraged to celebrate their birthdays with parties and modest gifts from friends. On Saturday afternoons, they were allowed to have coffee in their rooms. And in warm weather, "pleasure rides" were planned in which one room company at a time would be taken by wagon on a picnic to some interesting spot in the vicinity.

Because in the early years of the school the girls were not able to go home at Christmastime, extra effort was exerted to make the occasion both festive and meaningful for them.

One of the most moving of the traditional Moravian services—still observed today—is the Christmas Eve lovefeast, at which, amid music and following the customary serving of coffee and buns, hundreds of lighted beeswax candles are brought in and passed along the pews until every person present is holding one. The custom had started in Marienborn (Germany) on Christmas Eve in 1747 when Bishop Johannes von Watteville ended a children's service by distributing lighted tapers, which, he told the children, signified the "flame of love" kindled by Christ's birth and sufferings. The Brethren had brought the tradition to America and then down the long road from Pennsylvania to North Carolina.

For many years, only the children of the congregation were given candles. But the Moravians made no distinction between their own children and the girls in the boarding school; everyone in the school attended the Christmas Eve lovefeast, and pupils under twelve received candles along with the boys and girls of Salem. Lest the older pupils feel slighted by this, those over twelve were allowed to attend the New Year's Eve "watchnight" service, which meant that they could stay up until after midnight!

On Christmas morning when the girls scurried from the cold sleep hall down to their warm living rooms, each found at her place at the long study table a lighted taper, a small gift, cakes, nuts and other confections.

For weeks ahead of Christmas, the school girls were hard at work on their "dialogue," which they would perform for Salem's dignitaries and occasionally for visiting parents. These dialogues, written by the inspector, purportedly were a sort of conversation in which the girls discussed among themselves various aspects relative to the birth of Christ. But the inspector, being a minister, always seemed to let his inclination to preach get the better of dramatic instinct. And the texts of some of these Christmas dialogues tend to be a great deal more preoccupied with the death than with the birth of Jesus, describing the Crucifixion in rather gruesome detail—a carry-over, perhaps, from the latter years of Zinzendorf's influence, when the Unity had been temporarily caught up in an obsession with the wounds of Christ. Consequently, what came out of the mouths of eleven- and twelve-year-old girls as "conversation" is little short of astounding.

The dialogue presented in 1808,[3] for example, begins this way:

All being seated and two of the Pupils behind the scene.

SUNG: Still let me sing of love divine &c.

ALL SING: Come ye redeemed of the Lord
	Your grateful tribute bring.

Sally Murfree comes out from behind the scene, curtesies [sic] to the company, looks around as in amazement, and, standing before the company says:

SALLY MURFREE. What is that I see? Am I deceived? It seems to me you have a night of rejoicing. [*Keeps standing*]

At the latter part Becky Long comes out in the same manner, looks at the decorations and says:

BECKY LONG. I am amazed! What can the meaning of these decorations be on this night? [*Keeps standing*]

MARY JONES. Will you have the goodness to be seated, my dear! We will endeavor jointly to give an explanation, and I think you will join and help us along, for the history of this night, I conjecture, is familiar to you.

[*Both take their seats and Mary Jones continues:*]

We commemorate this night an highly interesting event—an event too great for our weak conception to reason upon—a miracle of God far beyond what the sages of the world could pretend to divine.

MARY LONG. What can you mean by this event, my dear! I am extremely anxious to be informed.

SARAH LOVE. It is the eventful birth of the Saviour of the world—The Son of God becoming the Son of man, and showing us the love of God to us his creatures in its fullest extent by the assumption of a relationship with us.

CYNTHIA COPELAND. I would be highly pleased to go a little into a conversation concerning the birth and life of this our Saviour—Will you be pleased to introduce the topic?

SARAH LOVE. With all my heart, as far as I am able, but we will ask the indulgence of the respected company, and we take it for granted they will judge favorably of our youthful essay, faulty as our performance may be. . . .

With that, the dialogue launches into a discussion, couched in similar language, of the events leading up to the birth of Christ, the birth itself, and the joy that it brought to the world. Then turning to a transparent painting of the Nativity scene—festooned in greenery and lighted from behind by a candle—the cast speaks of the smiling baby and the serenity of Mary's face. From there, the conversation moves quickly toward the Crucifixion, and dwells upon it graphically:

SARAH LOVE. Thus stood the meek, patient Jesus with a purple robe and crown of thorns, his soul tortured, his flesh lacerated by the lashes of the scourges, his head pierced with thorns, his face covered with blood mixed with the spittle of sinners, and his whole bruised body bedecked with gore. . . .

Finally, after the meaning of the death has been fully explained, the dialogue returns to the blessed event celebrated at Christmas and concludes with a song and this message:

MARY JONES. May the love wherewith we are all loved never escape our thoughts! May our meditation be continually fixed on Jesus' incarnation and death, and may we forever abide in him! So will he abide in us—and blessed—completely blessed will be all our days.

Whether the girls understood all of what they were saying, they nevertheless loved performing before an audience. And the dialogues were so popular with the townspeople that they were held in the *saal* of the old *Gemein Haus* to accommodate the crowds who came to hear them. Sometimes, too, it was necessary to give as many as three performances.

So it was that, despite the overall regimentation, there were moments of fun and excitement in school life. And apparently, after the first pangs of homesickness, most of the girls were quite happy and content. As one wrote to her parents on the eve of her departure:

Although I am so anxious to see my dear parents and friends, yet I always feel a deep regret when I think of leaving Salem. It seems as if I were leaving home, for I have become so attached to my friends and teachers that it appears almost heartrending to think of parting with them. . . .[4]

In all of the regulations so carefully spelled out for both teachers and pupils, however, nowhere is there ever a reference to the girls' behavior in regard to boys. Perhaps the school authorities felt that the girls were too young to be interested in boys. Or perhaps it was just that the separation of the sexes before marriage was so inherent

in Moravian thinking that the school never envisaged boy-girl relationships as a problem. Or it may be simply that those who drew
up the rules figured that they would deal with the situation when and
if it arose and that, in the meantime, the less said on the subject, the
better.

In any case, the problem did arise—fairly soon, in fact, after the
boarding school opened. On July 13, 1808, Inspector Steiner received
a letter from Thomas B. Hunt of Union District, South Carolina,
whose stepdaughter, Sarah Winters, was a student at Salem:

Am under necessity to acquaint you with painful circumstances. There's
in my neighborhood a young man, John Roachele, has taken attachment
to my poor girl in your charge & makes brags he'll take her from school in
all events. In Gods name hope you'll take every care as he is set out from
this for your part of Country & perhaps will come as Gentleman & only
intends to spite me & poor girl's mother & ruin name of y^r institution.
Therefor [sic] for y^r honor trust you will not be lacking on y^r part to give
Credit to y^r institution, honor to y^r self & satisfaction to friends.[5]

As Hunt had predicted, the young man arrived at the school. But
obviously the romance was not as one-sided as the girl's stepfather
had implied. And Steiner minced no words in informing him of that
fact:

John Roachele has hitherto behaved well. He disclaimed forcing or en-
ticing Miss Winter from here now. He has been in school & has behav^d
without exception. His intentions in future do not know and am afraid
Miss Winter would be glad for a chance to elope with him. Solicit you to
take Miss Winter home as soon as possible to relieve our anxiety. Have no
prison or nunnery to shut up young people, if they can not be seen by
anyone without watching they are not fit objects for our school.[6]

With that, Hunt changed his tune completely and begged that the
girl be permitted to remain in the school. Steiner consented, but only
"if R. does not come."[7]

As for the Salem boys, the tight pattern of school life allowed the
boarding school girls little opportunity to see them, except perhaps
at a distance during the daily walks. Even at the congregation worship services, the boys sat on the opposite side of the church.

The boys in Salem had had their own school since shortly after the town's school for little girls had begun, and by 1794 it was offering advanced work in writing, "reckoning," history, geography, geometry, Latin, and English, with music and "the drawing of landscapes and flowers" also a part of the curriculum.

As early as 1783, too, arrangements had been made for boys of Salem and the outlying Moravian communities to board in the school, which at that time was in the house later occupied by Abraham Steiner when he first became inspector of the Girls' Boarding School. Three years later, Frederic Marshall reported to Herrnhut that the school was increasing and "the snail is about to outgrow its little rented shell."[8] Consequently, a handsome new brick building for the Boys' School was completed in 1794. This building still stands, facing the northwest corner of Salem Square.

Encouraged by their success at the Girls' Boarding School, the Brethren in 1810 decided to open their Boys' School also to outsiders, but they were unable to recruit enough qualified teachers and those plans were never carried out. Another attempt was made in the 1820s, and a few boys from other places did enroll. But, probably because there were numerous other academies for boys in the South, the school never gained the reputation enjoyed by the Girls' Boarding School, and in less than two years it was returned to its original status as a school for Moravian boys only.

There were times, in fact, when the Boys' School was in financial difficulty. And in those times, the prosperous Girls' Boarding School generously shared some of its wealth, once donating two globes ("one of the earth and one of the heavens"[9]) and, in 1816, making a cash donation of $69.

When the Brethren had first begun to talk about opening the Boys' School to outside boarders, some of the parents of the girls in the Salem school at that time looked upon the prospect with less than enthusiasm. In one of Inspector Steiner's letter books is the digest of a letter written to Samuel Pannill of Green Hill, Virginia, in which he assured the apparently concerned father that he "need not be afraid of Male Academy, pupils will be young & number small."[10]

So if the Moravians seemed to go to extraordinary lengths to protect the innocence of the school girls during those early years, the impetus was not theirs alone. Even so, a minister of Raleigh, writing many years later,[11] was sharply critical of the cloistered atmosphere, which, he claimed, denied the girls "the privilege of society outside the institution." And as a case in point, he cited the plight of a "little, timid girl from the interior of Virginia" who, after being at the Girls' Boarding School in Salem for two years, "returned home, almost afraid to speak to a gentleman from her long seclusion from society."

But if such, indeed, were the girl's inhibitions, she must have managed to overcome them rather quickly, as soon after she left school, she was married. Her bridegroom, as it turned out, was the critical minister from Raleigh.

8

Inside the Classroom

I
N EARLY JANUARY, 1807, IT WAS BROUGHT TO THE
attention of the House Conference that the girls in several of the
room companies were asking to be put to bed too early in the evening.
The reason, the conference conceded, was that the Sisters did not
really know how to keep their charges occupied after supper, especially in winter when it was too dark and too cold to go outside for a
walk. They had tried to interest the girls in needlework, but as the
children had just spent three hours during the afternoon in sewing
and knitting classes, the suggestion had met with a notable lack of
enthusiasm. And after that, the Sisters—by this time of day probably
too tired to think—had run out of ideas.

Concluding that perhaps a little more varied daytime schedule
would help relieve the situation, the conference voted to divert one
hour in the afternoon from the usual handwork to reading instruction. "A trial is also to be made with keeping the children more occupied of an evening, in connection with which the reading of useful
books could be of help."[1]

The conference recognized, however, that "there are scarcely any
books for reading in the house,"[2] and that the school's small library
would have to be enlarged. Indeed, if the books on hand as listed in
the school's 1807 inventory[3] represented the selection of "bedtime
reading" offered the little girls at that time, the need for additional
material seems to have been rather dire:

Webster's Pronouncing Dictionary

1 Philadelphia School Dictionary

Murray's Grammar

Buchanan's regular English Syntax

Art of Speaking

American Spellingbooks

Scotts Lessons in Elocution

American accountant

American tutors assistant

Goughs arithmetic

Mitchel's Book keeping

Sharps universal history

Millots Elements of general History

Johnson's introduction to history

Rollins ancient history

Fanning on the Globe

Ferguson's introduction to Astronomy

Guthries Geography improved with an Atlas

Modern Geography by Davies

The World displayed

Jefferson's notes on Virginia

History of the Indian Mission by Loskiel

Bruce's Travels into Abyssinia

Tour thro' Canada

Michaux Travels in North America

Description of 300 Animals

Select Stories 2 Vols. one Vol. thereof missing, consequently worth nothing

Letters from a mother to her daughter

The Ladies friend

Minor Morals, by Charlotte Smith

The School for children

The Boarding school

Juvenile letters

Friend of Youth

Address to young persons

Present for a little girl

Premium

Ladies Pocket Library

Young Misses Magazine

Life of Joseph, the Son of Jacob

Robinson Crusoe

Sketches on the rotation of crops

Pilgrims Progress

Village Dialogues

Doddridge's Sermons

Rafael's Sermons

Acts of the days of the Son of Man

Liturgic Hymns of the United Brethren

Brotherly Agreement

Summary of Doctrine

English Tunebook

The melodist

6 musical books

Music, several printed
Copies

American Drawing Magazine

1 map of the United
States

1 Ditto of Europe

1 Ditto of Asia

1 Ditto of Africa

1 Ditto of America

1 pair Globes

Books in constant use in the
rooms

22 Scotts lessons in
elocution

3 Philadelphia School
Dictionaries

9 Preaching of the
Cross

5 Excursions into Bethlehem
& Nazareth

20 literary magazines or
thereabouts

The $5 entrance fee charged each new student had been earmarked for the support of the school library, and presumably it was out of this fund that the additional "books for reading" were purchased. Just what titles the inspector chose for this purpose we don't know, but we can be fairly certain that there was a strong thread of "usefulness" running through anything he selected. For although the education of girls in Salem was not as broad in scope as that offered the boys, it was no less serious in concept. Froth and frills had no place in it, and the idea of buying books merely for the school girls' entertainment would never have crossed the inspector's mind. At best, the time that the girls spent at the school was too short; he was determined that as little of it as possible should be wasted in any pursuit that did not improve the mind, strengthen the morals, beautify the spirit, or develop useful skills.

The school day, Monday through Friday, began at 8 A.M. and continued until 4 P.M., with a two-hour intermission from 11 A.M. until 1 P.M. for dinner (the day's main meal) and for allowing the girls time to get what they needed from their trunks in the sleep hall.

The class periods were one hour in length, and every girl had a different schedule, depending on her aptitude in each subject. As of January, 1808, for example, Elizabeth Simkins, almost thirteen, of Edgefield Courthouse, South Carolina, was in the "first" (highest)

Schedule of classes 1809

class in reading, the "second" classes in grammar and geography, and the "third" classes in cyphering and drawing. At the same time, Martha Powe of Chesterfield District, South Carolina, who had just turned thirteen, was in the "first" classes in reading and cyphering, the "second" in grammar and drawing, and the "third" in geography. As a girl mastered the work at one level in a given subject, she was immediately moved into a higher class in that subject. With this system of allowing each girl to advance at her own pace, the Salem Moravians must have been among the earliest Americans to practice a principle of education that later was to be widely preached. And when one considers the somewhat communal life that they themselves led at that time and the strict regimentation imposed on all other phases of boarding school life, this emphasis on the individual in the area of academics seems all the more progressive.

A girl's schedule of class work changed frequently as she advanced in one subject or the other. As of February, 1807, for instance, the week's study for Martha Rives, thirteen, of Columbia, South Carolina, was arranged as follows:

Monday: 8– 9 Writing
9–10 Cyphering
10–11 Grammar
3– 4 Drawing & Painting
(alternating every other week with music)

Tuesday: 8– 9 Writing
9–10 Cyphering
1– 2 Embroidery
2– 3 Embroidery
3– 4 Drawing & Painting
(alternating every other week with music)

Wednesday: 8– 9 History & Geography
9–10 Cyphering
1– 2 Embroidery
2– 3 Embroidery
3– 4 Drawing & Painting
(alternating every other week with music)

Thursday: 8– 9 Writing
9–10 Cyphering
10–11 History & Geography
1– 2 Embroidery
2– 3 Embroidery
3– 4 Embroidery
(alternating every other week with music)

Friday: 8– 9 Orthography
9–10 Cyphering
3– 4 Drawing & Painting
(alternating every other week with music)[4]

It is odd that there is no time in Martha's schedule allocated for reading, but it isn't likely that any girl escaped instruction in that very important subject. Martha appears to have had one or more class hours free every day except Thursday; no doubt at least several of those hours were spent in reading, if not in actual reading instruction. At any rate, we know that she was not left to her own devices during those periods, because it was a strict rule that any so-called "free" time was to be used for plain sewing, "marking" (pattern making), or knitting.

All of the girls were encouraged to make their own school dresses (usually of calico). Even so, much of the dressmaking chore fell to the teachers, who also made the caps worn by the pupils when they went outside the building. These caps were of bobinet and had round crowns edged by full double ruching. Eliza Vierling, who went to the boarding school as a teacher in 1826, recalled many years later that one Christmas she "had to make 21 of these caps, one for each girl in my room and often sat up until 12 o'clock working at them but did not receive a cent of pay for the extra work."[5]

As the House Conference had made clear at one of its first sessions, the teachers were expected to do this sewing despite the fact that all of them had demanding supervisory duties and carried heavy teaching loads besides. According to the 1807 class schedule, Sister Reichel, for example, did not have a single free class period from 8 A.M. until 4 P.M. on any one of the five school days. And she had to prepare lessons in an array of subjects: history and geography, grammar, globes, orthography, music, drawing, painting, and embroidery.

Particularly in embroidery, Sister Reichel perhaps was more skilled than any of the other teachers at that time, having learned the art firsthand at the Bethlehem Seminary, seat of the distinctive school of Moravian needlework which is recognized today as one of the finest in early America. "The scattered bits of [Moravian] needlework which remain to us are so fine, so clear, so thoroughly exhaustive of all excellence in technique that they are to the art of embroidery what the ivory miniature is to painting."[6]

Inventories of the Girls' Boarding School at Salem indicate that from the institution's earliest years an effort was made to teach some of the intricate forms of embroidery perfected in Bethlehem—tambour, ribbon work, crepe work, pictures worked in silk on satin. The inventory of 1805[7] lists such items on hand as "fine London silk," "White thick Sattin," "gold chord," "silver spangles," and "33 Embroidery frames." And Steiner's letter books are sprinkled with orders to an importing firm in Philadelphia for various colors of silk thread —an item that became increasingly hard to obtain in the years leading up to and during the War of 1812, when trade with England was cut off.

Ancestral Home of James Knox Polk

**Mourning embroidery done by Sarah Childress (Polk) while a student
at Salem Academy 1817–1818**

The extant samples of students' embroidery of that time testify to
the Salem school's success in carrying on the tradition of fine Moravian needlework. Among the most interesting of them are several
"mourning pieces"—a popular form in which silk embroidery was
combined with an inscription written in India ink to fashion a com-
memorative picture, usually one of mourners beside the grave of a
recently departed loved one.

In their painting classes, the girls concentrated largely on delicate
watercolor renditions of flowers, which were painted directly on the
pages of small autograph books or on single sheets of paper to be
framed. One of the remaining samples of the latter is a spray of spring
flowers dominated by a single pink rose—painted by Peggy Allison of
York District, South Carolina, and presented to Inspector Steiner on
his fifty-second birthday in 1810.

The girls taking piano lessons—and there appear to have been quite a number of them—did not lack for variety in sheet music. From its earliest years, the town of Salem had maintained an excellent music library, and undoubtedly the boarding school followed the tradition by constantly adding to its own store. Knowing the frugality of the early Moravians, though, we imagine that when the school acquired new printed music, it ordered only one copy of each piece and then assigned some teacher or older girl to the tedious task of making additional copies by hand. These would then have been sold to the boarding school pupils. In the account books for 1808,[8] for example, Nancy Pannill of Pittsylvania County, Virginia, was charged for the following pieces of music: "God save great Washington," "D° [Ditto] with Variations," "The Cottage in the Moor," "The Soldier's Return," "When pensive I thought," "Mary I believe thee true," "Anna Fare thee well," and "Andantino, primo & Secondo."

Music, painting, and fine needlework were all considered "special" courses and were given only to those girls whose parents paid an extra $2 per course each quarter. The same arrangement held true for town girls who attended these special classes in the boarding school. The Elders' Conference ruled that "the congregation children also shall pay a moderate fee when they take music or drawing,"[9] and, in the case of parents too poor to pay the fee, free lessons would be given only "if a child shows special talent and a promise of future usefulness."[10]

Ever since congregation parents had complained that girls in the town school were not receiving enough attention, a conscientious effort had been made not only to bolster the town school itself but also to integrate some of its class work with that of the boarding school. A certain amount of separation of the two schools was unavoidable, of course. For one thing, due to the Moravian practice of sending children to school when they were hardly more than infants, the age range of the town school was considerably lower than that of the boarding school, and instruction there necessarily had to be on a more elementary level. Also, there was the language difference; Salem families still spoke German in their homes, and although Moravian children were taught English, their parents expected the school to teach them to read and write in their own language as well. Samples of writing exercises done by town girls in 1809,[11] for instance, are in both English and German, and, incidentally, are as indicative of Moravian education in their subject matter as in their exquisite penmanship:

Love honest actions
Shame attends vice
Want accompanies sloth

MAY THE 19TH 1809   ANNA MARIA VOGLER
SALEM   AGED 7 YEARS

Make much of time
Nothing is certain
According to your pains will be your gains

MAY THE 19TH 1809   MARIA M. LANDMAN
SALEM   AGED 7 YEARS

Observe moral duties
Promise cautiously
Gentle and prudent deportment is very becoming

MAY THE 17TH 1809   MARIA THERESIA SHOBER
SALEM   AGED 10 YEARS

Even if he had not been nudged by parents' complaints, the inspector would have had reason enough to pay closer attention to the education of the town girls. For it had become evident quite early that the school would have to depend on the Single Sisters of Salem to supply its teachers. If this source were to be kept open, it was essential that girls of the Salem congregation be given advanced study in order that when they became old enough to join the Single Sisters' choir, they could qualify for the teaching positions. So gradually the better scholars among the town girls were brought into the boarding school classes. And by 1811, fifteen "day students" had joined the boarders for classes in reading, writing, arithmetic, English grammar, geography and history, music, drawing, and fine needlework.

Despite the Moravian bent for order and planning, it was some time after the boarding school opened before the school year would fall into any sort of pattern or schedule. With transportation so difficult in the early 1800s, the setting of definite dates for opening and closing a school term would have been impractical. Girls had to be accepted whenever their parents could find a way to get them to

**Watercolor done by a student, Peggy Allison, and presented to
Abraham Steiner on his fifty-second birthday**

Salem, which could be in the spring or the summer or the fall—or
even the winter, if the girls lived close by and the roads were passable. So the school was in continuous operation throughout the year,
and when a new pupil arrived, she was simply fitted into classes already in progress.

Departures were equally as erratic. Girls left school at any time that
their parents, from necessity or whim, chose to send for them, and
frequently the inspector had no inkling that a girl would be leaving
until her father or his emissary appeared in Salem to take her home.
Some girls stayed only a few months; others remained two or three
years. With such continual coming and going, a school calendar was
out of the question. And so was any prescribed course of study requisite to "graduation," although as early as 1807 the school was
issuing a diploma of sorts to girls upon their departure:

Be it known that Miss Mary M. Lewis, daughter of Major Richard Lewis, of Rutherford County, State of N.C., has for some time past, resided and been a pupil, in the Boarding School for Female Education, in Salem, N.C., and as she is now on the point of leaving the said Institution, the Inspector, and Tutoresses of the same cannot withhold from her the testimony of applause due her for her general good conduct, as a Pupil in said Institution. She has followed her studies with all assiduity and has made good progress therein, very willingly submitted to the rules of the school, and by her good conduct and strictly moral behavior, has gained the goodwill and esteem of those under whom she has been placed, and the sincere regard of the whole school.

Given at Salem, the 9th day of October, 1807, for myself, and in the name of the Tutoresses of the said Institution.

ABRAHAM STEINER, *Inspector* [12]

There is no evidence that the school girls at that time were graded individually in their various studies. But early in his term as inspector, Abraham Steiner instituted an annual "Examination," at which each girl, in the presence of an audience, was placed on her mettle to show what she had learned in the classroom.

The first of these Examinations—which were to evolve into gala entertainment events, attracting hundreds of visitors—was held in the early summer of 1808. And the Salem diary entry for June 18, 1808, reports it in some detail:

Today was the formal close of the Examination held this week in our Boarding and day school, in the presence of members of the Aeltesten Conferenz and the parents who were in town. In the first session, in the morning at eight o'clock, Br. Reichel heard the town girls read in English and in German, and catechised them on the selections in the reader on Jesus Christ our Saviour. In the following sessions, at eight and nine in the morning and at one in the afternoon, Br. Steiner examined the boarding pupils and the older congregation girls who are included in the higher classes according to their age and ability, in English reading, grammar, history, geography, and the use of the globes. Then specimens of writing, drawing, painting, knitting, tambour work, and other feminine handicrafts were taken around for inspection, while the music pupils played on the piano and songs were sung. This was the first such Examination held in our Boarding School and some shortcomings and errors were noted, but on the other hand there were many attractive evidences of industry and ability. These exercises were followed by a lovefeast, accompanied by music and singing.[13]

Copies of the questions asked the girls at some of these early Examinations have been preserved. And, perhaps more than any other source, they afford insight into not only the nature of what was being taught in the classrooms at that time but also the method by which the children learned.

Plainly, much of the learning was by rote. For under each of these questions is a carefully written answer so formal in its wording that no child of ten or twelve would possibly have produced it except by pure memorization:

Q. How many governments does the country of Louisiana contain?

A. The vast country of Louisiana contains the Territory of New Orleans in the South, and that of Louisiana in the North, the former of which is now to be created into a State.[14]

Q. How was our independence established?

A. A man was raised up by Providence to command our armies, who was able to make the best of our slender resources, & to supply their defeat by his extraordinary genius. George Washington, if any mortal man ever merited the appellation of Father of His Country, surely merits that name.[15]

True, such questions and answers were prepared for public hearing and were designed to impress an audience. In the private examinations, which the inspector conducted a few weeks beforehand, the girls no doubt were left to their own recall and rhetoric. Even so, preparation for this public display of their learning must have entailed prodigious memory work.

In the copies of questions and answers, the name of a pupil is written beside each. It is not clear whether this was merely a guide for the inspector or whether each girl was alerted beforehand as to which question would be asked her. At that, though, a girl would have had to memorize one or more of these stilted answers in every subject which she had been studying—plus, probably, a piano piece, a recitation, or a role in one of the dialogues. And we can imagine what stage fright a little girl must have suffered as she sat waiting, in her new white dress, to be called to the platform to spell a word, parse a sentence, work a problem in arithmetic, locate a foreign city on the globe, or answer a question in ancient history.

The questions themselves reflect something of the breadth and depth of classroom work by which the Salem school had earned its reputation as a pioneer in female education.

In history, for example, the questions ranged from the Creation all the way up to that asked Therese Shober in 1812: "How long is it that the United States are independent?"[16] (The answer: "It will be 36 years on the 4th of July."[17]) And at that same Examination, Elizabeth Bibb outlined the government of Egypt; Betsy Foll (probably Pfohl) gave the date for the building of Rome; Polly Hardeman told when the French Revolution began; and Mary Morton was called upon to answer: "In whose reign were St. Peter and St. Paul put to death?"

By 1823, questions were being asked about the Peruvian monarchy and various aspects of English, Greek, Roman, Mexican, and Scottish history.

In the grammar examination of 1813,[18] Amanda Nisbet declined the word "servant"; Mary Parrish was quizzed on the variations of adjectives; Eliza Wyly parsed the sentence, "My cousin Harriet has read too many novels for her benefit."

Arithmetic examinations covered the multiplication tables and such complicated problems as: "What is the Interest on 475 Dollars at 6 pr ct. Interest for 6 months?"[19] In orthography, the girls were asked to spell such words as "jeopardy," "defrauder," and "pentapetalous." And once Nancy Kain drew a question in which she was asked to spell "right," "rite," "ride," "write," and "wright."[20]

Geography was considered one of the more important areas of study. Among questions in that subject were: "What is an Isthmus?" "What is the boundary between New Hampshire & Vermont?" "What is the most important city on the banks of the Danube?" and "How are Paris and Rome situated in regard to each other, and what mountains are on the straight course between both cities?"[21] In the related subject, globes, pupils were asked to come to the front and "find the Places on the Globe that are under the same Meridian or in the same Longitude with us"[22] or determine "what o'clock is it at Copenhagen when we have 5 o'clock in the morning."[23]

There were questions on religion: "How is Faith brought about?"

For the Examination in the Boarding school
at Salem, the 26th of May 1810.

Hannah Christman — Qu. Into how many classes are the letters in the
Alphabet divided?
A. Into two: Vowels and Consonants.

Adeline Allison — Qu. What are Vowels?
A. Simple sounds, such as a, e, i, o, u.

~~Lucy Rives~~
Patsey George — Qu. What are Consonants?
A. Consonants are letters, that cannot be pronounced
without the help of a vowel. All letters which are
not vowels, are consonants, such as b, c, d.

Eliza Gahagan — Qu. What is Ch?
A. A compound consonant.

Polly Rives — Qu. How is it generally pronounced?
A. Like tch, as in church, chaff.

Fanny Shipman — Qu. How is the syllable arch pronounced?
A. Generally ark when it preceedes a vowel, as in
Archangel — and artch, when it stands before
a consonant, as in archbishop.

Qu. How many sounds has the simple vowel o?
A. Five principal sounds.
It sounds like o long — as in more.
like o short — as in love.
like oo — as in move.
like aw long — as in fork.
like aw short — as in not.

Qu.

Questions and answers for the Examination in 1810

and "What is wrought in man by the preaching of the gospel?"[24] And others on the history of music: "Was Music at first in the same perfection as we find it at present?" and "When was the Oratorio, or musical drama invented?"[25]

The examination in natural philosophy usually took the form of a dialogue in which a group of girls engaged in a learned "conversation" about gravity, heat, motion, and the like. In one of these, a girl named Fanny Coalter was assigned to contribute this nugget of knowledge:

> Everything that may be denominated body, is thus formed again or decomposed of cohesion, but may be dissolved again or decomposed by its grand antagonist principle, fire, or calorie in the language of chemistry. These two opposing powers keep nature in a state of perpetual motion, compose bodies, decompose them, and form the decomposed particles again into new bodies. It may be considered as an Axiom, that bodies are capable in certain circumstances, of three states of solidity, fluidity, and gas.[26]

Clearly, those who composed these dialogues were not striving for dramatic effects. And it is hard to say whether one's sympathy should be primarily with the school girls who had to memorize and speak this ponderosity or with the audience who had to sit on the hard church pews and listen to it. At any rate, it must have been following just such a dialogue that a teacher in the Boys' School was once moved to observe: "It was boring to listen to a dialogue on a hot day ... give me a nice algebra example, there is nothing so cooling and refreshing."[27]

9

Mushrooming Enrollment

OR THREE YEARS INSPECTOR STEINER HAD LIVED
with the inconvenience of having his residence too far from
his office. He had not complained, but now his daughters were growing up; Polly was sixteen, Sarah fourteen, and Elisabeth had just
turned nine. In his opinion, it was getting "dangerous" for the girls,
especially Polly and Sarah, to reside so close to the Single Brothers'
House. And he appealed to the Elders' Conference for another dwelling for his family.

At the time of his request—June, 1809—there was no other house
available for him. The Elders nevertheless fully appreciated Steiner's
problems, and by September of that year they had begun to consider
building an official residence for the inspector of the Girls' Boarding
School on the vacant lot just east of the Boys' School.

From the standpoint of convenience, the site was ideal, being directly across the street from the church and only a few steps away from
both the *Gemein Haus* and the Girls' Boarding School building.
True, the Elders conceded, the lot was not on the line by which water
was piped from springs northwest of town to the principal buildings
in Salem, but, in their view, it would be simple enough to dig a well
on the property. The Elders also acknowledged that money was generally scarce at that time; yet the boarding school itself was prosper-
ing and no doubt could assume the financing of a new building with
relatively little strain. Moreover, most of the major construction
needed in Salem in the foreseeable future had been finished; materials and labor thus should not be too difficult to obtain.

All in all, the Elders agreed, conditions were favorable enough to propose to the proper Salem boards that a house for the inspector be constructed. The proposal was approved by the *Aufseher Collegium* on October 3, 1809, and by the Congregation Council on October 19. Plans were drawn immediately, and by the end of the month, the Elders' Conference had given them final approval.

The house would be a one-story brick structure, forty-eight feet long and thirty-three feet wide, and would stand, facing the square, on the northwest corner of what are now Church and Academy streets. A hallway, nine feet wide, would bisect the building from front to back, separating a living room and a bedroom on the east side from another living room and a kitchen on the west side. The Elders noted that "another room can be arranged under the roof."[1]

A cellar with vaulted ceiling would extend only under the two west rooms, and would be accessible both by an outside door and by a stairway on the inside of the building.

It is not clear when construction actually began. But an undated document found in the Salem College Library and turned over to the Moravian archivist in 1953 appears to be a building contract between Steiner and a man named David Blum.

According to its provisions:

(1) for every thousand Bricks David Blum puts to the Walls to s^d house including Outside Walls, Middle or Partition Walls, Chimneys &c^a he is to have One Dollar & 50 cts.

(2) for each & every Arch over the Windows s^d Blum is to have 50 cents & for every Arch over the 2 house Doors One Dollar.

In consideration thereof s^d Blum promiseth to finish off the 4 outside Walls & two Gable ends & Chimney's above the roof Viz—

(1) to paint each Arch over the Windows & Door outside Colour or paint such as Mr. Steiner will furnish him with.

(2) Each & every Joint between each Brick to pencil white with Lime &c^a

(3) after finishing s^d Walls to take down the Scaffold, with the help of the hands working at the Building.

(4) s^d Blum also promises to help with his Men now in his employment at the raising of the Scaffold.

All and every of the above mentioned articles s^d David Blum promises to fulfill, & to have every thing done in a neat & workmanlike manner. Mr. Steiner will furnish s^d Blum with all the Tools, Boxes &c^a necessary for a Building, except such as the masons shall want for laying Bricks–Also find [supply] all the Workmen & attenders in Victuals & Drinks during the Time they are at Work at the Building.[2]

Blum and his men must have proved satisfactory workmen; or else, having authorized the construction, Salem's governing boards simply shifted the full responsibility to Steiner and concerned themselves with other town matters. At any rate, there is no further mention of the Inspector's House in their diaries and minutes until March 26, 1811, when the *Aufseher Collegium* expressed caution that "the steps leading up to the new living quarters of the Inspector shall not take too much room nor bar the footpath too much."[3]

Like all Salem buildings, the new house stood flush with the footpath, and, as its front door was some four or five feet from ground level, steps going straight up to the doorway would indeed have blocked the path for pedestrians. The builders solved the problem by making a small landing at door level, with a flight of steps leading off it on either side. In that way, the entrances extended over the footpath by only the width of the narrow landing.

By the summer of 1811, the building was nearing completion. Blum's men—supposedly well-supplied with tools, victuals, and drinks by Inspector Steiner—had gone about their work with dispatch. And the new house with its Flemish bond brickwork, its clay tile roof, the "eyebrow" arches over its windows, and the curving hood over its doorway presented quite an attractive addition to the buildings ringing Salem's square.

It was ready for occupancy by late summer, and on August 30 members of the Elders' Conference "had a happy lovefeast with Br. and Sr. Steiner, in honor of their moving into their new house."[4] From that day to the present, the Inspector's House has served as administrative headquarters for the institution, although the residence of the chief administrative officer long since has been located elsewhere in Salem.

The Steiners must have been delighted both with the conveniences of their new house and with the relief of having their daughters safely removed from the Single Brothers. But in exchange for these advantages, they were obliged to give up some of their family privacy. For every night, from the time they moved in, eight little girls from the boarding school came to their house to sleep.

Enrollment in the school had increased substantially. By the end of 1810, there were fifty pupils, which had necessitated the re-activation of the fourth room company. A year later, the number had grown to seventy. As the school building had been designed to accommodate only about sixty, sleeping space for the overflow had to be arranged in other houses in town. So the new Steiner house, with its large room "under the roof," was the first to be commandeered for this purpose.

Lack of space was to be a steadily mounting problem during the next fifteen years, as the popularity of Salem's school for girls spread over a broadening sphere of the South, leading more and more parents to seek admission for their daughters. As early as the summer of 1812, the Elders' Conference worriedly discussed the inadequacy of dining facilities. And a year later, because of "the all-too-great number of boarding pupils, which has continued in spite of efforts to reduce the number,"[5] the Elders explored the possibility of constructing a second sleep hall at the rear of the school building.

Plans for such an addition were actually drawn, and would include both a dormitory and a dining hall, but for some reason never mentioned in the records, these plans were not carried out. Whatever caused the change of mind, it certainly was not that the need for additional space had diminished. On the contrary, the problem of overcrowding became even more critical during the summer and early fall of 1813 when at times there were as many as ninety girls enrolled.

Steiner and members of the Helpers' Conference (who served as trustees of the school) did everything in their power to discourage the rush of applications. In the spring of 1814, an advertisement was placed in newspapers of several states, announcing "(1) that for the space of eight months no pupils can be received except those already accepted; (2) that in accordance with the published rules of the institution no girls will be received unless they have applied in advance and have been accepted."[6] And at the Examination that year, the assembled parents and other visitors were asked "that they would make known in the various places where they lived, or would confirm notice already given, that for the present it was impossible to receive more pupils, and that parents who were planning to send their daughters here would have to give up the idea."[7]

Applications nevertheless continued to pour in, and Steiner's letter books are filled with firm replies to persistent parents:

Can't be done now, are too full.[8]

School is too much filled & Measles are in parts.[9]

Promised you lately with hesitation to admit y[r] Daughter into Board[g] school, under impression that she had some previous promise. Find now, that this is mistake. Take therefore back promise, don't like to be trifled with & Trustees have resolved not to admit any at all for unlimited time. Can't admit her.[10]

Parents were not easily discouraged, however. If there was a chance that his daughter could be squeezed into the school— even though she would have to board with a family in town—a father seldom hesitated to bring her to Salem. Ludwig Eberhardt, a clockmaker, and Johann Gottlob Schroeter, the town's tailor, were among the Salem craftsmen who opened their homes to the young boarders. Most of these artisans, hard-pressed for cash, welcomed this opportunity to boost their income, but Steiner and other Salem leaders viewed the situation with growing concern.

With girls scattered all over town, it was impossible for the school to exercise proper supervision over them; already "undesirable results"[11] had been noted, "including the young men of the neighborhood seeking to make and maintain acquaintance with such girls."[12] Moreover, the fireplace in the Single Sisters' kitchen was taxed to its limit and the Sisters themselves exhausted by the burden of preparing meals for the constantly increasing numbers. The mushrooming classes usurped every available space in the school building, including the schoolroom of the town girls, who were moved to the *Gemein Haus*. And the inspector's proverbial problem of keeping qualified teachers became even more acute.

Already Steiner had lost three of his most reliable teachers to matrimony. Elisabeth Praezel, the talented musician, was married to Frederic Christian Meinung in the fall of 1808. The following spring, Sophia Dorothea Reichel, the capable head teacher of the boarding school since the day it opened, was married to Carl F. Seidel and moved with him to Nazareth. And a few months later, Johanna Sophia Schober was banished from the congregation (and the school) when she was married to Vaniman Zevely without proper congregational consent. Brother and Sister Zevely subsequently were re-instated as *auswartige* members (those living outside Salem), and one of their daughters, Sophia, was to become one of the school's most popular teachers. At the time, though, Sister Schober's abrupt departure, coming so close on the heels of the marriages of the Sisters Praezel and Reichel, left a gaping hole in the teaching ranks.

Fortunately for the school, Sister Reichel's move from Salem must have nudged her widowed father, Bishop Carl Gotthold Reichel, into remarrying. For soon after she left, he went to Pennsylvania and returned with a new wife, Catherine Fetter, who had been leader of the Single Sisters in Lititz. And as luck would have it, the Bishop's bride had two unmarried sisters who elected to come to North Carolina with her. One of them, Salome (Sally) Fetter, had been a teacher in the girls' school at Lititz. So, naturally, upon her arrival in Salem, she was at once pressed into service at the girls' school. Later the younger sister, Maria, also joined the teaching staff.

As always, however, the richest source of teacher potential for the Girls' Boarding School lay in the Single Sisters' House next door. And by the spring of 1811, Steiner's efforts to give extra training to promising congregation girls began to bear fruit. His own daughter, Maria (Polly), was then eighteen. At an early age, she had exhibited above-average scholastic aptitude, as attested by the fact that she had been chosen as one of the first two congregation girls to live and study at the boarding school, and she had continued to be a serious student. Henriette Friederica Vierling, then seventeen, also had been one of the better scholars among the congregation girls and had been selected for advanced training. Like Polly, she had grown up in an educated household; her father, Dr. Samuel Benjamin Vierling, had received his medical training in Berlin, and her mother, the former Martha Miksch, had been a teacher in the Little Girls' School in Salem.

At seventeen and eighteen, Friederica and Polly were scarcely older than many of the pupils in the school, but Steiner must have believed them mature enough for the responsibilities of teaching and engaged both in April, 1811. Thus began for Polly, particularly, a distinguished teaching career which, except for short intervals, was to last for more than half a century. Friederica's active teaching continued for only five years, ending with her marriage to Gotthold Benjamin Reichel. But as Reichel succeeded Steiner as inspector at that time, she remained closely associated with the boarding school until her untimely death at the age of thirty-five.

With the addition of Sisters Steiner and Vierling, the teaching staff—for a brief time anyway—was fairly solid, albeit young. Sally Fetter and Elisabeth Nissen had charge of the first room company; Susanna Praezel and Polly Steiner, the second; Susanna Peter and Friederica Vierling, the third; Philippine Christman and Rebecca Hartman, the fourth. But it wasn't long until the usual attrition set in. Sister Nissen was married to Wilhelm Fries and was replaced by Johanna Elisabeth Reuz, who left two years later because of ill health. Sister Hartman's health also soon failed, and she was retired on a pension of $12 a month. Elisabeth Transou taught for only a little over a year before leaving to be married. Of the recruits during those hectic latter years of Steiner's administration, only three remained for any appreciable length of time: Anna Paulina Schober served for eight years, Rebecca Holder for ten, and Louisa Kramsch for twenty-three.

The rush of applications and the necessity of lodging pupils with various families in town had added greatly to Steiner's already burdensome bookkeeping chores. Apparently he collected all fees from the parents of a girl who was boarding out in town and then compensated the householder with whom she was boarding. And we can imagine how he must have had to juggle funds when a parent was slow in paying while a Brother insisted on being paid on time and in full.

Recognizing that Steiner was overworked, the *Aufseher Collegium* suggested in the fall of 1813 that "a trustworthy and able person"[13] be sought to assist him. And in a letter to Bethlehem on November 1 of that year, Bishop Jacob Van Vleck, then pastor of the Salem congregation, reported that "Br. Steiner hopes to get in Chas. Bagge a much-needed help in the Girls Boarding School, in keeping books and getting out quarterly statements."[14]

From all indications, Charles Bagge was an engaging sort of fellow —intelligent, gregarious, and when it suited him, eager to oblige friends and strangers alike. But there was a rebellious streak in him which, despite his ability and disarming manner, often sorely tried the Brethren's patience.

A son of Traugott Bagge, Salem's prosperous storekeeper, he had been sent to Nazareth Hall to be educated. Upon his return to Salem in 1790, he went to work in his father's store—obviously with the dream that one day he would become head storekeeper. But when Traugott Bagge died in 1800, the congregation leaders chose someone else for the position. Bitterly disappointed, Charles wrote a letter to the town boards which displayed such an "unbecoming"[15] attitude that they made a determined effort to move him to some other congregation.

He refused to budge, however, and further irritated the Brethren by entering a "secret understanding"[16] with the Single Sister, Christina Holder. Rather than precipitate another unpleasant confrontation with the rebellious young man, the Elders considered it the better part of wisdom to see that the two were married as quickly as possible. So Charles Bagge and Christina Holder were married on August 20, 1801, and moved to Friedberg, where Bagge opened his own store.

He was never content living away from Salem, though, and time after time during the next dozen years, he tried to get permission to move back—occasionally using such direct means of persuasion as setting up a store so close to Salem's boundary that the congregation store was threatened with costly competition. Several times the question of his return was submitted to the Lot, but it was not until 1813 that the answer was "*Ja.*"

The Bagges moved back to Salem on October 27, 1813; their daughter, Eliza, already was there, attending the boarding school. It was then that the move was made to engage Bagge as an assistant to Inspector Steiner. But apparently he did not begin work at the school until the following spring. In the meantime, he had been appointed a Justice of the Peace, had been elected to the State Assembly, and had been named *Fremdendiener*, the congregation's official host to visitors.

Independently wealthy, at least by Salem standards, Bagge did not really have to work—which is probably why he could afford to be cantankerous. So within about a year after his return to Salem he resigned his positions as Justice of the Peace and Assemblyman and for the remainder of his life did what he enjoyed doing—"conducting visitors through the school, showing them objects of interest in the town, notifying the principal of the arrival of patrons with daughters or wards, taking the girls to the hotel when friends called to see them, carrying the mail and a thousand little acts of kindness besides."[17]

The school girls adored "Daddy Bagge," as they affectionately called him, and it was not uncommon to see him surrounded by girls who "buzzed about him with an air of proprietorship and camaraderie enjoyed by those only who sincerely love young people and children."[18]

The old rebel never fully mellowed, however. In 1826 when the attempt was made to start a boarding school for boys in Salem, Bagge, for some unexplained reason, did his best to undermine the enterprise. And as *Fremdendiener*, he was in an ideal position to accomplish his purpose. Not only did he fail to commend the school to visitors, as he had been instructed to do; on one occasion, he went so far as to tell a father of a prospective student that "it really would not be worthwhile to leave his son here since the whole matter [the school for boys] would cease to exist within a few months."[19]

As it turned out, Bagge was right. But his admitted bias resulted in his being relieved of the office of *Fremdendiener*. From then until his death in 1837, he lavished all his time and interest on the girls and their school. And at his funeral, the entire student body, all dressed in white, occupied the place of honor directly behind the casket as the procession moved from the church to God's Acre.

At the time Bagge began work at the school, the nation was deep in a second war with Great Britain. Like the rest of North Carolina, Salem was spared close contact with its bloody battles, but the town and its school for girls felt the effects of the War of 1812 both economically and emotionally. Correspondence with the Brethren in Europe was "sadly curtailed."[20] Many supplies for the school, especially such items as silk thread, were impossible to obtain. Occasionally passing companies of soldiers camped near Salem, their presence bringing the harsh reality of war close home to the townspeople. And to Inspector Steiner, the day's mail often brought the far-off war into sharp personal focus:

Son will settle with you for Daughter's Acct. Had prepared to come over myself, but re^d orders to take field at Norfolk to serve tour of duty in Country's service . . . Hope y^r attention to conduct of my child will not be neglected.[21]

Have deferred writing in expectation of having it in power to come to Salem to see you & to converse with you. Frontier of our state being object of attack by enemy has kept our forces constantly upon alert. At moment I was on start to visit you, was detailed to command company of militia in compliance with requisition of President & take field at moment's warning.[22]

Again the Moravians' scruples against bearing arms were respected by the authorities, and no men of Wachovia were among the thousands of North Carolinians who actively served in the conflict. But their traditional abhorrence of all wars, whatever the provocation and whoever the participants, moved them to heartfelt thanksgiving when on March 1, 1815, the news reached Salem that peace once more prevailed.

Today we had the desired pleasure of seeing in the public newspaper the proclamation of the President of the United States, which gave official notice that the treaty of peace and friendship between the United States and Great Britain was signed at Ghent on December 24, of last year, and that it had been signed by the President of the United States on the 18th of February. For not quite three years our beloved fatherland has been involved in war with England. All hearts were excited, and were filled with the warmest gratitude to the Giver of all good for this precious gift.

As a manifestation of that joy the entire town celebrated that evening by an illumination, which was possible because the weather was unusually beautiful and warm. There was no wind, so burning candles could be used in the open air in front of the houses and on the Square before the principal buildings. In some windows the word *Peace* gleamed happily in German and in English. The musicians did not fail to increase the rejoicing by playing appropriate melodies on the wind instruments, as they marched all over town; then they stopped on the green Square in front of the chief buildings where most of the Brethren and Sisters had gathered, and there in a true spirit of brotherly love and genuine thankfulness to the Lord they sang:

Now thank we all our God!

The Boarding School pupils and the rest of the children edified the congregation with their happy songs of praise. Then all those present joined in singing a number of verses from the English Hymn Book, the musicians playing the accompaniment; and Br. Reichel closed the celebration, by request, with a prayer of thanksgiving.[23]

On April 13, 1815, the girls of the Boarding School paraded through the town, singing hymns, as a part of "the solemn celebration which the President of the United States recommended as a festival of thanks and joy for the priceless mercy of the much desired restoration of peace in our beloved fatherland."[24]

Throughout the war years, Inspector Steiner had been fighting battles of his own—overcrowded conditions, an epidemic of measles, and then one of influenza, which swept through the school with vengeance, leaving many of the pupils with coughs that hung on for weeks. Worst of all, his own health was failing, and in the late fall of 1815 he notified the Helpers' Conference that "although he could not say that his present position was distasteful or too burdensome, still because of his attacks of illness, which especially affect his head, he doubted whether he should hold the position any longer."[25]

His condition must have grown rapidly worse. For not quite two months later, January 17, 1816, the Elders' Conference "heard with sympathy the announcement by Br. Van Vleck that our dear Br. Steiner, because of his frequent attacks of sickness, wishes to be relieved of his office as Inspector of the Girls Boarding School . . ."[26]

10

A Future 'First Lady'

SOLEMNLY THE HELPERS' CONFERENCE TURNED TO the Lord for guidance: "Did the Saviour approve that we try to secure Br. Gotthold Benjamin Reichel as inspector of the Boarding School?"[1] And the answer drawn from the Lot bowl was a gratifying "*Ja.*"

Benjamin Reichel was only thirty, a good fifteen years younger than either Kramsch or Steiner had been when they were tapped for the inspectorship. But in the essential requisites of teaching, record-keeping, and administration, his experience seemed tailor-made for the job.

Educated at Nazareth Hall, he had moved with his family from Nazareth to Salem when he was sixteen, and within a few years had earned such respect from his elders that he was chosen for a number of responsible positions in the congregation: instructor and then head teacher in the Boys' School, associate *pfleger* (leader) of the Single Brothers, secretary of the Helpers' Conference in Salem, and minute-keeper for the *Aufseher Collegium.*

Equally as important—perhaps more so in the eyes of the Brethren —young Reichel came of solid Moravian stock. As the son of Bishop Carl Gotthold Reichel, he had been reared in a home totally committed to the faith, and there is no evidence that he was ever disposed to stray from that upbringing. On the contrary, he had elected quite early to follow his father into the ministry, being ordained a deacon in the Unity of Brethren when he was twenty-six.

Further in his favor was the fact that, through his family, he already was more than casually acquainted with the operation of the boarding school; his father had served temporarily as inspector following the Kramsch unpleasantness, and his older sister, Sophia Dorothea, had been the school's first head teacher.

All in all, as far as the Helpers' Conference could see, Benjamin Reichel had only one shortcoming to speak of: he was not married. But this, of course, was a weakness which could easily be overcome through due Moravian process.

So, having secured the Lord's blessing on its selection, the conference lost no time in issuing the call to Reichel to become inspector of the Girls' Boarding School in Salem, and he readily accepted. The matter was then turned over to the Elders' Conference, which convened on Wednesday, January 17, 1816, and decided to notify the congregation of the appointment at the worship service on the following Sunday evening. Steiner would announce it separately to the school's teachers and pupils.

The Elders acknowledged, however, that the actual change in the inspector's office could not be effected immediately. For one thing, Reichel first had to be equipped with a wife. Too, the Elders were reluctant to move Steiner out of the Inspector's House, particularly in view of his poor health, until adequate living quarters could be arranged for him and his family. The latter consideration prompted the *Aufseher Collegium* "to proceed with the often discussed building of a home for retired ministers, so that a place of residence may be ready for Br. Steiner."[2] Accordingly construction was soon started on the lot just north of the church.

Meanwhile, Reichel, the Elders, and the Lord—presumably in that sequence—had settled upon Henriette Friederica Vierling, a teacher in the boarding school, as the most desirable candidate for the position of inspector's wife. Sister Vierling, who was then twenty-two, accepted the proposal on May 15, 1816, and on the evening of May 19 "after an impressive address by Br. Van Vleck,"[3] the marriage ceremony was performed. All parties agreed that until the Steiners could vacate the Inspector's House, the couple would make their home with the bride's parents, whose large brick house near God's Acre also served as a hospital for Dr. Vierling's patients.

Such high-level decisions, of course, were of little concern to the school girls. In this spring of 1816, with the annual Examination approaching, they faced their own moment of truth. And the exciting prospect of wearing new white dresses and seeing their parents again after many months was dampened more than a little by the drudgery of learning the answers to all those formidable questions—to say nothing of the dreadful thought that when their turn came to recite, memory might fail them!

The Examination began on May 29, and because by this time the number of pupils had grown to 109, it lasted three days.

The school year, which previously had followed no set schedule, now had fallen into a pattern of sorts. For the first time—at least, the first time such is mentioned in the records—there was a short vacation period at the conclusion of the Examination.

Nine of the pupils went home with their families. Others went to visit their parents and relatives. Of those who remained in the School the room groups made excursions during the two weeks of vacation for recreation and pleasure.[4]

Classes were resumed on June 17. And during the succeeding weeks it must have been increasingly burdensome for the Single Sisters and the families who kept boarding students to provide food for the girls.

The summer was partly very cool, partly so dry that in some neighborhoods practically no rain fell for fifteen weeks. Many mills could not run for lack of water; the gardens, meadows and fields looked pitiful; corn suffered greatly, so that it and all other foods rose unusually high in price.[5]

But somehow Salem, which had fewer than four hundred residents, managed to stretch its meager food supply to provide for the hundred or more hungry little school girls entrusted to its care.

Somehow, too, Abraham Steiner, sick as he obviously was, managed to carry on as inspector through the dry, dusty summer. In late August, though, the sympathetic Elders made arrangements for him to accompany a party that was going to Pennsylvania "in hope that the trip will benefit his impaired health."[6] Consequently on September 2, 1816—a week before Steiner was scheduled to leave— Gotthold Benjamin Reichel was installed as inspector of the Girls' Boarding School.

Gotthold Benjamin Reichel, Inspector 1816–1833

The burdens he assumed were no different from those which Steiner had borne so patiently for a decade. The new inspector had been in office less than three months when one of his most experienced teachers, Sister Susanna Praezel, left to be married. Fortunately for him in this first encounter with the perennial problem, Johanna Elisabeth Reuz was readily available as a replacement. Sister Reuz, it may be recalled, had been dismissed from the teaching staff in 1806 for accepting a present from a Single Brother. She had openly repented, however, had been duly forgiven, and had returned to the school in 1811, only to withdraw three years later because of ill health. Now fully recovered, she was able and willing to step into the vacancy.

The problem of overcrowding was not to be so easily resolved. Despite all efforts to halt the flow, girls continued to stream into Salem. Some came by stagecoach, and a few by private carriage. But many still arrived on horseback, "portmanteau slung to saddle bow."[7] As a rule, several girls of one family or of one community would arrive together, escorted by a father or an older brother. "The gentleman would then after entering his girls at school sell his superfluous horses while side-saddles and portmanteaus were hung up in a room set apart for that purpose till the young ladies had completed their school course and were ready to go home again."[8]

The arrival of new girls always stirred excitement among the pupils and the townspeople, but such occasions, of course, only compounded the inspector's dilemma. And one of Inspector Reichel's first challenges was to find—somehow, somewhere—space to accommodate the mounting numbers. Early in 1817, a large, year-round dining room was arranged in the cellar of the school building, which previously had been usable only in warm weather. This released the space on the first floor formerly used for wintertime dining, and it was immediately converted into a living room for a fifth room company.

The need for additional sleeping space remained desperate, however. Although no reason had been given for abandoning the plan to construct a new dormitory at the rear of the school, cost undoubtedly had been the main deterrent. For in May, 1817, when Reichel presented an alternate plan that "would not cost a great deal,"[9] the Elders' Conference, the *Aufseher Collegium*, and the Congregation Council accepted it with alacrity.

Reichel's plan would entail relatively little new construction; it would simply add a second story to the outbuilding behind the school then being used as a washhouse and woodshed. When the plan for a new dormitory had first been advanced in 1813, it included also the construction of a new washhouse to replace the one that had been built in 1805, and architectural evidence indicates that at least that portion of the plan was carried out. So the structure to which the second story would be added was relatively new and apparently sound. The long, low building, open on the side facing the school, already had three outside walls of solid stone. By installing stone columns and arches on the open side, it was believed, the structure could be made strong enough to support a second story of framework. "This together with several partition walls will take away all fears for eventual weakness of the whole structure,"[10] the *Collegium* concluded.

Discussing the plans again on June 2, the *Collegium* noted the "complaint on the part of the Single Sisters who take care of the laundry in the Girls School that there is lack of a pressing room, which, disadvantageous to their health, they had to do now in the [exposed] laundry room."[11] It was thus agreed that the renovation of the washhouse-woodshed would also include extending the southern eaves eight feet to allow for a pressing room on the ground floor.

At the end of June, Reichel was instructed to proceed with the construction. The new dormitory would not be ready for occupancy until the summer of 1818, but the Brethren's minds were eased by the fact that at last something concrete was being done to alleviate the overcrowded conditions.

The new house for retired ministers had been completed shortly before Christmas, 1816, and the Steiners had moved in soon after the holiday. This had freed the Inspector's House for the Reichels, who were able to get settled before the birth of the first of their nine children on March 1, 1817.

In late May of that year, Reichel conducted his first public Examination, which again, owing to the large number of pupils, lasted three days. Previously an advertisement had been posted in the tavern forbidding attendance at the Examination "except by those persons who are parents or guardians, or have received special invitations."[12] (Apparently already the Examinations had begun to attract the boisterous crowds who were to plague the peace-loving Moravians for many

Ancestral Home of James Knox Polk

Portrait of Sarah Childress Polk, c. 1830, by Ralph E. W. Earl

years.) Even so, Salem was crowded during the Examination, partly because an unusually large number of the pupils' relatives and friends attended and partly "because a lion and a lioness were on exhibit"[13] in town at the time.

The vacation following the Examination had barely begun when a young man, Anderson Childress, arrived in Salem with his two younger sisters, Susanna and Sarah, in tow. Traveling on horseback, they had ridden all the way from Murfreesborough, Tennessee, a journey of some four hundred miles, much of it across rugged mountain terrain. Other girls from other places were arriving at about the same time, so Salem took no special note of the party from Tennessee. For, of course, it could not have been known then that, as the wife of James Knox Polk, Sarah Childress would one day become First Lady of the Land.

Sarah and Susanna were the daughters of Joel Childress, who had made a great deal of money in land speculation, and they were accustomed to the finest of everything—including education—that wealth at that time could provide. When they were quite young, they had been given private lessons by a teacher in the boys' academy attended by their brother, later going to "a fashionable school at Nashville, where they were taught to play the piano and introduced into the most polished society Middle Tennessee afforded."[14] But Childress wanted more for his daughters, and so when Sarah was not quite fourteen, he had sent her and her sister to "the best girls' school in the South, the Female Academy conducted by the Moravians at Salem, North Carolina."[15]

According to the school's ledger,[16] the entrance fees for the Childress girls were due on June 1, 1817, and the student register of that time[17] also cites that date as the beginning of their stay in the school. They remained in Salem only a year, the register indicating that they left on May 27, 1818.

One of the favorite stories around Salem Academy and College, handed down through the years, tells of how young James Polk paid court to his future wife in the living room of the Inspector's House. And by a mighty stretch of the possible, it could be true that some sort of visit to Sarah by James did take place. Polk had been a classmate of Sarah's brother at the private academy back in Tennessee, and he may have been acquainted with the Childress family as early as

1817–18 when Sarah was in Salem. Also, during that same year, Polk was finishing his last term as a student at the University of North Carolina at Chapel Hill, some seventy or eighty miles away. So it would not have been too long a journey for him to come calling in Salem.

As of this writing, though, no evidence has turned up to substantiate the alleged visit or visits. And at the risk of spoiling a delightfully romantic story, it must be conceded that, judging by all available evidence and a little garden-variety logic, any courtship between these two at that time appears highly unlikely.

In the first place, James was twenty-two years old at the time, and his biographers point out that, especially during his last year at the university, he devoted himself zealously to his studies. It is thus hard to imagine that such a serious-minded young man would have any romantic interest in a girl of fourteen. And even if such an interest did flicker, the chances are that he would have considered it presumptuous to pay court; after all, Sarah was a wealthy girl, accustomed to the finest silks and satins, while he had as yet no means of supporting himself, much less a wife.

More to the point, most biographers of both President Polk and his wife agree that the two did not meet until both had finished their education in North Carolina and had returned to Tennessee. According to one account,[18] James first spotted the slender, dark-haired beauty at a Governor's reception in Murfreesborough in 1821, when he was just beginning the practice of law, and later that evening was overjoyed to find that she was the sister of his old classmate, Anderson Childress. Another account,[19] dramatizing Polk's proposal to Sarah in December, 1823, has him saying that they had known each other for "nearly three years," which would date their meeting two years after Sarah left Salem.

Whether or not Sarah Childress found romance in Salem, though, there is no question that she found much else there which would go with her to the White House and beyond. Ambitious and astute by nature, she had acquired at the Salem school the educational tools that would equip her to be not merely a President's wife but also his political adviser and colleague; she was, in fact, the first First Lady who had had a formal education. During Polk's term (1845–49), she served as his secretary, often working at the job twelve hours a day, and it was said that the President "relied upon her help and advice as he did on no other person."[20]

The Moravian influence on Sarah has been credited with (or, perhaps more accurately, blamed for) the fact that the White House during the Polk Administration was about as lively as a well-appointed mausoleum. Although Sarah always dressed elegantly for the customary social functions and was much admired both for her beauty and for her stimulating conversation, she and her husband allowed no drinking, card-playing, or dancing in the house, and they refused to receive visitors on the Sabbath, even those carrying important political or diplomatic credentials.

In all fairness, the responsibility for such strait-laced practices should not fall solely on the Moravians; Sarah's Calvinistic upbringing surely contributed to a large extent to the shaping of her attitudes. But the year spent in Salem did leave an indelible mark on her, and fond memories of it remained with her always. In 1886, five years before her death at the age of eighty-seven, she wrote to the school, acknowledging receipt of its alumnae publication:

> Please accept my sincere acknowledgments for the number of The Academy so kindly sent me. It is particularly interesting and acceptable as everything relating to my old and always revered and beloved Alma Mater attracts my attention and regard.
>
> There are probably no more than one or two living now who shared with me those bright and fleeting hours. Miss Louisa Kramsch, afterwards Mrs. Blickensderfer, was one of my teachers ever since gratefully remembered. . . .[21]

The summer of the Childress sisters' arrival in Salem had been relatively uneventful. On July 4, 1817, the boarding school girls joined the Brethren and Sisters of the congregation in a celebration at which "Br. Steiner made a short, suitable address to those present, which was followed by a lovefeast with wine and cakes, during which several toasts were read and fine music was rendered."[22] And on August 25, a brief excitement rippled through the town when Governor William Miller stopped in Salem for the night. Several people had contracted a fever which made them quite ill, but at the time the cases were too few to cause any great concern. So several of the congregation who had business of one sort of another in Pennsylvania decided to make the trip while the weather was still warm.

The wagon, accompanied by two Single Brothers on horseback, left Salem on August 31. Its passengers were the Single Sister, Salome Fetter, who was going to visit relatives, and Inspector Reichel, his wife, and their six-months-old daughter. Just why the Reichels made the trip at that time is not recorded. It may have been in the interest of recruiting teachers for the school. Or perhaps Reichel's health, which in later years would necessitate frequent recuperative trips, already had begun to fail. In any case, he was away from his post as inspector for nine weeks, and in his absence, the boarding school once more enjoyed the able leadership of Abraham Steiner, whose health apparently was sufficiently improved by that time to permit him to undertake the responsibility.

The Reichels' wagon had barely rumbled out of sight when the fever began to spread through Salem with epidemic vengeance. Undoubtedly it was typhoid, judging by the time of year and the symptoms of its victims, and few households in town, including the crowded boarding school, escaped.

Nearly a hundred cases, adult and children, were counted in town and surrounding county, and a considerable number of the pupils in the Boarding School suffered from this fever, through which the patients became uncommonly weak, and when the fever left them they regained their strength very, very slowly, and the least over-exertion caused a relapse. . . . In this time of sickness our dear Br. and Sr. Steiner did much for the school by their assistance while Br. and Sr. Reichel were away. . . .[23]

There had not been a death at the boarding school since the pathetic accident in 1807 in which the sea captain's daughter lost her life. But during those terrible weeks of the fever's crest, again it was Abraham Steiner who was called upon to give strength and solace to pupils and teachers when death came to their ranks. On October 17, Jane Jordan, a seventeen-year-old school girl from Greensville County, Virginia, died of the fever and the next day was buried among the Single Sisters in God's Acre. Less than a week later, fourteen-year-old Judith Hardeway of Nottaway County, Virginia, also "closed her journey here below."[24]

Almost sixty years old and far from robust, Steiner nevertheless rose to these crises with his customary calm, common sense, and unshakable faith. And the sheer strength of conviction that underlined his straightforward letters to frantic parents must have been blessedly reassuring:

DEAR SIR

In the absence of Mr. Reichel and wearied down by the incessant care of our female institution I have barely time to mention that your Daughter is in perfect health and has been so all during our late troubles and distress. We have had sad times indeed and are bowed down in humility before our God, but thanks be to Him the worst is over. No new cases have occurred these twelve days past. The greater part of the sick, who were numerous, have recovered their health. Some are convalescent and there are only two now that partly keep their bed. You may have heard reports enough which could have alarmed you and reports are the two [sic] most exaggerated the farther they spread. Our case was pitiful enough, at one time thirty odd pupils and half the tutoresses lying down at once and no assistance but within ourselves for in nearly all the houses in town there were some sick. Two of our beloved pupils have departed this life. Through the mercy of our God we are nearly all restored now so far that we can attend to our duties in the wanted regular manner. Do not be alarmed concerning your daughter. She is in health.

With most perfect esteem
I am
Your most obed^t
ABRAHAM STEINER[25]

II

The Spirited Sister Steiner

HE REICHELS RETURNED FROM PENNSYLVANIA
on November 5, 1817. By their long absence they had escaped both the fever itself and the dreadful strain which it had placed
on those left with responsibility for the school girls. And a weary
Abraham Steiner must have been greatly relieved when at last he
could relinquish the burden of inspectorship to its rightful and rested
owner.

Reichel had barely resumed his duties, though, when unwittingly
he plunged the school into a crisis of another sort. During the height
of the fever scare, many parents had taken their daughters away from
Salem. Upon his return, Reichel, finding what appeared to be a sharp
drop in enrollment, had accepted a large number of new applications—only to realize, too late, that these parents had had no intention of keeping their daughters out of school permanently; once the
danger of contagion was past, former students were returning to
Salem in a steady stream. The dismayed inspector could hardly turn
them away—not in good conscience, anyway. Nor, by the same token,
could he refuse to receive the new students whose applications had
been accepted without reservation. As a result, the school was trapped
in a space shortage that rapidly spread to alarming proportions.

Sickness and winter weather had slowed construction on the dormitory addition, and it was not nearly ready to absorb the overflow.
Consequently, beds were squeezed into the sleep hall of the main

building until there was barely walking space between them, and
school girls were lodged in every available nook in the houses out
in town. Conditions were no less congested in the dining hall, where
pupils took their meals pressed elbow to elbow along the backless
benches. And, most frustrating of all, teachers battled for their pupils'
attention in classrooms so crowded that there was scarcely room for
the girls to sit, much less settle down to concentrated study.

Yet almost every day more pupils arrived—excited little girls escorted by fathers who had traveled long distances fully confident that,
in the hands of these conscientious Moravians of Salem, their daughters would be given the tenderest of care and the finest education
offered to girls anywhere in the South.

Around the conference tables, beeswax candles burned long into the
night as the frantic Brethren and Sisters sought ways to cope with
the deluge. Dr. Vierling had died a few months previously, and it
was suggested that his big brick house be given over to the housing
and feeding of school girls. But the level-headed *Aufseher Collegium*
took a dim view of any such measure taken under the pressure of
expediency:

Generally the Collegium thinks that such an extension is against the
general plan of the school and harmful to the institution itself, because
good instruction and suitable supervision will suffer greatly from such
enlargement of the school, mainly since at present some of the best teachers are absent, and those teachers who are in school are partly rather weak,
partly without courage and partly not up to their service. . . .[1]

Under the circumstances, the *Collegium* concluded, the school's
only recourse was to throw itself on the mercy of "all those parents
whose children have to be expected here within a short time and
present to them our reasons of the impossibility for admitting them
all at one time."[2] To this end, a circular should be sent directly to
each parent, because, in the *Collegium*'s opinion, "an advertisement
which Br. Reichel is going to have put into the Raleigh and other
papers is not going to have the desired effect."[3]

The Elders' Conference instructed Inspector Reichel to dispatch
such a circular at once. Undaunted by the *Collegium*'s lack of faith,
he also went ahead with his advertisement, which appeared in the
Raleigh Register on February 20, 1818:

SALEM ACADEMY*

The friends and patrons of Salem Academy are respectfully informed, that the crowded state of this institution will not admit of our receiving new Pupils for some time hence. Two causes, in particular, have contributed in producing the present dilemma: 1st. The erroneous supposition that many of our pupils who were taken home last fall, would not re-enter this school; and 2d. The unforeseen delays in obtaining additional room for the convenient accommodation of even an inferior number than the present. If acquiescence in the wishes of parents and guardians, too liberally extended, as the result has shown, involves us in very serious difficulties, may we not with some measure of assurance, claim a generous return of a similar display of good will towards us? Those of our respected friends therefore who have already obtained leave to place one or more Scholars into this Academy are frankly requested not to avail themselves of this permission, until apprized of our ability to receive them. This Institution, thank God, is again blessed with general good health. Its worthy patrons will be pleased to accept our grateful acknowledgments, for their confidence and good will hitherto evinced and to assure themselves of our respectful consideration.

By order of the Board of Trustees

BENJAMIN REICHEL, ACTING INSPECTOR

Salem, N. C. Feb. 3, 1818[4]

The *Collegium,* it would seem, had had a point; Reichel's phrasing was too polished, his approach too oblique for the message to be driven home with much force. But apparently this was indicative of the man himself. Scholarly, sober-minded, and from all appearances, rather opinionated, Reichel seems to have been quite a contrast to his predecessor, Abraham Steiner, whose humor, warmth, and down-to-earth approach to both people and problems had made him so popular and so easy to work with. And if the impression of one young visitor in Salem was valid, even Reichel's sermons were somewhat less than spellbinding, being delivered, she wrote in her journal,[5] in a "monotonous singing tone of voice."

---

*This is one of the first instances in which the name "Salem Academy" appears in the school's own records. Although outsiders often referred to the institution as the "Academy" or "Female Academy," the Moravians themselves generally identified it simply as the "Girls' Boarding School."

It should be noted, though, that almost from the beginning of his term as inspector, Reichel was intermittently plagued by illness, which undoubtedly affected his personality, perhaps making him more remote than he normally would have been. And certainly the Elders had the highest regard for his ability; else they would hardly have retained him as inspector for so many years during which, time and again, his personal adversities created serious problems for the school.

If there was any resentment toward Reichel personally for all the troubles caused by his misreading of the enrollment figures, the feeling was never openly expressed—at least not among the congregation leaders; now that the damage was done, their only concern was how to pull the school out of its painful predicament. The circular sent directly to parents must have stemmed the flow of newcomers to some extent. But with enrollment already exceeding a hundred, the space shortage remained acute, making it necessary for Inspector Reichel to open a room in his own home for twelve of the youngest pupils. Fortunately work on the dormitory addition had proceeded rapidly during the spring of 1818, and by early June of that year its roomy sleep hall and two sickrooms on the second floor were ready for occupancy. Even so, Bishop Van Vleck reported in a letter to a Brother in Bethlehem[6] that there were "30–40 pupils placed with families in town."

The overcrowding had been particularly trying for the small staff of teachers, and in early July they presented a formal complaint to Bishop Van Vleck and Inspector Reichel, asking "urgently that their present difficult circumstances be considered and help be given them since, with the all-too-large number of students they are entirely unable to fulfill their duties with encouragement and success and their health is endangered."[7]

The trustees were only too well aware of the teachers' plight. For although forty or more girls had gone home after the Examination in May, some sixty new students had arrived—despite all efforts to discourage their parents—bringing the total enrollment to 116, larger than it had ever been. So another notice was inserted in the newspapers of the state, and this one was worded in such a way that no parent could possibly miss the point:

CIRCULAR

The Female Academy in Salem, Stokes County, N.C. being overcrowded to the great detriment of the Institution, as justice cannot be done by the Tutoresses to such a number of pupils not to mention the risk of endangering the health of the same, etc. The Trustees of the Academy deem it their duty, hereby to give notice to all, whom it may concern, that under twelve months at least no attention can be paid to any application for entering the names on the book as candidates for the school. Moreover the said Trustees find themselves under the imperious necessity to request those parents, relatives, guardians, etc. of young ladies, who upon former application have received the promise of their admission in the course of this year, to defer bringing or sending them until further notice from the Inspector of Salem Academy, there being no prospect of the possibility of their admittance in the present year.

JACOB VAN VLECK
In the name and in behalf of the Trustees

Salem, July 7[8]

The fact that the trustees themselves issued the notice was not so much a matter of their arbitrarily taking the responsibility out of Reichel's hands; the sad truth was that Reichel simply had become incapable of handling his obligations. For the illness that was to cause so much distress for the Brethren had surfaced in the summer of 1818, and for the first of what was to be many times, the aging Abraham Steiner had to be called upon to take over some of the inspector's duties. The exact cause of Reichel's poor health is never made clear in the records; there is indication that, in the minds of at least some of the Brethren, his ailments were not altogether of a physical nature. In his memoir,[9] Reichel himself described one of the early symptoms as a "nervous disease" in his hand, which prevented him from playing the organ. And there are references in later correspondence to his losing the use of both hands.

Whatever its origin, Reichel's disability dumped an extra burden onto his wife, who in this summer of 1818 was caring for one baby barely a year old, was expecting another, and at the same time was trying to carry her share of school responsibilities, including supervision of the laundry.

Ever since the boarding school opened, the laundry for the pupils, teachers, and the school itself had been done by Single Sisters. During the early years, the Sisters, accustomed to manual labor, had managed to do the job with little strain. But when the school's enrollment mushroomed, the chore of washing and ironing clothing and bed linen for more than a hundred persons each week had turned into such back-breaking drudgery that Sister Reichel was finding it increasingly difficult to recruit enough Single Sisters who were strong enough, not to mention willing enough, to undertake the work. So partly to relieve her and partly to provide gainful employment for an impecunious Brother named Johann Christian Burkhard, the Elders' Conference and the *Aufseher Collegium* decided to remove the laundry operation from the school completely and to set it up elsewhere in town as a business for Burkhard. The new laundry, installed in the old stillhouse a short distance west of the square, was opened in October, 1818.

Meanwhile, late that summer, typhoid fever again had struck Salem, sweeping through the boarding school with particular severity and taking the life of a young teacher, Maria Fetter. Sister Fetter's death left a big gap in the teachers' ranks and, worse, another dent in their morale—badly riddled already by the overwork, the weariness and worry of the epidemic, and the lack of strong leadership caused by Reichel's illness. In October, Sister Philippine Christman, who had served the school for more than a decade, asked to be relieved "because of her increasing weakness."[10] And the following spring, Sister Salome Fetter was forced to retire from full-time teaching because of bad health.

Salome Fetter, older sister of the deceased Maria, was the sort of teacher—mature and professionally well qualified—that the school could ill afford to lose, particularly at that time, and she was persuaded to continue to teach a few classes, for which she was paid four cents an hour. In addition, as a reward for her faithful service, she was given, rent free, living quarters in the old pressing room in the building at the rear of the school, free candles and firewood, and a dollar a week in cash.

During this same spring of 1819, Reichel's worsening health so impaired his work that the Elders found it necessary: "a. to ask Br. Reichel to give up his duties for so long as the state of his health indicated and transfer them to Br. Steiner; b. to ask Br. Steiner, if Br. Reichel agrees to this, whether he would take over all the duties of the Inspector for the time."[11] Reichel was reluctant to give up, but finally agreed "to relinquish his duties, at least until the end of July."[12] The Elders also considerately relieved Sister Reichel of all obligations in connection with the school.

So again it fell to the lot of Abraham Steiner, then sixty-one and not himself in the best of health, to conduct the Examination in May and to wrestle with the boarding school's ever-present problems of finances, parent relations, student welfare, and staff recruitment. The depression of 1819, rather severe throughout the country, had served to reduce enrollment to a little over eighty, thus sparing him at least the dilemmas caused by overcrowding. But the school still was sorely understaffed, and, in desperation, he had had to employ an immature Older Girl, Henrietta Kluge, to fill in. The situation improved slightly a few months later when Sister Susanna Elisabeth Lösch, who had been living with her father in Raleigh, asked for permission to return to Salem and agreed to accept a teaching position.

In October, 1819, however, the school lost the services of the semi-retired Salome Fetter, when at the age of forty-one, she accepted the marriage proposal of the widowed Brother Eberhard Freytag of Bethlehem. Evidently the poor health which had forced her to retire had taken a turn for the better! In any event, hers was among the first marriages in Salem that were not previously submitted to the Lot for the Lord's approval; the Unity Synod, meeting the previous year in Herrnhut, had ruled that, except in the cases of ministers, use of the Lot in marriages was no longer required.

Little by little, the Brethren of Salem were also relaxing some of the rigid rules by which the congregation had lived since the town was founded half a century before. Essentially the church still exercised control over the material as well as the spiritual affairs of its communicants. And the time had not yet come when it was willing to let down the bars to non-members who wanted to live or work in Salem, including teachers for the Girls' Boarding School. Despite the school's dire need for teachers, the *Aufseher Collegium* in 1820 turned down the application of a qualified young woman:

We are completely convinced of the fact that Mary Rea's character is without flaw. We also know that the school suffers from a definite lack of teachers. However, the Collegium unanimously holds the view that it would be better not to employ such a person, who knows so little about the reason of our living together in one community, about our orders, yes, and in this case, has often looked with contempt at our belief and sworn never to belong to our group. . . . If Mary Rea, however, should show her serious desire of becoming a member of the Brethren Unity, our consideration of her case would be quite different from the ones above stated.[13]

Times and circumstances nevertheless were changing. Salem was no longer an isolated little community in the middle of a wilderness; civilization long since had closed in around it. And whether they chose or not, the Moravians were becoming more and more involved with people from other places and of other faiths. This growing exposure to outside influences could hardly be expected to leave Salem untouched—either its sternly regulated way of life or the attitudes of its residents, especially the young people. More significantly, the congregation leaders themselves were showing signs that the bolts which once had fastened them so tightly to the doctrine of their fathers were beginning to work loose.

In matters basic to the faith itself, they remained uncompromising. But being discerning men, they were able to distinguish between what was fundamental and what was merely institutional. And when changing conditions rendered an old community custom useless or unpalatable to the congregation, they did not hesitate to let it go: "The proposal to stop ringing the bell for stopping work was approved, for everybody knows when the sun goes down."[14]

A departure much more far-reaching came in 1822 when Rebecca Martin, a student in the Academy and a Methodist, asked for and received permission to participate with the Moravians in the Holy Communion. To be sure, the Salem people regarded the boarding students as more or less their own, and a similar request by any other professing Methodist might not have been quite so readily granted. Nevertheless, this is the first instance on record of a break by the Salem Moravians in the hitherto closely regulated admission to Holy Communion, and, as such, reflects the depth of change that was seeping into the community.

A year later—and again without stirring a furor—the Elders' Conference voted to dismantle an institution cherished by the Unity since the early years of Herrnhut, the Single Brothers' House.

Perhaps if the *vorsteher* (business manager) of the house had been a different sort of man, the system of communal living for the unmarried men and boys of Salem might have lasted a little longer. But the younger Single Brothers had begun to see something of the world outside Salem, and what they saw was vastly more attractive to them than that offered by the austere, confined way of life in a choir house. Already they were rebelling, scandalizing the Elders by openly flirting with the Single Sisters and by decorating the walls of their rooms and toilets with most "improper . . . drawings and inscriptions."[15] The *vorsteher*, Brother Mangus Hulthin—a gentle, unworldly soul—simply had been unable to maintain discipline. And the Elders must have foreseen that, in truth, the task would soon become too much for any man. So after prayerful consideration, they had turned the Single Brothers' House over to the community for whatever uses it chose and had advised the building's occupants to find lodging either with their families or in other private homes in town.

The common housekeeping of the Single Sisters, on the other hand, was to continue even after other and more fundamental practices in Salem fell victim to the changing times. For, of course, the status of spinsters in early nineteenth century America was altogether different from that of bachelors; opportunities for unmarried women to have any sort of life of their own were few. And in a way, the Single Sisters of Salem were luckier than most; by maintaining their own joint living quarters and business operation, they enjoyed companionship and a measure of independence not always open to "maiden ladies" of that time, whose unhappy lot often was to live out their days as virtual servants in the homes of relatives.

So there really was little incentive for the Single Sisters to rebel against choir house living. Besides, the shrewd town fathers had every reason to see that the Single Sisters' Diacony was kept intact; it was a highly profitable business—thanks to the boarding school—and, as such, a handy source of revenue for the community itself. By 1820, the Single Sisters had paid off the mortgage on their choir house, and from then on, their net profit, derived mainly from providing board for the school girls ($557.86 in 1820, for example; $699.00 in 1821), was appropriated either to support such worthy causes as the "Heathen Mission" and sustenance for a needy widow or to pay off the Community Diaconate's indebtedness, including liabilities of the defunct Single Brothers' House.

Apparently the Sisters did not resent these inroads on their nest egg; sharing was the accepted way in Salem. But, as Dr. Adelaide Fries observed in 1914: "Had all the surplus profits been held for the S.S. [Single Sisters'] Diacony, and safely invested, the Sisters' House today would be handsomely endowed."[16]

In other respects, though, the Sisters were not nearly so docile. Collectively and individually, they had minds of their own, and in more than one argument the Brethren managed to have the last word only by giving them their own way.

Not the least spirited among the Single Sisters at that time was Abraham Steiner's daughter, Maria (Polly), who, as it turned out, was perhaps the most outstanding teacher in the entire first century of girls' education in Salem. In many ways, she must have been much like her father: outspoken but kindly, deeply devout but down-to-earth in her relationships with other people, conscientious but never meek in carrying out her duties, a natural leader. Her formal education had been acquired solely in the schools at Salem, but "she gave evidence of a mind of no ordinary calibre, studiously using every opportunity for improving herself."[17] And, like all good teachers, she had the patience and the power to instill in others a desire to learn. As one of her pupils, Maria Crockett, wrote in a letter home: "She takes great pains to explain everything to us that we may understand what we learn and not forget it."[18]

Following her death half a century later, a former minister in Salem paid her high tribute both as a woman and as a teacher:

> She had indeed rare tact and ability in dealing with young people. Hers was the happy faculty possessed by so few of knowing when to keep silence and when to speak. Joined to the intuitive perception of a woman, she had a logical way of arriving at conclusions. At the proper time she would press home her views with convincing power. . . . Her work in the Academy was indeed a labor of loyalty and love. To the last she prepared herself carefully and conscientiously to meet her classes. There was nothing slipshod in her teaching. Her pupils could scarcely fail to appreciate her faithfulness and from her example gain inspiration for work. . . .[19]

Because Polly Steiner was a woman of such strong character and ability, she was chosen, in 1820, for the larger responsibility of *pflegerin* (leader) of the Single Sisters. This meant, of course, that she had to give up her work at the boarding school, and, with teachers of any calibre in short supply, the loss of such a stalwart was felt all the more keenly. Fortunately—at least for the school—her absence turned out to be temporary. She was simply too much of an individualist to fit comfortably into the garb of piety and propriety designed for a *pflegerin*. And whether or not there was any truth in the rumors that she was too friendly with the widowed Dr. Friedrich Heinrich Schumann, the town physician, the matter came to a head in the late fall of 1823. "For the sake of her office," Sister Steiner had been asked to give up "a recreational trip"[20] which she had planned to make in the company of Dr. Schumann, two other Single Sisters, and a Single Brother, Ludwig Benzien, who at the time was a teacher in the Boys' School. She refused to cancel the trip; furthermore, she let it be known that she would not listen to any further discussion of the subject. And in what must have been a strained confrontation with the Elders, she resigned as *pflegerin*.

She indicated, though, that she was "willing to serve [the congregation] in the Girls Boarding School."[21] The Elders, being both charitable and fully cognizant of the needs of the school, permitted her to return to teaching. Not in the least chastened by the experience, she had been back at the school only a few months when she again stepped out of line by giving private music lessons "without having asked the Elders Conference for permission."[22] The *Aufseher Collegium* ruled that any such teaching for private gain "has to cease immediately."[23] But the year was not over when the willful young teacher again was taken to task:

> Sr. Dorothea Warner will tell the Anstalt Srs. L. Kramsch, Polly Steiner and S. Peter, in no uncertain way of the displeasure of Eld. Conf. over their behavior of yesterday—contrary to Regulations—when they, without asking permission of the Inspector, went to a meeting in Waughtown last evening and remained there over night. . . .[24]

If the Elders had not been fond of Polly Steiner or had not had so much respect for her ability, they might have been less patient with these occasional wayward streaks. As it was, they never took any more serious action than a stern reprimand, after which, as far as we know, she went right on with her teaching as though nothing had happened. And, as the Elders fully realized, the school was fortunate to have her.

In 1828, when Sister Steiner was almost thirty-six, she was married

to the Reverend Christian Friedrich Denke, a fifty-three-year-old widower, and moved with him to Friedberg, where he was the pastor.
They returned to Salem five years later, taking up residence in a new
clapboard house which Denke had had built on a lot on the western
edge of town. After her husband's death in 1838, she continued to
live in the house, sharing it first with others in the community who
needed lodging and in later years with her two sisters.

Although she spent a great deal of time teaching singing and giving
religious instruction to black children of the community, she did not
resume her academic career until 1845, when she became governess
for two girls from Macon, Georgia (former pupils in the boarding
school), whose parents asked her to accompany them to the Brethren's school at Montauban in southern France. She remained with
the girls in France for two years, during which she herself became
so proficient in French that she could, and did, teach it at Salem
Academy many years afterwards.

In 1848, shortly after her return from Europe, Maria Steiner Denke
was asked to be "directoress" of the Academy, and not until a few
months before her death did she again interrupt her work at the
school which she had entered as a pupil with the first class in 1804.

No one could see her, during the later years of her life, wending her
way at the appointed hour to the academy, her body bent & frail, but her
mind active & strong, without feeling a deep respect for a laborer in the
Lord's vineyard, who had not only borne the burden & heat of the day,
but was busy, even at eventide, to do what she knew was duty, but what
has been to her a pleasure & a delight. . . .[25]

She was not quite seventy-six when she died on November 27, 1868.

12

Slavery and the Space Shortage

A S ECONOMIC CONDITIONS IMPROVED FOLLOWING the depression of 1819, enrollment at the Academy began to climb again. By the end of 1819, there were 109 girls in school; three years later, the number had grown to 125, the highest to date.

The three months of rest during the late spring and summer of 1819 had restored Reichel's health—temporarily, at least. And if ever an inspector needed to be strong in mind and body, this was the time. For with the mounting enrollment, the old problem of trying to fit too many girls into too little space had reared again. Moreover, it fell to Reichel's lot to guide the school through the emotional turmoil of the death of a pupil, thirteen-year-old Elizabeth Bacot of Darlington District in South Carolina, and to make the final sad accounting to her parents:

expenditures for nurses	2.00
other funeral expenses	2.60
Dr. Shuman's [sic] bill	36.00
1 cherry coffin	8.00
marble tombstone	5.50
engraving for same	3.10[1]

Too, there was the obligation—perennial since the boarding school had opened—of mollifying the Salem parents who complained, with valid reason, that in re-arranging space and assigning teachers, the school had shortchanged the town girls. And on that matter, Reichel had to answer to the town boards as well. As the *Aufseher Collegium* sternly reminded him: "Our own children will always be our first concern and be nearer to our heart than those children who are sent here for the sake of education from other communities, though the latter are of course of advantage in economic respects."[2]

When Samuel Kramsch's failing eyesight made it necessary for him and his wife to be brought back to Salem from Hope in the fall of 1819, the schoolroom for the town girls in the *Gemein Haus* was taken for the Kramsches' living quarters and the town girls' school moved to the old pressing room in the building at the rear of the boarding school recently vacated by Salome Fetter. But as there were twenty-two little girls attending the town school, it was immediately clear that this space was much too small. So in the early spring of 1820, the town girls' school was moved back to the *Gemein Haus*, this time to the room which the various town boards had been using for conferences. The arrangement allowed more elbow room for the girls, but it was rather inhibiting for their teachers, who were cautioned by the Elders' Conference that the school activities must "create the least possible disturbance to those living in the Gemein Haus."[3]

At the same time, the Elders "considered with sorrowful concern the difficult situation in the Boarding School in regard to filling vacancies among the teaching force."[4] On one pretext or another, it seems, every one of the Single Sisters in Salem who were asked to serve had refused. And it isn't hard to see why: the demands made on a teacher at that time were relentless. Writing of the hardships many years later, Eliza Vierling Kremer, who taught at the school in the 1820s, said that she "cried every day for the first six months."[5] The wonder, though, is that she had any time even for tears. For in those crowded times, the classes were almost unmanageably large, and in addition to trying to prepare for and teach the subjects assigned to her, each teacher still was expected to alternate with another, day and night, in overseeing a room company, which now numbered as many as twenty or twenty-five girls—entirely too many for either effective discipline or proper personal care. As though that weren't enough to exhaust the hardiest, every day one teacher or the other was responsible for cleaning the company's living room: straightening, dusting, sweeping the lint from the sandy floors. Furthermore:

Every Friday afternoon at 2 o'clock the teacher who was not on duty took all the girls into another room and the duty teacher and two of the girls scrubbed the floor. At 11 o'clock [that same day] they had washed the sand for the floor quite white and cleaned the dirty greasy candlesticks. . . .[6]

And if, by rare chance, a teacher did have a free hour, according to Mrs. Kremer, "we were not allowed to leave the house, for we were supposed to spend every spare minute in study."[7]

It is hardly surprising, then, that, one after another, the Sisters asked to be relieved from teaching on a plea of poor health: Elisabeth Lösch in 1820, Caritas Schneider in 1822, Lisetta Schulz in 1824. And apparently, if offered the opportunity, others rushed to escape via the matrimonial route.

In view of the total lack of prospects among the Sisters in Salem, the Elders concluded that "the only remaining hope [for staffing the school] is to send an urgent request to Pennsylvania."[8] The appeal bore fruit, and in September, 1820, Abraham Steiner, still faithfully serving the school, left with the stage for Pennsylvania to escort the Northern recruits to Salem. He returned in mid-November with four Single Sisters: Mary and Sarah Louisa Towle from Nazareth and Wilhelmina Böhler and Sibylla Dull from Bethlehem. But within only a few months, Paulina Schober, who earlier that year had been persuaded to return to teaching, deserted the ranks by marrying Johann Gottlieb Herman and moving to the small congregation at Newport, Rhode Island. So the net gain was only three, and within two years, two of those had left to be married.

In late May, 1823, another Single Sister, Sophia Kitschell, arrived from Pennsylvania for service in the school, and shortly afterwards was assigned to the town girls' school—with, as it turned out, rather unfortunate results. According to the minutes of the *Aufseher Collegium* on December 15, 1823, "one of our members made the remark that ever since Sr. Kitschelt [sic] is in charge of the local Girls School, the children learn backwards rather than forwards."[9] This led the *Collegium* to note on the record that it "wished very much to have the school provided with a good teacher, and not with one who is not able to meet our requirements and standards."[10] The harried Inspector Reichel promised to find a better qualified teacher for the post.

This and other evidences of the deteriorating quality of instruction seemed to worry Reichel most of all the problems caused by over-crowding in the school. And he appealed for more space in order not only to have smaller classes among the boarding pupils but also to divide the growing number of town girls into two classes. The *Collegium* was sympathetic, but it was equally concerned about the undesirable situation in which, for lack of room at the school, many students were boarding with families in town; some of its members seemed to think that Reichel had not done all he could have in reducing the enrollment.

Whether or not the *Collegium* put pressure on Reichel about the matter at this particular time is not known. In any event, the stresses of the job must have taken their toll, and in the early summer of 1823, he was forced to give up, leaving on June 15 for Pennsylvania with the hope that the trip would restore his health. He returned on August 7, reportedly much improved.

The dismantling of the Single Brothers' House that summer started a logistical chain that helped alleviate at least a measure of the school's space shortage. The local boys' school was moved from the Boys' School building to the Brothers' House, and Bishop Andreas Benade, pastor of the Salem congregation, and his wife moved their residence from the *Gemein Haus* to the vacated Boys' School. This released enough space in the *Gemein Haus* for Reichel to be given the two classrooms for the town girls which he had so long desired. He was also permitted to use the old *saal* in the *Gemein Haus* for the boarding school's embroidery classes.

At best, though, this was only improvised relief, neither entirely adequate nor necessarily permanent. Reichel realized this, and being a persistent man, for all his ailments, he let scarcely three months elapse before he went back to the *Collegium* with another proposition: to build an addition to the Girls' Boarding School building. That was on February 22, 1824. Less than two weeks later, the *Collegium* gave its formal consent, but with one proviso: "that the number of students is not going to be increased, after the construction has been carried out."[11]

The new brick wing, measuring the same height and depth as the 1805 section, extended the boarding school building northward by about twenty-five feet, leaving only a twelve-foot driveway between the school and the *Gemein Haus*. In fact, because the structure would come so close to the *Gemein Haus*, the chimney at its north gable was a false one—put there for appearances only—since a working chimney would have created a fire hazard. Such fire-consciousness among the planners is evident in much of their design. Attractive though the arched front doorway of the addition turned out to be, it was not intended so much for looks as to provide another exit from the building "in case of fire (from which may God preserve us!)."[12] And there were sturdy stairs leading from the upper floors to the ground floor lest "there might be serious consequences, when so many occupy the upper story, if there should be some unforeseen necessity requiring them to hurry down and there would be but one way to go."[13]

Like the original part of the building, the addition included an ample attic, which was connected to the old sleep hall, thereby expanding the dormitory space. The first and second floors of the new wing also were accessible to the old building by connecting doors, "so that both houses appear to be one,"[14] the combined frontage being ninety feet. The first, or ground, floor room, twenty-four by forty feet, was planned for use in embroidery and sewing instruction. On the second floor was the chapel, the entrance to which was through a small room "to be used by the teachers in their free hours, but for classes also."[15]

The Chapel has 9 windows, 3 on each side. Light from the Chapel falls into the first children's room [living room] where the gable window remains unchanged. On the west side of the Chapel, 3 steps high, stands the lectern, or pulpit, very ornamentally constructed. Benches are placed round about, the center section of benches provided with back-rests. One hundred eighty people can be comfortably accommodated. There are 2 pretty chandeliers, each with 6 lights, which show up beautifully at night when lit. In winter the chapel can be provided with a stove.[16]

By late September, construction was complete except for finishing touches in the embroidery room. Already the new dormitory section was occupied, presumably by some of the girls who had been boarding out in town. It was the new chapel, though, that pleased the inspector most. The school girls had never before had a place of worship all their own, and, zealous missionary that he was, Reichel could see it as a golden setting in which to·spread the Word among them. Con-

sequently, he set Friday, September 24, 1824, as the date for a cere-
monial dedication, at which prayers, music, and addresses would be
tailored expressly to appeal to little girls.

Reichel also asked for and received permission of the Elders to
designate September 24 as the festival day for the Academy, to be
observed each year thereafter. Up to that time, the boarding school
girls had had no separate religious day but had shared the festival day
of the Little Girls' choir in Salem. The Brethren had become increasingly aware, however, that the religious background of their
own daughters was quite different from that of the girls who came to
Salem from widely varied religious experience; it was hard to reach
both groups in a single observance. So already they had agreed that it
would be "more to the purpose to set a special festival day for our
Boarding School."[17] Reichel's suggestion of September 24 seemed
most appropriate.

Accordingly, our foster daughters [boarding school pupils] assembled
on Thursday, September 23 at 5 P.M. in the church. Br. Reichel led them
to think, first of all, of the fitness of the transfer of their festival day to
the morrow. . . . They were, therefore, to make ready for this day, particularly by preparing their hearts through prayer and meditation. . . .[18]

In Moravian tradition, the Dedication Day was announced early in
the morning of September 24 by a trombone choir, playing in the
windows of the new chapel. The ceremonies began at 9 A.M. with
an address by Bishop Andreas Benade "stressing the happy occasion
for this celebration."[19] Then Inspector Reichel "spoke to the hearts
of his pupils, the teachers, and visitors on the text, 'Whom having not
seen, ye love; in whom, though now ye see him not, yet believing ye
rejoice with joy unspeakable and full of glory,' I Peter 1:8."[20]

The lovefeast at 2 P.M., attended by 230 persons, among whom were the
little school girls in town, part of whom had to be seated in adjoining
rooms, was especially lovely. A printed ode arranged for the occasion was
sung from full hearts. The choir, composed of pupils, was particularly
effective by reason of heartiness of expression in singing, which, accompanied by grand piano and stringed instruments in an adjoining room,
made a deep and moving impression. . . . In the festival ode, among other
notes, it had been printed—and it was this the children sang, standing,
with particular emphasis—that more had taken place in this Anstalt since

its founding, through the grace of the Lord, than the first pupils, 20 years ago, could imagine or anticipate, and that, in a certain respect, 100 scholars present today represented 1,000 educated here, appearing before God in a fellowship of prayer. . . .

In the morning the weather was cloudy and seemed to indicate rain. During the lovefeast the sun's rays greeted us all at once and pleasant warmth followed the damp cold. How that bright sun gladdened the hearts of the young people! At once they wished to use the pleasant weather for the extension of their festivities and asked of their teachers, as a special favor, that they might have a procession through the town, singing songs of praise and thanksgiving. Since, however, it is hardly possible to keep singing in such a long procession, they formed a circle at 6 different places and Br. Reichel repeated the verses which they sang happily. . . .[21]

In the evening service, attended by many visitors who happened to have arrived in town that day, Reichel "commended our educational institution to the congregation," reminding its members "that, although the Anstalt has existed here for over 20 years, the foster daughters of it, groups that enter and depart, are here mostly for a short time only, and we could show our interests in their welfare in no better way than to remember them in our intercessions frequently that they may receive here good impressions of the love of Jesus so that, when they leave this Salem they may not only keep it in affectionate remembrance, but also retain the radiance of peace in their hearts until they and we meet some day in the Salem Above and unite in the new song to the Lamb of God Who bought us."[22]

From that time on, the Academy girls joined the congregation for worship only on such occasions as the "singing meetings," liturgical services and, once a month, when the church sermon was in English. Otherwise, their devotional life centered in their own chapel. Each Wednesday evening, they assembled there for a Bible lesson, and there were always three services on Sundays: "10 A.M., English sermon; 1 P.M., reading of some edifying devotional literature; in the evening, singing meeting."[23]

For fidgety little girls, many Sundays must have seemed endless— especially if, indeed, Inspector Reichel's delivery was as singsong as it was once reported to be. But there is no evidence that either the girls or their parents registered any serious objections to the heavy religious emphasis at the school. As one student who attended the Academy during Reichel's regime was to recall many years later, "Our school life was so intimately blended with our religious life that it was in the true spirit of worship that we joined in the simple ritual of the old church."[24]

The total cost of the school building's new wing was $2,050. But paying off this indebtedness promised to be no great strain on the Academy; so healthy was its treasury at the time that $1,500 of the amount could be retired immediately out of profits from the previous year.

The Single Sisters, on the other hand, had not been nearly so prosperous; instead of the $500–$600 annual profit which they had been realizing of late—chiefly from providing board for the Academy girls —their surplus for the fiscal year 1823–24 amounted to only $155.06½. The cause of the sharp drop was readily apparent to all concerned: because more and more of the school girls who were lodging in homes out in town had begun to take their meals also with these families, the Single Sisters simply weren't being called upon to feed as many as before. Naturally they were unhappy about the situation, but no more so than the *Aufseher Collegium*; the community had come to depend on the Sisters' profits for funds to meet its own obligations, and the *Collegium* did not like to see such a handy source of revenue drying up.

The Collegium considers it therefore its duty to point out to the School Inspector . . . that as long as the number of 90 students attends the school, this number will have to take their meals in the Sisters House.[25]

Reichel had little difficulty meeting this quota when the new wing opened and he was able to bring many of the out-boarders into the school building. But the enrollment at the end of 1824 was 101, and by the end of 1825, it had climbed to 114. So even with the expanded sleep hall, there still was not room for all the students within the building itself, and it remained necessary for a number to board with families in town.

Obviously members of the *Collegium* had made little headway in their efforts to persuade Reichel to reduce the enrollment so that outboarding could be eliminated altogether. One reason he was dragging his feet, they suspected, was that he dreaded to face the opposition of certain Brethren who had been enjoying the income derived from keeping students in their homes and who surely would not suffer the loss of it in silence. As early as the summer of 1823, the *Collegium* had concluded that "boarding of the girls in the community will only be stopped, if the Community Direction advises the Inspector to take the necessary steps for this."[26] In that way, the community leaders would share the blame with Reichel.

The months wore on, however, and neither the community leadership nor Reichel made any firm move in that direction. But shortly after Christmas, the problem of out-boarding began to sprout new implications so undesirable that even the hesitant Reichel could not afford to stall much longer.

Wilhelm Fries, a joiner in whose home several Academy girls were boarding, had purchased a Negro slave woman without asking permission of the town boards. Any such willful conduct by a Brother would have been troubling enough, of course, but in this case, it was all the more disturbing because it was woven into the sensitive question of slavery, which was an especially painful one for the Salem Brethren.

For some years, the Moravians throughout Wachovia had been holding special services for Negroes in the neighborhood, and in 1823—through the efforts of Susannah Kramsch (wife of the former inspector), Polly Steiner, and others of the Salem Female Missionary Society—a separate church for Negroes was built at the southern edge of town. Abraham Steiner conducted regular services there, and several Negro men and women, in fact, had been received as communicant members of the Unity. But these efforts stemmed solely from the traditional Moravian zeal to tell the Gospel to the heathen, and the question of slavery that otherwise troubled the Brethren had no bearing on the mission.

Oddly enough, perhaps, it wasn't the moral aspect of slavery that seemed to bother them. "The laws of our state are in favor of holding slaves,"[27] they conceded, and there is nothing in the records to indicate that, publicly or privately, they ever voiced any strong protest against them. On the contrary, they willingly permitted the keeping of slaves on Moravian-owned farms outside of town. But the bringing of slaves into Salem was an altogether different matter. To the Brethren's way of thinking, the presence of slaves inside the town itself posed a serious threat to Salem's strictly regulated and morally oriented way of life:

> It was pointed out that there was reason to fear that our congregation rules would be broken often, or there would be complaints about them. Attention was also drawn to the point that our residents should watch their services from outside. It might easily follow that the young women in the congregation would become work-shy and ashamed of work; and there would be increasing difficulty in holding growing boys to the learning of a profession, in restraining them into outward morality and inward growth in good; and that this would affect the children as well as the growing youth.[28]

Consequently, early in the century the Congregation Council had ruled that "no one may or shall be permitted to keep in this congregation town Negro slaves of either sex which they may own," and that exceptions to this rule could be made "only in special cases and under certain circumstances, and with the approval of the Aufseher Collegium and Aeltesten Conferenz."[29] From time to time, exceptions had been granted, although always with reluctance—among them, the purchase, by Abraham Steiner in 1810, of a slave girl for work in the boarding school.

The rule, never universally popular with the rank and file of Salem residents, had become increasingly less so through the years as various Brethren, traveling about the state, had observed how cheap and how useful slave labor could be in the home as well as on the farm. And though the general rule against slave-holding in Salem was re-affirmed periodically, the town boards had let themselves be persuaded into making more and more exceptions.

Wilhelm Fries had been among the more persistent applicants. An aggressive businessman, he had purchased several slaves for his farm and already had one Negro girl working in his home when he ruffled the town leaders, including Inspector Reichel, by acquiring another without permission.

> Br. Reichel has declared that if Br. Fries needs two negro women on account of the school children boarded in his house he would rather take the children into the school. Br. Reichel does not like the idea that more negroes come into the community on account of the boarding school.[30]

This was the catalyst that finally stirred Reichel and the community leaders into decisive action. On September 20, 1824, they served notice that, after a grace period of one year, all out-boarding of Academy girls would be stopped. As expected, Fries and other Brethren fought the ruling vigorously, pleading "adverse and straitened circumstances"[31] that would befall them as a result. But the town boards were not to be moved, and by late 1825 or early 1826, all of the boarding school girls presumably were at last housed under one roof—where neither their manners nor their morals could escape the sharp eyes of Inspector Reichel and his corps of conscientious teachers.

13

A Chieftain's Daughter

A S OF AUGUST, 1826, SIXTEEN SINGLE SISTERS WERE
employed by the Academy as tutoresses for the boarding students and town girls. Among them were two veterans: Polly Steiner, who had been there since 1811, and Louisa Kramsch, whose service dated back to 1814. And four others—Regina Leinbach, Lydia Stauber, Charlotte Pfohl, and Anna Leinbach—had just begun careers that would turn out to be also long and faithful. But just that month, Susanna Elisabeth Peter had left the school, after nineteen years, to marry the widowed Vaniman Zevely, and, especially among the younger teachers, the turnover was as constant as ever.

Earlier in the year, the school had had to fill a vacancy with Inspector Reichel's sister-in-law and ward, Eliza Vierling. She was only fifteen at the time, younger than some of her pupils, and for this reason Reichel had been dubious about employing her. But Polly Steiner, speaking her mind as usual, had insisted that she be given a chance and had at once taken the young girl under her wing. As noted earlier, Eliza cried every day for the first six months, though by the end of that tearful term, she had fitted herself into the stringent confines of a teacher's lot and, in her reminiscences written half a century later, recalled those years with evident pleasure:

The girls were all in bed by 9 o'clock, then for an hour the teachers would enjoy themselves, generally retiring about 10. The senior teacher always went at 10, no matter what the rest of us were doing. One night she came down to the room where we were enjoying ourselves and said to me, "Are you here or are you upstairs?" I said, "Why I think I am here." "Well," said she, "are you here in the spirit or in the body, for if you are here in the body, your spirit is up in your bed, covered up as you lie." "I suppose it must be my spirit, then," I said, and we went upstairs to see and found one of the girls asleep in my bed. Then I had to wake her up, make up my bed and let it cool off before I could retire.[1]

Student life in the Academy had not changed essentially in the twenty years since girls first came to live in the school building. The room company was still the hub of all activity outside the classroom, although each company was somewhat larger than in earlier years, and by February of 1826, the number of companies had increased to six. With the larger companies, space within the living room assigned to each became even more cramped. Sometimes in the evening as many as twenty girls would he crowded around the study tables in a single room, preparing their lessons by the light of tallow candles— "about one candle to every four girls."[2]

For their meals—still brought from the Single Sisters' kitchen—the girls and teachers now filled two rooms in the cellar.

Girls sat on benches on each side of the table, teachers on stools at the end. When all had taken their places, the teachers at the table nearest the door began to sing the blessing—all present joining in:

> "Leave thy place divine
> with us – We are thine."[3]

The fare was still plain—soups, meats and potatoes, for the most part, with pie for supper occasionally. And the table appointments were no fancier—pewter plates, "bowls without handles"[4] for milk or coffee, and tablecloths of coarse tow linen; neither teachers nor pupils were provided napkins.

Because of the generally cramped conditions, facilities for indoor recreation were almost nonexistent. But a short distance south of the school building (just beyond the lot on which Gramley Dormitory now stands) was an area which the Academy had developed as a "pleasure garden" for the school girls. It must have been quite a masterly piece of landscaping, for a visitor from Connecticut was so impressed that he recorded a description of the garden in topographical detail:

Eliza Vierling Kremer, teacher in the Girls' Boarding School
1826–1832

It is situated on a hill, the East end of which is high & abrupt; some distance down this, they had dug down right in the earth, & drawing the dirt forward threw it on rock, etc., thereby forming a horizontal plane of about thirty feet in circumference; & on the back, rose a perpendicular terrace of some height, which was entirely covered over with a grass peculiar to that vicinage. At the bottom of this terrace was arranged circular seats, which, from the height of the hill in the rear were protected from the sun in an early hour in the afternoon. From the extremity of this plane descended in different directions, two rows of steps, & joined again at the bottom, of the hill, where was a beautiful spring, from which issued a brisk current, winding in a serpentine course through a handsome meadow, 'til it reached a brook about a quarter of a mile distant. . . .[5]

Each room company was assigned a plot in the garden where the girls planted and tended their own flowers, the room companies vying with one another to produce the largest and most beautiful blossoms. It was usually the "second" room company that carried off first prize, though—due to the happy circumstance of having its efforts directed by the gifted botany teacher, Polly Steiner. In later years, a large pavilion was erected on the upper level of the garden and climbing roses planted around it. "Here such as did not take interest in gardening, would sit in clusters, with book in hand."[6]

It would be many years before transportation facilities progressed to the point where most of the school girls could go home for the summer vacation. But they looked forward to the two weeks in early June when classes were suspended and remembered them fondly long afterwards:

What a glorious time the girls had that remained in vacation. I think the teachers exerted themselves in every way to make us happy. They would charter the four-horse stage and take us into the country to dine and spend the day. . . .[7]

But all too soon the holiday was over, and for the remainder of the sultry summer, the girls struggled to keep their minds on their lessons, enjoying only the brief respites of a few hours in the pleasure garden, late afternoon walks to an old bridge south of town, skipping rope in the school yard, and on Saturdays, an excursion to the store to spend their pocket money for fruits, cakes, and candies.

Yet, judging by the tone of their letters, most of them must have been content. There was, in fact, such an openly happy atmosphere in the school that Juliana Margaret Connor, a visitor in Salem in 1827, remarked on it in her diary:

I was much pleased with the general appearance of content and happiness which beamed in the countenances of all the pupils—their instructress's treat them with maternal kindness and are rewarded by their warm attachment, punishment is unknown, reasoning and persuasion are the only means employed to correct and convince. . . .[8]

There were moments, of course, when all was not serene within the school building's walls, and occasionally reverberations of an incident involving a student could be heard as far away as the chambers of the august congregation boards. The Elders' Conference, sitting in session on January 30, 1827, noted with much displeasure that a young man in town "has secretly made the acquaintance with one of the pupils in the Girls School, and they have exchanged silhouettes and a pocket book."[9] Equally concerned over the same incident, the *Aufseher Collegium* two months later demanded the "quick removal" of the brash young man "who becomes so dangerous to the good reputation of our school."[10] And at the monthly prayer meeting of the congregation, "Br. Benade offered special petitions for our two educational institutions, as things have happened recently which threatened to disturb the inner life of our Girls School, through the forbidding acquaintance of a young Brother with a boarding pupil."[11]

The boy was sent away, but there is no evidence that the school girl involved received any punishment, although certainly she had not been an altogether unwilling accomplice. Perhaps her teachers simply administered an extra-heavy dose of the "reasoning and persuasion" which had so impressed the visiting Mrs. Connor—and which, coming from idolized teachers, probably hurt worse than any tangible measures could have.

Overworked as all the teachers were, it is rather remarkable that any of them could consistently find the time, the energy, and the patience to maintain such an affectionate rapport with their charges. But somehow they managed, and on occasions of sickness or sorrow, they were ready with a little pampering to help ease the loneliness. Once one of the girls, Louisa Lenoir of Fort Defiance (then in

Wilkes County), was confined to the sickroom for many weeks with what must have been pneumonia. When she was well enough to write to her worried mother, she described the thoughtful attention shown her, especially by Charles Bagge, the inspector's assistant:

O if you could only have been here to see how kind he [Bagge] has been to me during my sickness, he seemed just like a father. he would come to see me every day sometimes twice & was always sending or bringing me some little nice thing that he thought I would eat; one day after I had got a great deal better, he came up and said he had a present for me, he gave me a fine large apple & an orange. I found out afterwards that he had sent to Salisbury for the latter on purpose for me, there are a great many other acts of kindness I could mention but they are too numerous to put in a letter; I hope I shall not be so ungrateful as to forget them soon. . . . But while I am telling you of the kindness of daddy Baggy [sic] I must not forget the kindness of others; if I had been at home surrounded by my nearest relations I could not have been treated more tenderly or have had more attention paid me. . . .[12]

Appended to Louisa's letter was a note from her teacher, Louisa Kramsch, assuring the girl's mother that "there can be no room for further anxiety."[13]

The school girls were especially happy at Christmas when, after weeks of preparation, they presented their special dialogue for the townspeople and such parents and other visitors as happened to be in Salem at the time. These dialogues still were so well-attended that it was necessary to present several performances, though just how much the audiences actually enjoyed the so-called dramas may be questionable; with the sober-sided Benjamin Reichel as author, the lines written for the little girls to speak must have been, if anything, even more ponderous than those in Steiner's day. Certainly, George Frederick Bahnson, the new minister at Bethania in the early 1830s, found them so. After hearing his first dialogue, he wrote in his diary that Reichel's composition was "rather strange of content, being a kind of dogmatic exposition of the whole christian doctrine, from the manger to the cross," and, in his opinion, "could not be called a Christmas dialogue."[14]

For the girls themselves, though, the chance to appear before an audience of their elders was a thrill that none wanted to miss, no matter how dull or dogmatic were the speeches they had been asked to deliver. And the occasion was even more exciting now that the Academy had its own chapel, which was festooned elaborately for the performances, with the dominant decoration always a large transparent painting of the Nativity, framed in greenery and lighted from behind by candles.

On Christmas Eve in 1826, a full-blooded Indian chief, Major Ridge, arrived in Salem to enter his daughter, Sarah (Sally), in the boarding school. They had come from Oochgelogy in Georgia, where a few years before, the Moravians had established a second mission among the Cherokees. A decade later, Major Ridge (or "The Ridge," as he was called by his tribesmen) would enrage many of his own people by signing the treaty with the federal government by which the Cherokees were forced to give up their lands and move West. But in 1826, he was one of the most influential and genuinely respected chiefs, not only among the Cherokees themselves but also among such national leaders as General Andrew Jackson, with whom he had fought, side by side, in the Creek War. And he had been friendly with the Moravians from the earliest days of their missionary effort among his people, his wife, Susanna, having become a communicant member of the Moravian Indian congregation.

Although himself illiterate and never able to speak English with any fluency, Major Ridge had long believed that the salvation of the Indian in a white man's world rested on education. So he had encouraged the Moravian missionaries to open a school for Cherokee children—indeed, insisted that they do so—and had sent two of his older children, Nancy and John, to the Brethren's school at Springplace.

When Sally was old enough, she also was sent to Springplace. By this time (about 1821), the Ridge family had come to adopt more and more of the white man's ways. Major Ridge had prospered, his holdings including large farms, a store, and a ferry. He now owned some thirty Negro slaves and was soon to build a spacious home—two stories high, with broad verandas and with a room for Sally that was finished with the finest wainscoting and panelings. By this time, too, his son John had gone to Cornwall in Connecticut for further study, had married a white girl, and had returned to the Cherokee country to assume his own position of leadership.

So the background out of which Sally Ridge came to Salem Academy was, in many ways, little more primitive than that of her white schoolmates. The truth is, she had moved in circles far more cosmopolitan, probably, than any of them had experienced. For Ridge had become increasingly ambitious for his children, and in 1823, when he went to Washington as a part of a delegation sent to plead for the Cherokees' right to hold their lands in Georgia, he took Sally along, hoping that "the War Department would now send her . . . to some good finishing school in the East."[15] The War Department refused the request, but Sally remained with her father in Washington while he completed his mission on behalf of the Cherokees, staying at Tennison's Hotel in the heart of the city and conceivably accompanying him when he and other members of the delegation were entertained at the receptions of Mrs. John Quincy Adams and at parties at both the White House and the home of John C. Calhoun.

Upon their return, Ridge had applied to Salem Academy for Sally's admission there, but J. Renatus Schmidt, the Brother then in charge of the Moravian school at Springplace, had advised the school not to accept her "on the grounds that it spoiled Indians to educate them away from home."[16] So Sally had entered a school at Turnip Mountain, not far from her father's ferry.

Just what changed the Brethren's minds about accepting her is not clear; probably it was simply that in 1826 Susanna Ridge applied for her daughter's admission and they did not feel they could turn down a member of their own faith. At any rate, Sally was accepted. And though it was December, when trails were treacherous and the winds bitter cold, Ridge brought her down the rugged mountains to Salem.

Shortly after arriving on Christmas Eve, the chief visited the school's chapel:

He was a magnificent man, tall and handsome with small hands with tapering fingers and small feet. When taken into the chapel he stood with clasped hands and silent awe before the transparency while his Negro slave told him in Cherokee the meaning of it. He could speak only Cherokee and his attendant who spoke English, Cherokee and Creek was also his interpreter. . . .[17]

Little is known of how Sally Ridge fared either in her studies or in her relationship with her teachers and schoolmates. She was sixteen

Major Ridge, a Cherokee chief

when she entered the school—older than most of the pupils, as old as some of her teachers—and, very dark in coloring, was said to be quite striking in appearance. No doubt she was (and felt herself to be) a curiosity, both because of her "different" looks and because, despite her education and command of the English language, she still clung to some of her native ways: "At night she undressed as did the others but wrapped herself in a blanket before retiring."[18]

When the visiting Mrs. Connor and her party toured the school, Sally, who was in a sewing class, was pointed out to them. "I vainly endeavored to catch her eye and the expression of her countenance," Mrs. Connor wrote, "but she manifested not the slightest degree of curiosity at the entree of so many strangers—never raised her head from the garment at which she was busily employed, presenting a strong contrast to the gazing looks of those by whom she was surrounded displaying most fully the indian character."[19]

During the time Sally was a student at the Academy, Ridge contracted with Daniel Welfare, the best-known of the early Salem artists, to paint her portrait, and Sister Eliza Vierling was assigned to accompany the Indian girl to Welfare's gallery for the sittings.

Sally's mother, also a full-blooded Cherokee and quite an intelligent woman in her own right, attended one of the Examinations in which her daughter participated.

She wore a man's fur hat without ornament and dressed very plainly although neatly, but it was observed that the white ladies in their silks and satins left the seat of honor beside the principal on the front row for her.[20]

When Sally Ridge left the Academy following the Examination in May, 1828, she returned to a Cherokee Nation in brewing turmoil. Late that year, President Jackson, her father's old friend, served notice that he would support an act calling for the removal of all Indians to lands beyond the Mississippi. In the valiant fight for Cherokee rights that ensued, Major Ridge worked alongside another staunch friend of the Moravians, John Ross, a man of mixed Scottish-Cherokee blood, who was principal chief of the Nation. The two chiefs eventually came to a bitter parting, Ridge signing the controversial treaty and Ross refusing to give up—not, however, before Ross had sent his own daughter, Jane, to Salem Academy.

In 1837, Major Ridge and his son John Ridge, with their families, voluntarily left Georgia for new homes in the West. Just before they departed, Sally had married a Georgian, George W. Paschal, a lawyer who had been living among the Cherokees for many years, and some months later, they, too, set out for the West.

Jane Ross remained in Salem throughout her father's last determined but futile attempts to save the Cherokee lands, leaving in 1838 just as the first bands of men, women, and children who had sided with John Ross in his lost cause began their long, sorrowful "Trail of Tears."

So far as is known, neither ever returned to Salem, though during the Civil War, Jane became a member of the Moravian Church in Bethlehem.

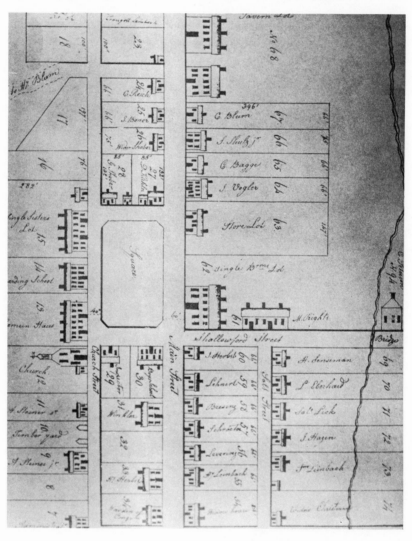

Diagram of Salem Square from an 1822 drawing by Frederic Meinung

14

Reichel's
Illness

I N THE LATE 1820s, SALEM BEGAN TO FEEL THE PINCH
of the economic depression then spreading across the nation. "The
times are very bad," wrote Wilhelm Fries to his son at Nazareth Hall,
"little is sold in the shop, and prices have fallen very low."[1]

At first, the Academy seemed to be weathering these conditions
relatively well: "In spite of the bad commercial situation in the southern and western states, our Boarding School for Girls has received
new pupils to take the place of nearly all of those who have gone
home."[2] Even so, the prospects were not encouraging. And when
Polly Steiner and another teacher, Carolina Friederica Eberhard, left
the school to be married, Reichel made no effort to fill the vacancies;
he simply discontinued the sixth room company and regrouped
teachers and pupils among the five remaining companies.

In view of the worsening economy, Reichel also asked for and
received permission of the Provincial Helpers' Conference to reduce
the school fees from $161 a year to $147, and (because of the lower
food prices) to cut the rate paid to the Single Sisters for meals from
14 2/7¢ a day per pupil to 12½¢.

He also wishes to be allowed to pay the [Single Sisters'] kitchen when
he has the money, not monthly, for the parents of children never pay in
advance, and often not until they come to take the daughter home. The
same situation exists with regard to the shoemaker, whose account has
been paid by the Inspector semi-annually, and often he must wait a long
time to get the money from the parents. . . .[3]

During succeeding months, though, the economy deteriorated so drastically that fewer and fewer parents throughout the region could afford even the reduced school fees. By late May, 1829, the Academy enrollment had plummeted to fifty—less than half of what it had been just three years previously—and the room companies had been decreased to four. At the end of 1831, there were only forty-eight boarders at the school; the following year, the number dropped to thirty-seven, the lowest since 1809.

Yet, lean as the times were, the Salem Brethren never once considered either closing the boarding school or altering its basic character in any way. If anything, the few girls who were in the Academy at the time probably received even closer personal attention and more thorough instruction than those who had come to Salem in the prosperous years. For, of course, classes and room companies were much smaller, and with fewer teachers needed to carry the load, the school could afford only the best qualified among the Single Sisters. During that time, Louisa Kramsch left Salem to make her home in Rhode Island, but even the loss of such a popular and competent teacher did not hurt the school nearly as much as it might have several years previously when the enrollment was so large.

The industrious Salem residents likewise took the austerity in stride. Though money was as scarce in Salem as elsewhere in 1829, Johann Christian Blum chose that time to found the town's first newspaper, *The Weekly Gleaner*, which, he promised, would be "of a miscellaneous character, devoted to the diffusion of general intelligence, instructive and amusing...."[4] As it turned out, Blum's newspaper was not nearly so durable as his *Almanac*, which he had started in 1828 and which is still being published today; the paper folded at the end of a year. But while it lasted, the *Gleaner* did indeed diffuse numerous items of general intelligence, including a report on the invention of the typewriter:

A gentleman of Michigan has invented a machine for printing letters, &c. It is furnished with keys, and played upon after the manner of a forte piano, and a young lady seated at it, and employed in printing a letter or card of invitation, would appear in the same attitude as in playing upon a forte piano.[5]

And it was in the columns of the *Gleaner* that public notice was given to an event which would be written into the musical history of America:

NOTICE

The friends of Music are herewith informed that the famous ORATO-RIO of *Joseph Haydn* called "THE CREATION" will be performed in the village Church on July 4th next by the full corps of Instrumental and Vocal Musicians of Salem. The doors will be open at 1 P.M. and the music commence at 2 P.M.

Entrance tickets, at 50 cents, may be had on application at the Printing Office, Tavern and Store.

MUSICAL COMMITTEE

Salem, June 1st, 1829 [6]

Eighteen years earlier (in 1811), the Moravians of Bethlehem had presented the first performance of *The Creation* ever to be heard in America.[7] The performance by the Moravians of Salem on July 4, 1829, would be the first presentation of the renowned oratorio in the South, and the orchestral parts used on that occasion were copies of the copies that John Frederik Peter (former minister at Salem) had made for the historic performance at Bethlehem.[8]

Rehearsals had been in progress in Salem since late March, taking place (by special permission of the Elders' Conference) on Sunday afternoons in the chapel of the old Single Brothers' House. Some thirty or forty singers and instrumentalists were participating, and as the date for the performance drew near, excitement mounted throughout the town. A "Friend to Music," writing in *The Weekly Gleaner*, predicted that the oratorio would "surely create in every bosom a sensation of awe, adoration and delight, and a desire one day in heaven to behold the consequences of the creation. . . ."[9]

As always when there were important public events in Salem, the Academy girls had been given a special invitation to attend the performance, and, dressed in their best, they were among those assembled in the church on the Fourth of July afternoon. The day undoubtedly was hot, and, for restless little girls, the music, however sublime, must have seemed uncommonly long. But one of them was impressed enough by the pageantry of the occasion to describe it later in a letter to her cousin:

... Dear Cousin I will now give you a slight information how the fourth of July was celebrated here, which was something very different from the method that I have formerly been accustomed to, which we had a very friendly invitation from the inhabitants of this town who were assembled together about one o'clock; there was something similar to a platform or stage built, on which there were a couple of rows of very elegant singers first formed of the ladies, second of the gentlemen, further back and all around were the musicians with all kinds of instruments which continued till about five o'clock in the evening. . . .[10]

Much more to the students' liking, probably, was the Fourth of July celebration two years later (1831) when the Salem Light Infantry Company appeared for the first time in full uniform. With the band playing and the handsome young men stepping smartly to drill orders, it must have been a thrilling experience for the school girls. But for many of the older members of the congregation, also gathered around the town square to watch, the colorful exhibition was but a painful reminder that at last the end had come to Salem's long-held resistance to bearing arms.

At its last session, the General Assembly of North Carolina had repealed the old act by which Moravians and certain other religious groups were exempt from military service. Evidently convinced that a protest would be futile, Salem's leaders had bowed to the authority of the state, though it must have bruised many a conscience to do so. A volunteer company had been organized in Salem, and, to the disgust of oldtimers like Wilhelm Fries, the young Brethren had entered into the military drills with enthusiasm. The Fourth of July observance in 1831 afforded them their first opportunity for a public appearance. And they strutted out that day in their new uniforms, their caps (ordered from Philadelphia) splendidly adorned with red ostrich plumes, to parade before the congregation, Academy girls, and visitors and to fire "thirteen rounds in honour of the thirteen good old States."[11]

Three months later, the town—and the school—had more sober reasons to observe the readiness of the military company when on September 24, the Academy's festival day, a report reached Salem "that a considerable number of Negroes were on the way here to commit excesses against the white people, as it happened in Virginia a few weeks ago, where they murdered and pillaged."[12] The report turned out to be false, but the festival lovefeast was canceled and the school girls kept behind barred doors while members of the volunteer company stood watch at various posts all over town throughout the day and night.

The depression years had not been easy for the people of Salem, and to compound their straitened circumstances, a prolonged drought in the summer of 1830 had so damaged the corn and wheat crops that many families were forced to substitute potatoes for bread. Yet when news reached Salem of the disastrous fire in Fayetteville on May 29, 1831, the whole congregation was so distressed by the plight of the hundreds left homeless that the Congregation Diacony contributed $25.50 for their aid; the Single Sisters' Diacony gave $25 and the Girls' Boarding School, $50. In addition:

Mr. Reichel was so filled with compassion for the sufferers that he called the entire school together in the Chapel, and telling them the sad story asked if they would not like to make up a purse to be sent to the burned and ruined city. Nearly all contributed something, and two of the teachers each gave five dollars, a whole month's salary, although it envolved much self-sacrifice for the ensuing four weeks.[13]

In all, the pupils and teachers of the Academy contributed $120.

Reichel's open concern for the misfortunes of others seems to indicate that, at that particular time anyway, he was well in command of his own troubles. But less than two years before, such had been far from the case, and only the patience and compassion and generosity of the Brethren saved him from what surely would have been a total breakdown. For during the latter years of the 1820s, the old nervous ailments which had plagued him almost from the start of his term as inspector had grown steadily worse. Fortunately the decreased enrollment resulting from the economic depression had relieved him of many of the old pressures—the overcrowded classes, the overworked teachers, the deluge of applications from persistent parents. But it was evident to everyone that he was becoming less and less able to cope even with the lighter work load, and, particularly in his preaching duties, others had been obliged to absorb some of the strain.

Then on March 18, 1829, came the final shattering blow: his wife, on whom he had leaned heavily, died at childbirth, leaving nine children, the oldest of whom had just turned thirteen.

Henriette Friederica Reichel was only thirty-five, and her untimely death was grievous enough to the school itself, where she had been beloved as a teacher and where in later years, as the wife of the inspector, she had been "the maternal guardian of nearly eight hundred daughters from various places, whose best interest she had always at heart. . . ."[14] But the immediate, crushing impact of her death fell on her own home where, among the nine children suddenly left motherless, were a ten-months-old baby and three others under the age of six.

Mrs. Reichel's sister, Eliza Vierling, at once gave up her work as teacher in the Academy and moved into the Inspector's House to try, as best she could, to care for the children. She was not quite eighteen—utterly inexperienced in managing a large family—and she had little or no help in the formidable task from the children's father. For Reichel, already a sick man, had been devastated by his wife's death.

He is in mind and body entirely unable to attend to anything. Without having pain or a so-called sickness he is so nerve-weak that he can use his feet only with difficulty, and his hands are entirely useless as of one who is paralyzed. He has for some time sought to regain his health by pleasure rides, often for several days journeys, but without good results. He has himself said that his work and his family (because he just cannot drive himself to it) make it impossible for him to get a hold of himself. . . .[15]

Throughout the spring and summer of 1829, Reichel struggled to overcome the terrible despondency, but by late July, his condition still had not improved. In desperation, the Elders decided to send him to Pennsylvania—presumably to stay with his sister, Dorothea, and her husband—with the hope that the change might help him. Miserable and discouraged, Reichel insisted on resigning as inspector before he left, but the Elders realized that if they let him give up, his chances of recovery could be even slimmer. So they persuaded him to reconsider, to look upon the trip merely as a short leave of absence. Fortunately Abraham Steiner, then in his seventies, agreed again to take over supervision of the boarding school temporarily, and Reichel was assured "that everything in Salem would be taken care of with the utmost fidelity and he was not to be anxious."[16]

The Brethren, though, were a great deal more worried than they let him know. In a letter to Bishop John Daniel Anders in Bethlehem, the Reverend Johann Christian Bechler, then chairman of the Provincial Helpers' Conference in Salem, confided that "more than just a visit is necessary to reach the wished-for results,"[17] and he appealed for Anders' help:

Br. Reichel must not set a terminal date for his journey home until he is fully recovered according to his and your judgment, dear Brother. . . . It is now our request to you and to all our fellow workers in Pennsylvania . . . that you treat our poor Br. Reichel with counsel and comfort and cheer as long as he needs it. . . .[18]

Reichel left Salem on August 3, 1829. Exactly one week later, Abraham Steiner's own wife, Catharine, died after a lingering illness. But Steiner had always been a man of strong spirit, and, despite his bereavement, he did not falter in his commitment to the Academy, carrying on the work for the remainder of that summer and fall while Reichel was away.

Meanwhile, Reichel's condition was the subject of frequent concerned correspondence between Bechler in Salem and Anders in Bethlehem. Reichel had been in Pennsylvania only a few weeks when he began to talk of going home, and again Bechler insisted that he be kept North until he was completely cured; otherwise, Bechler wrote, it would only mean that Reichel would have to make another trip.

The two sensible ministers nevertheless were looking ahead; at the proper time, they agreed, Reichel should remarry, so that when he returned to work, he would have help in coping with the demands of his large family as well as those of the boarding school. To be sure, Bechler wrote, it would be unfair to ask any "noble (that she must be) Sister"[19] to marry Reichel in his present state of health, but they should begin considering possible candidates. In Bechler's opinion, none of the relatively few eligible Sisters in Salem would be suitable; besides, Reichel himself had indicated before he left on his trip that he did not want to marry anyone in Salem. The preferred course, then, Bechler wrote, was for the Brethren in Bethlehem to select a wife for Reichel from among the Pennsylvania congregations, and, when Reichel had recovered sufficiently, make sure that he married her before returning to Salem.

Perhaps thinking that the prospect of a new wife might cheer Reichel, Anders told him what they had in mind. But to Anders' dismay, Reichel was anything but pleased; he would go home and marry a Salem Sister, he said. This was such an about-face that, upon being apprised of it, Bechler dispatched a sharp retort: if that was what Brother Reichel was thinking, then plainly he was not well enough to come home!

Bechler's letter was dated September 26, 1829. Less than two weeks later, Reichel turned up in Salem, unannounced and without a wife, explaining that he first wanted "to stay as he is and see what then to do further."[20] The Brethren were dumfounded, but there was nothing they could do but make him welcome and hope for the best. Indeed, Reichel did appear "spry and comparatively strong"[21] as he resumed his work at the school. Within only a few weeks, however, he began to notice "all sort of symptoms of recurrences of his former bad condition,"[22] and Bechler minced no words in reporting that development to Anders: "I must say that I am disappointed that you, dear Brother, and the worthy P.H.C. [Provincial Helpers' Conference] did not do at our request and in brotherly aid all that could be done in the circumstances to carry out our wish."[23]

But the damage was done. And again, as had happened time and again before, others stepped in to ease some of the ailing Reichel's load, Bechler himself assuming most of the preaching duties.

Meanwhile, there had been a flurry of activity in Pennsylvania; perhaps Bechler's reprimand had goaded the Brethren there into action, or it could well be that Reichel had had his own plans all along. In any event, the Elders' Conference in Salem noted on February 24, 1830, that Inspector Reichel would marry Mary Parsons, a Single Sister of Lancaster, Pennsylvania. (Mary Parsons was the sister of his brother's wife.) And on March 23, Reichel and his nine-year-old son, Edward, set out for Pennsylvania. The Salem Diary made no mention of a pending marriage, reporting only that the trip was "in hope of recovery of his health."[24] But the wedding did take place, and either the trip or the marriage, or both, wrought recuperative wonders—at least temporarily.

Reichel brought his bride back to Salem, and one Sunday shortly thereafter preached the morning sermon at the church. Apparently his happiness at being married was plain for all the congregation to see—too much so, in the opinion of Johann Heinrich Leinbach, a shoemaker: "Mr. Reichel preached & he is yet in his Honeymoon days; I don't care much to hear a person preach thus situated."[25]

With a new Mrs. Reichel now installed in the Inspector's House and caring for the children, Eliza Vierling moved back to the Academy and resumed her teaching. And with a new wife now to share the burden, Reichel was able to discharge his own responsibilities again, both as preacher and as inspector. Although by late June his associates had begun to notice that he seemed "to be getting weaker in his hands again,"[26] the records show that during the next three years he conducted the school's annual Examinations, recruited teachers when necessary, led the chapel services on festival days, preached on frequent occasions, composed the Christmas dialogues, and evidently withstood the strain of such emergencies as the report of the Negro uprising in 1831 and the severe windstorm in August, 1833, which overturned one of the Academy's outbuildings.

Reichel's return to the school released the faithful Abraham Steiner from his duties there, although he continued to work in the Sunday school at the Negro church and to hold church services from time to time both in Salem and in the outlying congregations. But his health was failing. "Dropsy of the heart set in,"[27] and on May 22, 1833, "in the evening of the 6th hour . . . [he] fell asleep in his 76th year."[28]

It was appropriate that at his funeral three days later, the English address should be delivered by Benjamin Reichel, who, of all the Brethren touched by the life and work of Abraham Steiner, probably owed him the greatest personal debt.

Before the year ended, Reichel himself was dead, having succumbed to "dropsy of the chest"[29] on December 20, 1833, at the age of forty-eight. And the sermon at his funeral on December 22 was preached by another Brother who had devotedly supported him through his sorrows and afflictions, Johann Christian Bechler. Because it was "particularly applicable to the late Brother,"[30] Bechler said, he chose as his text the regular Unity text for December 22, 1833—the Old Testament verse previously chosen in Herrnhut and sent to Moravians everywhere to be read on that day: *Say ye to the righteous, that it shall be well with him: for they shall eat the fruit of their doings.* (Isaiah 3:10)

Both Steiner and Reichel were buried near the crest of the grassy hill of God's Acre in Salem, where still today their flat gravestones rest almost side by side—separated only by that of Rudolph Christ, whose wife, Elisabeth Oesterlein, was the first teacher of little girls in Salem.

15

An Unpopular Choice

BECHLER HIMSELF ASSUMED SUPERVISION OF THE Academy until a new inspector could be appointed. He was an experienced educator, having once been a professor at Nazareth. But as president of the Provincial Helpers, he had heavy enough responsibilities as it was; it was imperative that a full-time inspector be selected and installed as soon as possible. So on January 20, 1834, the Provincial Helpers' Conference convened to begin the prayerful process of choosing a "talented, true Brother"[1] for the position.

Preferably, members agreed, the inspector should be an American— or at least a man who had been educated in this country and consequently was fluent in the English language. Noting also that there would soon be a need for a preacher for the Salem congregation, the conference concluded that an effort should be made to find a man capable of serving both as inspector and preacher.

One such man who came readily to mind was Peter Wolle. Wolle was an ordained minister and a composer who later would edit the first Moravian hymnbook to be printed in America. At the time he was being considered for the Academy post, he was serving a pastorate in Philadelphia, but he was well known in Wachovia, having been head teacher in the Boys' School at Salem, *pfleger* of the Single Brothers there, and minister at Bethania. Also strongly in his favor, as far as the Wachovians were concerned, was the fact that his wife was the former Maria Theresia Schober, who was the daughter of the prominent Salemite, Gottlieb Schober, and who had been a teacher at the Academy before her marriage.

Another name mentioned that day was that of John Christian Jacobson. Jacobson had been pastor of the small congregation at Bethania for seven years, and, the Helpers conceded, he merited a more prestigious and remunerative appointment. But Jacobson was a native Dane, and although he had been in America nearly eighteen years, he still spoke English with a noticeable accent. It would be more desirable, the Helpers decided, if Wolle could come to Salem as inspector and preacher, Jacobson could be sent to Philadelphia as minister, and a younger man, George Frederick Bahnson, then of Nazareth, could be brought to Wachovia to fill the vacancy at Bethania.

Because this plan would involve changes in the Northern Province, it was sent to the Provincial Helpers' Conference at Bethlehem for consideration. Before that conference could come to any decision, however, there was an unexpected death in the ranks of the Northern ministers, which necessitated emergency changes in ministerial appointments in that province. It was late March before Bechler and his associates in Salem received a report from Bethlehem relative to their own situation.

Having consulted the Lot, the Northern conference had arrived at six acceptable combinations. Each would fill the inspector's post at Salem, would offer a promotion to Jacobson, and would provide for the other vacancies created by the changes. Three of the six combinations named Peter Wolle as inspector of the Academy. The fourth proposed Carl Van Vleck; the fifth, Samuel Reinecke; the sixth, John Christian Jacobson.

Members of the Provincial Helpers' Conference of Wachovia were far from pleased with the report. To be sure, they said, they were grateful to their Northern Brethren for the time and concern given Salem's problems, but, after all, they themselves were in a better position to know what their own school needed, and, to their way of thinking, two of the proposals sent down from the North were totally unacceptable. Furthermore, there were several others about which they had serious reservations.

Apparently at some point while waiting to hear from Bethlehem, the conference had concluded that the same man—even one of Peter Wolle's proven abilities—could not effectively handle the duties of both the inspector and the principal preacher in Salem; it would be more practical if the inspector were only the associate preacher. Also in the interim, the name of one of the Wachovia Brethren, young August Heinrich Schulz—then minister at Friedberg—had been suggested for the inspectorship, and his candidacy had attracted rather widespread favor. So in the light of these later developments, the conference countered with four combinations of its own.

One combination would make Wolle inspector and associate preacher at Salem and would send Jacobson to Newport, Rhode Island. The second would name Wolle to the Salem positions and would assign Jacobson to Graceham, Maryland. The third would offer the inspector/associate preacher post to young Schulz and, for the time being, leave Jacobson at Bethania. And the fourth would make Jacobson himself inspector and associate preacher, filling the vacancy at Bethania with George Frederick Bahnson.

Clearly, Peter Wolle was the first choice of both Helpers' Conferences; as the conference in Wachovia had frankly noted, "there are to be found few qualified Brothers who can come next to Br. Peter Wolle in the propositions."[2] But the appointment was too important for the Brethren to make without guidance from the Lord. Thus the Helpers in Bethlehem once more submitted the matter to the Lot. And the Lord's choice—to the surprise of many, no doubt—was John Christian Jacobson.

Whether Wolle knew that he was being considered is not known. But certainly he was one of the first to learn the outcome of the Lot, and he wasted no time in writing the news to his relatives in Salem. Unfortunately his letter arrived in the same mailbag that brought the official report. As a result, word leaked out and spread rapidly through the Salem congregation before the Helpers' Conference had had time, even, to notify Jacobson of his appointment.

The letters had reached Salem late in the evening on Saturday, April 19. So, as Bechler later reported to Bishop Anders in Bethlehem, the entire congregation "had the whole blessed Sunday's time to get themselves heated up over it, while *we* were at a loss to be able to arrange the calling, etc. in an orderly way, and to pour oil on the turbulent water."[3]

Indeed, the news seems to have stirred up quite a tempest, for Jacobson, at the time, was not at all popular with the Salem residents, although just why they disliked him is not altogether clear. George Frederick Bahnson, who was also a Dane, attributed much of their

John Christian Jacobson, Inspector 1834–1844

antipathy to the fact that Jacobson was foreign-born; in Bahnson's outspoken (and hardly unbiased) opinion, "the Salemites are prejudiced against everyone that is not raised among them."[4] According to Bahnson, even Bechler, who was born on the island of Oesel in the Baltic Sea, was "quite misunderstood & whatever he does or says is taken amiss."[5] In his diary, Bahnson noted on another occasion that the Brethren and Sisters of Salem regarded "Jacobson & his lady . . . [as] slovenly"[6]—a criticism unfairly based, in his disgusted opinion, on the fact that when Jacobson came to Salem for the monthly meeting of Wachovia ministers, he did not wear the customary black suit. "They forgot that his income did not permit it."[7]

Members of the Helpers' Conference must not have shared these views, however. Or if they did, they must have felt that Jacobson's ability outweighed any personal shortcomings; else they would never have nominated him for the inspectorship in the first place. And in a letter to Bishop Anders, Bechler did not disguise his indignation at the unfair disadvantage in which the premature disclosure of the news had placed Jacobson both at the moment and later in his relationship with the Academy teachers and with the Salem congregation as a whole: "Why did Br. Wolle have to bring on such an indeseratica! Was he not bound to secrecy, if indeed he had to be let in on our affairs?"[8] If only the announcement could have been made to the Academy staff "in a proper and affectionate manner," Bechler lamented, misunderstandings could have been prevented, and Jacobson would not have had to begin his work in an atmosphere of "disappointment fever."[9]

Presumably Jacobson was at his home in Bethania during the height of Salem's stormy reaction to his appointment, but he could hardly have been unaware of it, and he must have faced the prospect of moving to Salem with more than a little trepidation. It was nevertheless the Lord's wish that he take the position. And when at last the offer could be made to him, Jacobson—faithful disciple that he was—accepted without a moment's hesitation.

Actually, despite his accented English, Jacobson was eminently suited, both in background and in ability, to head a Moravian school. The son of a Moravian missionary, he was born in 1795 at Burkall in Denmark, where his father was then serving. The family soon moved to the village of Skiern, on the west coast of Jutland, and when John

Christian was six, he was sent to the Moravian boarding school at Christiansfeld, later attending the Brethren's school at Niesky (not far from Herrnhut), where he completed theological training.

In 1816, Jacobson, then twenty-one, was called to America to teach at Nazareth Hall. After serving at that school for ten years, he accepted a call to become pastor at Bethania, and following his marriage to Lisetta Schnall, he arrived in North Carolina shortly before Christmas in 1826.

His seven years at Bethania had not been easy. The congregation was small and scattered; the pay, meager. Because it was difficult to keep schoolmasters in such a small, outlying community, Jacobson frequently had to add teaching to his other duties. And because he could not afford a horse, he had to make most of his pastoral calls on foot—often, also, walking all the way to Salem for the various provincial meetings he was expected to attend. Dusty or muddy as the road invariably was, it is small wonder the Salemites found his grooming less than immaculate!

Jacobson accepted the appointment as inspector of Salem Academy on Sunday, April 20, 1834. But it was nearly two months before he could move his family to Salem and assume his new duties. First, George Frederick Bahnson, who had accepted the call to replace Jacobson at Bethania but who was a Single Brother, must acquire a wife (Hortensia Frueauf); then the couple had to make the long journey to North Carolina. Also, arrangements had to be made for Reichel's widow to vacate the Inspector's House in Salem and, in accordance with her request, to take the Reichel children to Pennsylvania. So it was not until June 11 that all of these preliminaries had been disposed of and the Jacobsons were able to move to Salem. In the interim, Bechler had continued to supervise the boarding school and had conducted the Examinations on May 22–23.

Just how much hostility, if any, greeted Jacobson as he began his work can only be conjectured. But the atmosphere must not have been altogether friendly, judging by the June 29 entry in Bahnson's diary in which he reported that Jacobson had preached in English at the Salem church for the first time, "which was no easy task under present circumstances."[10] Bahnson himself later was to admit that "Br. Jacobson speaks sometimes so low [and] at other times so loud & fast that it is a very difficult matter to understand properly."[11] So, in all fairness, the "circumstances" of Jacobson's first sermon in Salem probably were no more comfortable for the congregation than for the new preacher.

Jacobson nevertheless plunged into his responsibilities at the Academy with what has been described as "characteristic zeal and energy."[12] Reichel's long illness, the depression, and finally Reichel's death followed by the six-month period with a temporary inspector combined to hold the Academy more or less at a standstill for several years. Few changes had been made either in the physical plant or in the order of school life itself, and both were showing signs of wear, if not outright neglect. The pleasure garden, for example, had gone so long untended that it was virtually a jungle, and one of Jacobson's first moves was to have it cleared so that once again the school girls could plant and care for their favorite flowers.

In other ways, one student recalled many years later: "Mr. Jacobson turned over a new leaf. We saw no more pewter mugs and dishes ... [but now] had white porcelain mugs from which to drink our milk. ... The white sand was no more sprinkled on the floor."[13] And both he and Mrs. Jacobson apparently had the rare faculty of being able to administer firm discipline but at the same time to treat the students with such sincere warmth and kindness that they easily won the girls' affection as well as their respect. As one was to write of them long afterwards:

Busy, energetic, quick to detect error, loving and sympathetic, how we girls all loved him. Dear Mrs. Jacobson, amiable and gentle but dignified and authoritative, we all remember as she went about her morning and evening rounds, always wrapped in a large plaid and wearing a becoming cap trimmed in colored ribbon. . . .[14]

The Academy teachers, on the other hand, were not so readily won over. The records fail to mention who had been their choice for the inspector's position, but clearly it had not been Jacobson. And they had not hesitated to vent their displeasure. As Bahnson wrote in his diary on November 6, 1834, "I had the great honor of being introduced to the bluestockings of the Academy, those very same ladies, who influenced by own or inspired prejudices, have so much to say against my clever & talented countryman."[15]

Many of the town people, too, were slow to become reconciled. As late as July 2, 1835, Bahnson noted that some refused to give Jacobson credit for any of the progress at the Academy, reminding him that it was not due to *his* efforts and prayers but "solely to the supplications formerly offered by the worthy Br. Reichel."[16]

Considering that brotherly love was one of the foundation stones of the Moravian way of life, such an uncharitable attitude seems oddly out of character. But this was a troubled period for the people of Salem, and the heavy smog of insecurity hanging over them appears to have thrown the whole temper of the town somewhat off balance.

The depression had struck Salem at a time when it already was rankling under a severe case of growing pains. From a total of 466 residents at the close of 1832, its population had mushroomed to "700 souls"[17] by the late spring of 1835—a 40 per cent rise in a little over two years. And its list of businesses now included:

Hotels, 1, 2 merchants, 1 book store and 1 toy shop, 2 confectionaries, 2 jewelers, 1 candle manufactory, 2 clock makers, 3 hatters, 4 cabinet makers, 5 shoemakers, 3 gun-smiths, 1 copper-smith, 1 tin-plate worker, 2 black-smiths, 1 tanner, 1 skin-dresser, 1 saddler, 2 coopers, 2 potters, 1 tobacconist, 1 baker and 2 milliners.[18]

With money so scarce, there simply wasn't enough business to go around, and the resultant financial worries eroded men's tolerance, shortened their tempers, and often caused even the most conscientious to wink at time-honored congregation rules. "Times are hard," Johann Heinrich Leinbach, a shoemaker, wrote in his journal, "& many people do not do as they want others to do unto them."[19] With the town now so large, the congregation leaders, who once had been able to control behavior, were hard-pressed to keep their usual cautionary eye on everyone, and heated squabbles frequently erupted among Brethren before differences could be detected and properly mediated.

Nor were the Single Sisters immune from the general unrest. Owing to the sharp drop in enrollment at the boarding school, their income from providing meals for the pupils was sharply curtailed, and instead of substantial annual profits—always a source of great pride for the Sisters—they had ended the fiscal year 1832–33 with an embarrassing $200 deficit. Their chagrin was hardly salved when the *Aufseher Collegium* sternly suggested that they had not managed their business affairs as efficiently as they might have.

And underlying these surface frustrations was the uneasy realization that, little by little, Salem's cherished old way of life had been slipping away. The tightly controlled, family-like system of congregation living—for so long the Moravians' fortress—now was being buffeted on all sides both by the changing times and by changing attitudes within the congregation itself, particularly the young people, among whom a "new dynasty"[20] of outspoken independents was gathering force. "I never yet beheld a place," Bahnson observed, "where the youngsters act such a sass as at Salem."[21]

So Salem already was on edge when the disappointing news broke that John Christian Jacobson had been chosen inspector of the boarding school. And one suspects that in this highly charged atmosphere his unpopularity became magnified to abnormal proportions. Certainly there could not have been very much basically amiss in either Jacobson's ability or his personality, for he went on to serve one of the most productive terms in the Academy's history. And when he left Salem after ten years at the school to become inspector at Nazareth Hall, the congregation bade him and his wife farewell with "heartfelt thanks."[22]

The animosity of those first years nevertheless must have deeply concerned him. But if so, he had little time to brood over it, for by the summer of 1834, when he began his work, economic conditions in the South had taken a turn for the better, bringing a rapid increase in the school's enrollment, and Jacobson soon was battling the same space problem that had beset his predecessors. Every month brought more girls to Salem from throughout the region until, by the Examination of 1835, there were a hundred boarders at the Academy. Jacobson was forced to open his own home to lodge some of the overflow from the main school building, and assemblies were now held in the *Gemein Haus* because the school's chapel had had to be converted into quarters for a room company. Even so, there still was not room enough to accommodate the steadily growing number of pupils.

On July 14, 1835, the *Aufseher Collegium* convened in special session to consider Jacobson's dilemma. Although no workable solution was reached that day, the *Collegium* did strongly recommend that Jacobson try to dam the flood of new arrivals by inserting notices in a number of newspapers. So in succeeding weeks the following item appeared in three consecutive issues of newspapers in Salem, Raleigh, Salisbury, Milledgeville, Georgia, Columbia, South Carolina, Lynchburg, Virginia, Danville, Virginia, Knoxville, Tennessee and Tuscaloosa, Alabama:

Salem, N. C. Boarding School

FOR YOUNG LADIES

The Trustees of this well known Establishment for the education of Young Ladies, feeling truly grateful for the very great and increasing confidence of parents, guardians, and other patrons of their Institution, are, at the same time, solicitous to preserve that high confidence, by endeavoring to accomplish their duties towards their pupils, and each individual among them, in the most conscientious manner. In order to attain to this object, they must be enabled to keep up a due proportion between the *number* of their pupils and their own *means* for accommodating and instructing them.

It is therefore most respectfully requested, that all those persons who wish to place young ladies under their care, will please give *previous notice* of such intention, and make application for a place in the Institution; to the subscriber.

By order of the Board of Trustees

JNO. C. JACOBSON, *Inspector*

Salem, Stokes County, N.C.
July 20, 1835[23]

Jacobson had hoped that more room for the school could be arranged without going to the expense of additional construction, but after exploring all possibilities for space in existing buildings, he and the *Aufseher Collegium* were forced to conclude that some sort of new construction would be the only practical solution. The least expensive building, they decided, would be a two-story connector between the main school building and the rear outbuilding which had been enlarged in 1818. The new structure would completely fill the space (about forty by ninety feet) between the two standing buildings except at ground level, where "an arched passage way wide enough for a wagon to pass through"[24] would be left open. In approving these plans, the *Collegium* "recommended all possible precautions for fire protection."[25]

The records are not clear either as to when the addition was completed or as to the specific uses made of it. It is known, however, that a part of the building served as a chapel for the school, off and on, for nearly twenty years. Whatever other relief it offered to the space shortage, though, was, at best, only partial. For, despite all efforts to control enrollment, the number of pupils had increased to 136 by the end of 1836. If anything, parents seemed more insistent than ever that their daughters be admitted, and many turned to influential friends or relatives whose pressure, they hoped, might be more persuasive with Jacobson and the trustees:

Mr. Spragens is very desirous to place her [his daughter] in your accademy [sic] and having no acquaintance with you has requested me to address you on the subject which I shall be oblige to you to reply as soon as it may suit your convenience.[26]

... my Sister, Mrs Susan Galloway wishes to get her daughter May Galloway in your Academy next June & fearing from the great number of applicants she would not be able to do so, requested me to apply to you for her admission. . . .[27]

Following the summer vacation in 1837, so many new students arrived that another room company had to be formed. There were now seven companies, each made up of twenty-two girls and two teachers. In desperation, Jacobson asked for permission to use the small *saal* in the *Gemein Haus* temporarily as an embroidery room. In the middle of July, he again appealed to the Elders' Conference and *Aufseher Collegium* for help, this time for permission to utilize a part of the *Gemein Haus* as a dormitory until other arrangements could be made. Consequently, two storage rooms in the attic, formerly used for sleeping, were converted into dormitory space.

Those were only makeshift measures, however. In early August, the Provincial Helpers' Conference conferred with the *Collegium* on the urgent question of what could be done to provide more permanent relief from the overcrowded conditions. The result was a recommendation that sleeping space in the main school building be expanded by adding a half-story and by replacing the existing sharply pitched roof with a much flatter one. This clerestory was indeed built, as is evidenced by a drawing of the Girls' Boarding School made

Moravian Archives, Winston-Salem, North Carolina

Drawing of Girls' Boarding School, c. 1840, by Gustavius Grunewald

in the early 1840s.[28] The building now had a row of windows across the front of the third story, thus improving the ventilation of the girls' sleeping quarters as well as increasing the space.

The stream of new arrivals continued unabated throughout the summer and fall of 1837; by the end of the year, the number of pupils stood at 170, the highest to date. An eighth room company had been added, but with the total enrollment so high, each company still had twenty or more girls in it—at least five more than the preferred maximum. And the two Sisters charged with constant supervision of so many lively, often mischievous, little girls must have trudged to their beds each night limp with exhaustion. But if Henriette Schober is typical of the Sisters working at the Academy at that time, they seemed to accept their lot with reasonably good humor. Writing to a friend in

Bethlehem about the various worship services of the Academy's festival day in September, 1837, Sister Schober merely commented, without complaint, that "the girls were very happy, but I don't think it
[the religious occasion] did some of them much good, for they are
as bad again as ever today. . . ."[29]

In addition to Henriette Schober, there were fifteen Single Sisters
employed as teachers at the Academy in that September of 1837:
Lydia Stauber, Charlotte Pfohl, Anna Leinbach, Anna Elisabeth
Christ, Dorothea Sophia Rüde, Lisette Schulz, Clara Reichel (daughter of the late inspector), Theresa Belo, Maria Lavinia Blum, Henrietta Schnall, Louisa Hagen, Antoinette Bagge, Louisa Rüde, Lisetta
Meinung, and Louisa Belo.

Just that month, the school had lost the services of Louisa Kramsch,
who had accepted a call to become leader of the Single Sisters in Bethlehem. She had spent the greater part of her forty-two years within
the walls of the Academy building, having first moved there with her
mother and father, who was then inspector, on the day the building
opened in 1805. She attended school there, and in 1814, when she was
nineteen, was employed as a teacher. Except for a few months following her mother's death in 1831, when she left to live with relatives in
Rhode Island, she had served the Academy faithfully and was one
of its most popular teachers, admired and beloved by both staff and
pupils.

"Miss Louisa's having to leave us so soon, marred my pleasure some
yesterday," Sister Schober wrote in her account of the festival day,
"& when in the lovefeast Mr Jacobson spoke of her departing & of the
many services she had rendered to this institution for more than twenty years, there were tears shed by a good many. . . ."[30]

The Academy's farewell gift to Sister Kramsch was "a beautiful
worked framing piece by all the girls & also an album in which all
the girls had written."[31]

16

The Annual Examination

INSPECTOR JACOBSON CONDUCTED HIS FIRST PUBLIC Examination on May 21–22, 1835. As had been necessary for a number of years, the exercises were held in the church sanctuary, because it was the only hall in town large enough to accommodate the crowds of spectators. And, as usual, the church galleries were splendidly decorated with exhibits of the girls' embroidery and painting.

Among the audience on the opening morning was Jacobson's good friend from Bethania, George Frederick Bahnson, who noted that the inspector entered the church with "astonishing nonchalance . . . as if he had directed such ceremonies for at least 15 years."[1] Jacobson offered a few introductory remarks, in the course of which he reported that since the boarding school was established, a total of 1,560 pupils "had been placed under its care and instruction."[2]

The program itself opened with a roll call, each girl rising and curtsying as her name was read, "it being considered a proper introduction to the audience in view of the part each should take later."[3] Then Jacobson began the long process of calling the various classes to the front to recite their memorized answers to questions about what they had studied in history, geography, arithmetic, astronomy, and all the other "branches" then included in the school's curriculum.

If this Examination of 1835 followed the traditional pattern (and there is no evidence to the contrary), these question-and-answer periods were interspersed with vocal and instrumental selections and demonstrations of elocution bearing such titles as "Ode to Content,"

"The Nightingale and the Glow-worm," "On Procrastination" and "Nothing Formed in Vain."[4] There were also dialogues centering on certain studies such as, say, botany, in which "a group of girls would surround a table profusely decorated with flowers, and taking up leaves and blossoms talk about them, naming their parts...."[5]

The weather in Salem that day, more than likely, was hot and humid. (At the Examination in 1823, the thermometer had stood at a sweltering ninety-five degrees!) Inside the crowded church, the air was close and the wooden benches hard. Bahnson confessed that he, for one, "got tired tol^y [tolerably] soon"[6] after the exercises began; as he explained, "whoever are not either parent brother &ct or any how at least single would not feel as much interest in them as the generality of people showed."[7]

Over the years, though, these annual Academy Examinations had come to be some of the most popular entertainment events in that entire area of the state. Parents of the school girls, of course, came in great numbers, often from as far away as Alabama, Georgia, and Tennessee.

Weeks before, great family coaches began to come, drawn by two or four horses, and accompanied by a retinue of servants with baggage wagons; the old Hotel would be full to overflowing, and many families in town would throw their doors wide open, considering the patrons of the Academy the guests of the town....[8]

True, the accommodations offered by the hospitable Moravians often left much to be desired. As one guest wrote to Inspector Jacobson:

Having been so unfortunate last year in your Village as to be crowd^d into a garret filled with all sorts of men, I am anxious to Secure during the approaching examination a lodging, at least where I can be retired, and have Some room to call my own for the time I shall be there....[9]

But, by and large, the inconveniences did not seem to deter many from returning year after year—especially the young men from surrounding towns and from the state university at Chapel Hill, who, dapper in their tight-fitting black suits and carrying the black umbrellas so fashionable at that time, made the most of this opportunity to ogle the pretty school girls.

Fifty years afterwards, one of them was to recall the event in vivid detail:

My first, and, so far as I can now recall, my only visit to the old Moravian town was as early as 1829, now a full fifty years ago. It was on the occasion of what was then known as the annual public Examination of the Academy, and occurred about the last of the month of May. Such an occasion then attracted an immense concourse of people. Approaching the town by the old stage-road leading to it from Greensboro, my first view of the curious old place was from a hill eastward of the town. From every direction the people were pouring in, crowding the hotel, filling the streets, thronging the square in front of the Academy. Every fence corner had a horse hitched to it. German manners and customs prevailed. The German language was spoken to a great extent. . . .

The great centre of attraction was the Academy. At an early hour, the girls, in their uniform, the distinguishing feature of which was their neat little white caps, fitting closely over the ears, and tied with ribbons under the chin. Then, there were their flowing sashes and white dresses, investing the procession from the Academy to the church with a charm that attracted all eyes.

The public Examination in those days was more for spectacular display than for anything else. I have reason to know now what I did not know then—that everything was "cut and dried" for the occasion. There had been the previous drill. The public examination was a sort of "dress parade." The impression upon the spectators, who were not admitted behind the curtain, was that the girls were prodigiously smart, and that they were prepared to answer any questions that might be propounded in History, Botany, Chemistry, or anything else comprehended in the scope of a scientific and finished education. . . .

As soon as the public Examination closed, the girls that were going to leave for a short vacation, or were leaving to return no more, were turned over to their fathers, or other members of the family who had come to take them home, and ere the sun had gone down, they were rolling away with hearts as merry as the birds that were singing in the wild woods, and hastening homewards. Comparative silence came over the quaint little old town. The persons left behind were sad and lonesome. A few lights gleamed at night from the Academy windows. Scarcely a note of music was heard. The girls left behind were homesick. But the vacation was

short. New scholars came in and soon the same old routine was established. . . .[10]

Salem had never really relished having the large crowds who filled
the town for the Examination. And at one time the date for the event
had been "purposely set in the week of the Salisbury and Greensboro
Court in order to avoid so great a thronging here of outside young
people from these neighboring towns."[11] But the court officials had
complained, as they themselves were prevented from attending. So in
1832, the date was changed, and Salem resigned itself to the not-
always-easy task of maintaining order during this overcrowded time.

Two Brethren were employed as doorkeepers at the church to act
both as sergeants at arms and as "Map & Globe carriers."[12] They were
paid $3 each for the two days of work. Despite their efforts to main-
tain order, there must have been a great deal of milling around during the course of the program, for many parents brought their entire
families, including infants who were constantly being carried in and
out by their slave nurses. Bahnson observed that one "little baby attracted general notice by the nicest red cheeks ever seen, but close examination said to have shown them to be painted!"[13]

It was in the evenings, however—after the school exercises were
over—that the serious troubles began. Visitors, accustomed to a gayer
social life than sober-sided Salem had to offer, soon become bored,
and the forms of diversion that they initiated often caused the town
leaders no little concern. In 1831, for example, several visiting gentlemen approached Johann Heinrich Leinbach with an offer to pay the
band if it would present a program of military music. Virtually certain that Benjamin Reichel, then Academy inspector, would disap-
prove, Leinbach at first politely declined. But the next evening the
gentlemen again made the request. Feeling that it would be inhos-
pitable to refuse a second time (also he liked the idea of receiving
money), Leinbach ventured to speak to Reichel about the matter:

Mr. Reichel said he should certainly not have any objection, if only the
Pupils of the School could be kept away; upon the strength of this I informed the gentlemen that we would make music, but that the Inspector
did not wish any of the girls to be present as it would be too late for them
to be out, accordingly the music took place, & we received thirteen dollars
& fifty cents.[14]

By 1841, it had become an accepted practice for the Salem band to present a concert for the entertainment of visitors in town for the Examination. But by 1845, the Examination had spawned another and much more disturbing diversion: dancing and drinking in the Tavern. If such goings-on were not stopped, the Elders declared, "the reputation of Salem as a religious community will have suffered and the welfare of the Girls' Boarding School endangered."[15] And the Provincial Helpers' Conference, no less dismayed by the dancing and drinking—not to mention the behavior of "a lot of folk who were disorderly and hard to keep in check"[16]—was moved to question whether the annual Examination ought, indeed, to be held.

It was to be some years, though, before the Examination was discontinued. Meanwhile, untouched by all the attendant problems, the Academy students regarded the occasion, as one described it, as "one of the most pleasing, & also exciting periods in a school girl's life!"[17] Excitement began to mount months in advance. As early as February one year, Missouri Alston was writing to her mother in Halifax County with a detailed account of her needs for the big event:

I shall want a white dress, a collar, some handkerchiefs, two pair of stockings, a pair of gloves, a small tucking comb, and any thing else you think I shall want. . . . I want my dress made plain and nothing fine about it. I mean I do not want any of those flounces and big bows that Mrs Tyner (if she makes it) will want to put on it. . . .[18]

Before the "dress parade," of course, Missouri and her schoolmates faced the ordeal of private examinations, at which, according to Eliza Vierling, "the answers were not cut and dried"[19]—just dreadfully dry.

Private examinations were commenced some weeks before the public occasion and were held in the chapel where the whole school had to be present day after day until every class had been examined in every study. It may well be supposed that it became somewhat tiresome . . . and that no one was especially delighted to attend, least of all the principal [inspector] who had all the examining to do.[20]

Apparently much of the classroom work during Jacobson's term still followed the old method of learning by rote. Even so, there is evidence that by the early 1830s the Academy girls were being encouraged not only to read independently but also to make their own assessments of what they had read. And judging by letters written by several girls to their relatives, some of the books that they chose (or, more probably, were chosen for them) presented rather formidable fare for a twelve- or thirteen-year-old:

I have finished reading "Erwing's History of Columbus" and the first volume of Plutarch's "Lives" and am now reading the second. I am very desirous to finish all the volumes before I go home, but I fear I cannot as there are eight. I have also had the history of Charles XII of Sweden out of the library and have read nearly through it. It gives a good account of Peter the Great also. I admire Charles for his bravery but Peter did more for his country than Charles. . . .[21]

I am now reading the reign of Henry the eighth; but I am very much pleased with the character of Cranmer Archbishop of Canterbury. Perhaps I may be influenced by pity (for I believe we often are). How I wish I had some person to read with me so I could dispute with them about what I liked and what I disliked, I would enjoy it so much more. . . .[22]

Since I wrote last, I have read the reign of Edward the 6th, also the cruel & bloody reign of the bigoted & imperious Mary. I am now reading the reign of Elizabeth. I have heard some persons say they loved Elizabeth, but I don't know how they can, for although I may admire her talents, whenever I think of her deceitful transactions with, & her cruel treatment of Mary, queen of Scots I never could love her. . . . I have also been reading another book since I wrote you, entitled Germany. . . . I am very interested in it now, although I thought it dry at first. . . .[23]

Most of the reading and the studying took place by the light of tallow candles set on the long tables in the various living rooms— and after a strenuous day that had begun before dawn with the clang of the rising bell.

The day's schedule had not changed essentially from the pattern established in the early years of the Academy:

. . . we rise in the morning at half after 5 and breakfast at half after 6, and study until 8 and and then go to our different classes, and continue until 11 and we dine at half after 11, and we have sewing school at 1 until 4 and then go to bread, then we go to walk if the weather will permit, and when we come back, we go to supper at 5. . . .[24]

Original owned by Rondthaler family

**Sepia drawing of Salem Square, looking east, c. 1830s, by
John Christian Jacobson**

In the spring and summer, when the days were longer, there was usually another walk after supper before the girls settled down to their study. Bedtime was 8:30.

Singing school was held once a week, and, in addition to going to church on Sundays, all pupils were required to attend religious services on several evenings during the week.

As for the schedule of classroom work, Heziah I. Sullivan wrote to her aunt in 1838 that "we have Grammar monday, wednesday and friday, and History, wednesday, and Drawing, tuesday and thursday and Cyphering, monday, and friday. . . ."[25] That same year, Sarah Davis wrote to her brother that she had "not commenced Latin or French but expect to commence in a very short time."[26] In a letter to the same brother, Sarah wrote that she took music lessons several times a week and currently was working on a piece called *Brattleboro Waltz.*[27]

That fine embroidery was still being taught in the Academy is evidenced in a letter from Jacobson to a firm in Boston in 1836[28] inquiring about such items as "English & German worsteds," "Chenille cords," "marking silk," "Rug and Marking Canvass" and "patterns for worsted work."

With the hours spent in the classrooms and at embroidery, music lessons, extra reading, daily housekeeping chores, and the many church services, pupils at the Academy in the late 1830s had no more leisure time than had the girls who were there before them. Regimentation still was the order of the day—too much so, according to reports that reached one parent: ".... There is an opinion abroad in this State, how extensive, I know not, it however *exists*, that the discipline of your school is too *rough* for the tenderness of the female constitution!"[29] By and large, though, parents seemed to endorse the strict discipline:

Having been Educated in the Salem Institution 26 years ago I still feel partial to the rule and regulations of the Institution which you will readily acknowledge by my having sent 2 of my Daughters to the same place....[30]

I wish you to see that she attends her classes reagularly [*sic*]. I shall hold you honerably [*sic*] responsible for her good conduct and her prompt attention to her studies.[31]

One thing I have allways [*sic*] understood. That Injunction is held over the virtuous morals of all whom may be trusted to your Charge. This confidence cherished will give the Parents or Guardians a calm repose either by day or by night.[32]

I know from having one daughter heretofore educated there, that every attention is paid to the students both in sickness and in health, and that the institution is conducted with more order and regularity than is to be found in some others....[33]

My mind is quieted, when on inquiry I am informed that no man has ever lost his child at Salem, and had her taken in marriage by miscreants....[34]

For the conscientious Moravians of Salem, such expressions of trust were treasures to be safeguarded; under no circumstances must the good name of their boarding school be subject to question. To that end, the town leaders did not hesitate to volunteer advice to the Academy administration at any time they felt so moved. And especially in the early years of Jacobson's term, they were moved rather often.

Perhaps in view of the unhappiness over Jacobson's appointment, the Brethren watched him more closely than they might have otherwise, lest he fall into mistakes that would only aggravate his unpopularity among the Salemites. Also in the general unrest in Salem at that time, the town leaders, feeling their control slipping, probably were trying to assert themselves in every way possible. On the other hand, Jacobson gave them some reason to be uneasy; he was inclined to be more permissive with both his teachers and his pupils than his predecessors had been—certainly more so than the Brethren thought wise and proper. Even his old friend, George Frederick Bahnson, was shocked that the Academy teachers, on the school's festival day in 1836, were allowed to be "dressed in rather too fanciful a style, with singular yellow, pink, green or blue ribboned caps to describe which my pen is too unskilfull [*sic*] but which did not please me at all."[35]

So during those early years of his term, Jacobson was the recipient of a great deal of gratuitous advice, some of it indirect but nonetheless clear in its intent:

The landlord, Br. Senseman, allowed a ball to be held in the tavern last Saturday night. Since all such events are wholly against the honored and well known precepts of our Brotherhood, it seemed very strange to Auf. Col. [*Aufseher Collegium*] that several Sisters from the Girls Boarding School and a number of their charges attended. Auf. Col. hopes that events of this kind in the future will be carefully avoided.[36]

Whether Jacobson resented all this surveillance can only be conjectured. But as evidenced by the way he weathered the antagonism of those first years in Salem, he surely was blessed with a goodly portion of tolerance, and the chances are that he listened to the well-meaning, though probably irritating, advice with respectful attention. Then, being an independent sort, he simply elected in some instances to disregard it; e.g. one report by an obviously miffed *Collegium*:

Auf. Col. has heard that not only a large number of the residents in town but also the children in the Girls Boarding School are affronted because certain young men, strangers of whose background one knows nothing, continue to have unhindered access to the schoolhouse. Since such actions would not only have a detrimental effect on the name of the institution among strangers but is also very bad practice for us at home, Auf. Col. is very sorry that its well-meant advice formerly given concerning this matter had not been taken and followed. Although Auf. Col. is well aware that it has nothing to do with the immediate direction of the school, it also knows that the whole town takes a lively interest in its welfare and that the welfare of the institution depends largely on the good and strict discipline which has hitherto been maintained in it. Auf. Col. is minded—if it is necessary—to leave nothing undone to keep this pearl unspotted and to maintain the school house as a *sanctum sanctorum*.[37]

There is no record of Jacobson's response.

17

A Capital Loss

T HE DECADE FROM 1830 TO 1840 SAW MAJOR DEVEL-
opments in the realm of higher education in North Carolina.
The state's university, which had opened in 1795 and which for many
years had been the only institution of higher learning in North Carolina, began a marked expansion in both curriculum and enrollment
under the administration of David L. Swain, who assumed the presidency in 1835. Two years earlier, the Quakers had opened a coeducational school, New Garden Boarding School (later Guilford College),
in Guilford County, and in 1834 the Baptists had started an institution
in Wake County, which, as Wake Forest College, would flourish in
that location for 122 years and then would move to Winston-Salem
and become Wake Forest University. The Presbyterians opened
Davidson College in 1837, and a year or so later a Methodist minister
in Trinity in Randolph County established a school that was the forerunner of Duke University.

It was in this same decade (in 1838) that North Carolina issued for
the first time a charter to a college for women, Greensborough Female
College, now Greensboro College. Meanwhile, Salem Female Academy, now thirty-six years old, maintained its reputation as "one of
the best schools for women in the South,"[1] attracting students in growing numbers.

Leaders of the congregation in Salem watched this mushrooming
enrollment at the Academy with a concern bordering on alarm. How,
they reasoned, could Inspector Jacobson and his small staff possibly

exert proper discipline among such a large number of girls? With the classrooms becoming more and more crowded, how could they hope to maintain the high standards of instruction for which the school had so long been reputed?

Yet even these worried men recognized that the situation at the Academy was not a total liability; from the pecuniary standpoint, at least, it was proving to be quite profitable for Salem as well as for the boarding school. For as the number of pupils had increased, so, of course, had the income from tuition fees, with the pleasant result that the Academy now ended each fiscal year with a substantial surplus in its treasury. And such a source of ready cash in this time of tight money came in handy when community needs arose.

So it was that in 1836, when stock was being peddled to capitalize a cotton mill in Salem, the "Aufseher Collegium was very happy to hear that the administration of the Girls Boarding School was minded to take a very liberal subscription."[2]

This was the period, it will be recalled, when Salem was struggling to keep its head above the troubled waters of town growth, depressed economic conditions, and unsettling changes in the old order of congregational life. Moreover, sparks from the industrial revolution then igniting the New England states had begun to float southward, carrying with them the threat of further encroachment on Salem's old ways and old trades; already in nearby Greensboro, steam-powered machines were spinning cotton and weaving cloth at a rate of speed that a Moravian Sister, treadling her small wheel, found hard to fathom.

Worried about the worsening economic situation in Salem and "lured . . . by the reports that other cotton mills were getting as high as twenty per cent on their investment,"[3] several of the more venturesome Brethren, with the congregation's blessings, organized the Salem Cotton Manufacturing Company and "drafted a preliminary plan in what way such a cotton mill could be built in the Salem vicinity for the advantage of the entire Community."[4]

The plan called for the installation of "1000 to 2000 spindles with the corresponding weaving apparatus which is to be steam-driven."[5] For this and other capital expenses, it was calculated, a stock issue of $50,000 (250 shares at $200 each) would be necessary.

The company's enthusiasm for the new enterprise was not unanimously shared by the congregation leaders, particularly members of the Elders' Conference, who expressed grave misgivings about the harmful effect that such a factory—bringing to Salem, as it must, many non-Moravians—might have on the Brethren's morale. And it was at the insistence of these more cautious Elders that a clause was inserted into the lease for the mill site stipulating that "nothing is to be permitted on the premises of the cotton factory which is counter to the letter and the spirit of the Cong. [Congregation] Regulations of the settlement of Salem."[6] To insure that control of the mill would rest in Moravian hands, congregation leaders decreed that the majority of its stock be held within Salem itself—by individual Brethren and such institutions as the Congregation Diacony and the Girls' Boarding School.

An entry in the Academy's "Day Book" indicates that the school subscribed to $3,000 (fifteen shares) of cotton mill stock, the first installment of which was paid on August 11, 1836. As it turned out, the Academy lost every penny of its investment and a great deal more. For Salem's first attempt at industrialization was a miserable failure. Under-capitalization, inexperienced management, a glutted market for yarn caused by the rush of so many in the area to get into the cotton manufacturing business—all these damaging factors combined to dash Salem's hopes for profit, although for more than ten years the company made a valiant effort to keep the mill running. Finally, deeply in debt and unable to secure additional bank loans, the company was dissolved, and in 1854 such assets as remained were sold to John Motley Morehead of Leaksville—but not before the major stockholders such as the Girls' Boarding School had made good all debts to non-stockholding creditors. Just how much the Academy lost in the ill-fated venture is unclear, but its ledger for 1854 notes a $9,000 "Reserve for Cotton Factory Losses."

In the late 1830s, however, when hopes for the cotton mill still hung high, Inspector Jacobson was more concerned with internal problems. Even with the addition of the clerestory to the school building, there still was not space enough to accommodate the nearly two hundred pupils who had been accepted, and in the summer of 1838 he applied to the *Aufseher Collegium* for permission to house a number of girls in the old Single Brothers' House. His proposal was accepted, though the *Collegium* plainly was acting against its better judgment:

The Collegium finds many a doubt in this problem, since the house [Single Brothers' House] is situated along a public street and at a place where most of our youngsters from the Community usually gather. We would rather have the Inspector help himself in another way. For the time being, the Collegium grants him use of the rooms, rent free, under the following conditions:

1) The Inspector is to have all damages repaired which the house might suffer from his students
2) On Dec. 1 the rooms will have to be vacated again
3) This enlargement of his space shall not be reason for him to admit new students and thus create new problems.

The Collegium does not want to assume any right to judge the Girls Boarding School, however, we consider it our responsibility to look after the welfare of the mentioned school as well as the whole Community, and therefore have to express our doubt concerning the immense increase of students . . . and we have to fear that such a number of girls cannot be supervised adequately. This may mean a loss of reputation and actual value of the Salem Girls Boarding School. The Collegium considers it necessary therefore to remind the trustees of the school to try to reduce the institution to normal limits. The trustees will also have to consider the health and capacity of the instructors, who are heaped with work and who will not be able to do their best, if so many children are in one class room.

We agreed that the number of students should not surpass 120 judging from the space at hand.[7]

So with characteristic candor, the *Collegium* again registered its disapproval of the situation that Jacobson and his trustees had allowed to develop at the school. But, rightly or wrongly, the situation had developed, and faced with it, Jacobson had no choice other than to act on the *Collegium's* grudging acceptance of his proposal. Thus in August of 1838, a room company, the ninth, was temporarily housed in the Single Brothers' House, diagonally across the square from the school building.

Earlier that year, Jacobson had been obliged to build an addition to his own house to alleviate crowded conditions there. For with the rise in enrollment, the inspector's work load had grown too heavy for one man to handle, and an assistant had been employed to keep the school's books. The only available working space for the bookkeeper, however, was in the one small room in the inspector's home which he had been using for his own office. Consequently, as early as 1836, Jacobson had presented plans for the addition of two rooms on the west side of the Inspector's House, one to be utilized as his private office and the other as a reception room for parents and other visitors. But it was not until two years later that the wing was completed.

Early references to the inspector's assistant mention no names— only that the bookkeeper would be "paid a certain sum and then is to receive an additional 5 or 6 cents a month for each student because the work varies greatly from month to month and with the number of pupils."[8] But it is known that as of late April, 1839, the position was held by Joshua Boner. For about that time, Boner, an accomplished organist and former teacher in the Boys' School, had requested permission to marry, and the *Aufseher Collegium*, weighing his potential for supporting a wife, decided that Boner "could make a living by keeping books of the Boarding School and his business [started earlier that month] in pianos and musical instruments."[9]

Although Joshua Boner was primarily a musician and businessman, a string of coincidences had tied him rather closely to girls' education in Salem and would continue to do so for most of his life—indeed, to the present day. He was, for instance, the son of a former teacher in the Little Girls' School—Dorothea Meyer, who, it will be remembered, scandalized the congregation in 1797 by eloping with Isaac Boner in the dead of night. His wife, Anna Elisabeth Christ, was the daughter of the first teacher in the Little Girls' School—Elisabeth Oesterlein, who married Rudolph Christ. The house that Boner built in 1844 on Salem's main street would be restored nearly 130 years afterwards for use as the official home of the president of Salem Academy and College. And, as will be seen later, he figured prominently in one of the more colorful incidents involving the Academy during the Civil War.

Boner's assistance with the bookkeeping afforded a measure of relief to the overburdened inspector. Even so, Jacobson was confronted daily with obligations that he could not properly delegate, not the least of them being the correspondence with parents or guardians, which, in view of the nearly two hundred girls in his care, had grown to mountainous proportions.

By now, girls were coming to Salem Academy from places as distant as Tuscaloosa and Demopolis, Alabama, Tallahassee, Florida, and Arkansas Territory, not to mention remote sections of eastern North Carolina, South Carolina, Virginia, Georgia, and the mountains of Tennessee. Every post brought letters from anxious parents with questions that must be answered promptly, reassuringly, and often with the utmost tact:

I received your address two days ago informing me of the indisposition of my children in Salem, which I was sorry to hear. I am rightly at a loss to know what course to take for before I could go out and return it would be some time in late February—and a question consequently arises would the exposure in travelling at this season of the year for three weeks not be as dangerous as to let her [sic] remain until Spring? . . . I must request you to drop me further information respecting their health—as often as you can find time—and hope the solicitude of a Parent for the welfare of a child will be a sufficient apology on my part for troubling you in this matter. . . .[10]

When I left Salem my daughter had quite a sore throat. I hoped to have heard from her before this. I beg of you if she is sick at any time to let me know it immediately. . . .[11]

You have enclosed five dollars which you will please divide between Marth and Carnelia I do not like to Indulge children in having money at their disposal it gets them into habits of *Extravagance*-I want If you please to see those children whom I have left in your charge to get nothing but what actual necessity requires . . . one great Inducement I had for sending them to your institution was the well known reputation that your people have for prudence & *Economy*. . . .[12]

My poor Louisa is a very weakly, delicate child; her constitution has been severely wrack'd by the frequent attacks of chill and fever, which she has had in this sickly clime. I think all that is really necessary, is to have her warmly clad, and keep her close, until the severe weather is over, also to give her tonics to strengthen her. I would recommend flannel drawr's under her other garments, and I will be quite obliged to you, Sir, if you would be so kind as to request her tutoresses to have them made for her. . . . I shall feel very thankful to you, if you would, agreeable to promise, write again, and let us know every particular respecting the health of our poor afflicted child. . . .[13]

I am truly sorry to hear of my daughter using improper language to her Teacher; I trust the expressions of the Mistress was not designed to cast any reflections. . . .[14]

If Jacobson kept a record of his replies to the many letters that poured into his office, it has not yet been unearthed. The chances are that, in those days before the common use of typewriters and carbon paper, he simply did not have time to make copies of his correspondence. But judging by the tone of his incoming mail, we can surmise that his letters lacked none of the courtesy and personal concern so necessary to inspire a parent's trust in him and in the school:

She is a diffident young lady, but I need not instruct you in the plan of her exercises or in the manner of your Treatment toward her having the utmost confidence in your willingness & ability in these matters.[15]

We feel truly grateful to you, sir, for the kindness which you have showed, in letting us know, so particularly, the situation of our children, in regard to their health. I am well assured, that were any thing serious the matter with our child, you would not conceal it from us. . . .[16]

My Dear sir the charge I commit into your hands is a great one, but I have the fullest confidence that proper care will be taken of my children. . . .[17]

Jacobson had been at the school less than two years when, as had happened to Inspector Steiner, it fell his sad duty to notify a girl's family of her death at the Academy. Sixteen-year-old Martha Ross King of Knox County, East Tennessee, had died on December 28, 1835, "after a short but severe illness (convulsions)."[18] Martha had been buried in God's Acre at Salem for more than a month when Jacobson's letter reached her guardian, and he wrote his grieving but grateful reply:

Big Meadows, Knox County, Ten.
Feb. 8, 1836

REV. JOHN C. JACOBSON
DEAR SIR

The sad intelligence of my daughters death has just reached me, ! ! &
I take the earliest opportunity of acknowledging your goodness. From
what you write, I have no doubt everything was done for my daughter
that was in your power or those who had anything to do with her and that
is our only comfort. How true Sir "we know not what a day may bring
fourth [sic, also other misspelled words]." That God, who can do all
things, and sais to the richious come up higher; & *Martha* my Lovely
Martha, has obayed that command. Marth was born the 9th day of January 1821. I wish you to have a tomb stone such as you have on your graves
put on hers, with her age and so forth. I have just writin to Caroline, in-
curageing her to stay. You will please talk with her, I will bring her other
sister in the summer to stay with her, and bring her mother to see her also.
Sir please accept for your self, and others the best wishes of

Your *friend* &c
W. P. WRIGHT[19]

The tragedy occurred only seven months after George Frederick
Bahnson had noted[20] that resentment over Jacobson's appointment
was still stirring in Salem. So whether the inspector faced it without
the full confidence of his own teachers is a matter of conjecture. In
any event, their earlier ill feeling must have dissipated by the late
1830s; at least, there is no evidence of it in extant personal letters
written by several of the teachers at that time, most of which are
taken up with the trials of being mother hen to a brood of lively
school girls:

Ding dong bell, disturbed already, four o'clock. I have to go and give the
girls bread, so it goes, friday evening washing going on, one minute,
please mam, can I have a needle, next thread, then corset string. . . .[21]

. . . after getting through the schoolhouse, I generally have a thousand
little things to which to attend, & beside, am so glad to get away from
the noise and bustle of an academy life, that I am inclined to leave every
thing undone that does not require immediate attention. . . .[22]

Time is very precious to us, as we have to be very busy & constantly engaged
while in the house, that I at least feel as if I would rather lay down & go
to sleep when I am free, than to do anything. . . .[23]

The recipient of many of these letters was Sophia A. Herman, whose
mother, Paulina Schober Herman, had been one of the first two girls
of the Salem congregation to attend the boarding school. At the time,
Sophia had just entered the Bethlehem Female Seminary as a teacher
—a situation that drew empathetic comments from her "sister sufferers" at the Academy in Salem.

How do you like it to be engaged that way? I for my part like it tolerably
well, but you have no doubt found yourself that it is not an easy task. . . .[24]

. . . dear Sophy are you really & actually an inmate of Bethlehem Female
Institute [sic] and "teaching the young idea how to shoot"? I hope you
have no rebellious girls to give you any trouble. That is according to my
opinion the most trying part of the whole. . . .[25]

As the decade of the 1830s neared its close, the congregation, like
the teachers, seems to have become reconciled to having the Danish-
born John Christian Jacobson at the head of its beloved Girls' Boarding School. Certainly if there was any lingering animosity among
individuals, the school itself remained an "unspotted pearl" in the
eyes of all in Salem—an object of unbounded pride, a blessing for
which, at each year's end, eloquent thanks were offered:

The Boarding School for Girls here has had cause to rejoice throughout
the year in a distinguished manner over the blessing of the Lord in external
and internal matters. Regardless of the generally prevailing lack of money
the throng of pupils has been so large that a considerable number had to
be turned away. It is certainly for every true member of the congregation
a matter of gratitude that we are deemed worthy to cherish in our midst
such a school plant in which through instruction and training not only
so many young hearts are directed to all Good but through them far and
wide so wholesome an effect can be made on coming generations. That
with such a large number the health of teachers and pupils has been
maintained in such a degree, that also not one case of serious illness has
occurred, that we have been protected the whole year through from all
disaster and harm, that the Lord has always been able to make hearts will-

Salem July 15th 1840

Dear Sophia,

I have determined not to let this opportunity pass without writing a few lines to you, although my time is so much occupied that I can not write much but only prove to you that I still think of you all, often, yes very often & that, with a great deal of affection, for your many kindness attention to me last Summer; I suppose you have seen the Miss Bagg's & also become acquainted with them. You can enjoy yourself much with Miss A. by playing & singing together, more than you could with either of us. Last Wednesday our school commenced again, so that we have just now properly got into the way. & in consequence have much to do, we have a great many new Scholars & will doubtless have a very full school this Session as they have not yet all returned that went home to spend their vacation; the number present now is about 160.

We have a great many apples this Summer, but not so many peaches, yet we have some & shall probably get more later in the season as it is rather early yet. Do you still keep music school, or rather have you not yet entered the Academy as a regular

Letter to Sophia Herman (de Schweinitz) from Maria Lavinia Blum, a
teacher in the Girls' Boarding School 1835–1841

ing to be trained for the service so difficult for faithful souls but also so fine and indescribably important for the youth, that we have lacked nothing good deserves at the end of the year a joyous consideration at the feet of our Lord and Master.

At the examination held usually at the end of May were shown the beautiful fruits of the efforts of the teachers and the industry of the pupils and there is reason to believe that on many hearts there has remained a lasting impression of the spiritual blessing enjoyed here. . . .[26]

18

New Quarters, New Inspector

O
VER THE YEARS, THE SINGLE SISTERS HAD BE-
come increasingly dissatisfied with conditions in their kitch-
en. The room was small, and during the summer the heat from the
fire, which burned all day as the Sisters cooked meals both for themselves and for the boarding school, made the rest of the house un-
comfortable and the kitchen itself almost unbearable. So in July, 1840,
they proposed that the laundry house at the rear of the Sisters' House
be enlarged and that the kitchen, including the bake oven, be moved
to this outbuilding.

Both the *Aufseher Collegium* and the Elders' Conference endorsed
the proposal, and plans for the new kitchen were progressing rapidly
when Inspector Jacobson entered a strong objection. The school also
needed more space, he argued, and he, too, had planned to build an
addition at the rear of the school building. As the Single Sisters'
House and the Girls' Boarding School stood side by side with relatively little space between, the Sisters' new kitchen would "materially
harm the intended building of the Girls' Boarding School."[1]

Agreeing that Jacobson's point was well taken, the *Collegium* and
the Elders worked out a compromise: the Sisters' kitchen would be
built as planned, but, instead of constructing an addition to the school
building, the Academy would be given use of the entire *Gemein Haus*.
In exchange for this space, the school would finance the construction
of a dwelling for the ministers who customarily resided in the *Gemein
Haus* and also the construction of a small *saal* to replace the *saal* in

the *Gemein Haus* which the congregation had been using for meetings and small worship services.

Jacobson readily agreed to the plan—as well he might, for the *Gemein Haus* offered a great deal more space than he could have hoped for in an addition to the school building. He was warned, however, that if the Congregation Council turned over the *Gemein Haus* to the school, he must not take advantage of the space gained to increase the number of students. Jacobson promised to hold the enrollment at its current level and further guaranteed that "two rooms as customary remain for the use of the Salem Girls School [town girls' school]."[2]

Final approval of the project was given by the Congregation Council on November 26, 1840, and by December 14, plans for both of the new buildings to be underwritten by the school had been drawn. The new *saal*, measuring thirty-eight by thirty feet, would be added to the north side of the church. The new home for ministers, to be located on a lot just north of the church, would be a brick structure: "two stories with four rooms in each story, cellar and laundry, a small porch in front, a larger one behind the house."[3]

By December of the following year, both structures had been completed. The ministers then living in the *Gemein Haus* moved into their new quarters, and on December 9, 1841, Jacobson took possession of the vacated building, beginning at once to convert it to school use. With the removal of partition walls, the second story was turned into a dormitory. Renovation of the lower floor created living rooms for the two room companies made up of the youngest school girls. And a porch was constructed connecting the *Gemein Haus* to the boarding school building "so that children and teachers can go from one building to the other without getting their feet wet."[4]

So now the "campus" of the Girls' Boarding School consisted of three buildings rimming the northeast corner of the town square: the original 1805 building, which had been enlarged twice in the thirty-six years since it was built; the 1811 Inspector's House, which also had been enlarged; and the renovated 1771 *Gemein Haus*.

At the end of the fiscal year (May 31, 1841), the school accounts showed an item of $3,020.25½ "for the erection of new buildings [ministers' house and new *saal*] and repairs."[5] But as the Academy had closed that fiscal year with a surplus of more than $7,000, it was able to meet this obligation easily and still have funds to spare for such worthy causes as "the needy Diaconies in Europe," the parsonage at Hope, the Nazareth Hall library, street improvements in Salem, and clothing and transportation for Jacobson's oldest son, William, to enter the school at Nazareth.[6]

By the end of the following fiscal year, however, the school's financial health had begun to fail a little—largely because of the fact that so many parents were either slow in paying for their daughters' tuition and board or else failed to pay altogether. Jacobson reported to the Provincial Helpers' Conference on December 5, 1842, that his books showed $4,948 in "debts owed for children who have left school this year without payment."[7] With this cash income missing, he was finding it harder and harder to pay the school's debts and had been obliged to borrow $3,000 that year "to meet the usual outlays for food, laundry, shoemaker, etc."[8]

The Helpers recommended that the inspector "reduce the current and extraordinary expenses in every way possible" and further advised him

to take every conceivable measure to collect and safeguard the debts, and to this end send out a suitable brother, such as Joshua or Thomas Boner, as agent, but to give the debtors advance notice of this. The collector would have to try to collect the money in accordance with the accounts and notes which he should take with him, and obtain well-secured notes in lieu of the book accounts. In the case of those who are unwilling to pay and are not reliable people it should be seriously urged that they take their children home again.[9]

Whether it was the result of these measures or general economic conditions—or, perhaps, the fact that there were now other schools available to Southern girls—the enrollment at the Academy began to drop. From a total of 171 students at the end of 1841, the number had fallen to 135 at the close of 1842 and to 126 the following year. So Jacobson had no difficulty keeping his promise that the addition of the *Gemein Haus* would not precipitate an increase in enrollment.

But he had other problems. In the spring of 1843, an epidemic of measles spread through the school, and before it subsided late that summer, between seventy and eighty girls had contracted it. Half a century later, a woman who had been one of the epidemic's victims recalled those terrible weeks:

When we were sick, oh so sick with measles, the loving kindness and tender ministration of one teacher [unidentified] won the heart of this lonely orphan girl. Her watchful care during those long weary nights when she and Miss [Lisetta] Brietz took turns in waiting on and caring for us will never be forgotten. I was in the chapel with nineteen other girls. The sick room was full. At least forty girls were down at that time with measles. What a time those long suffering, patient, noble-hearted teachers had with forty sick, impatient girls.[10]

One fifteen-year-old girl, Eliza Agnes Shaw of South Carolina, died during the epidemic. And in noting the sad event, the Salem diarist wrote: "In this hard blow which has hit our Br. and Sr. Jacobson we sympathize with sorrow and ask that the Lord will turn all for the best."[11] The school had barely recovered from measles when an epidemic of influenza swept through both the town and the school, raging throughout the fall and early winter of 1843 and taking the lives of a teacher, Maria Lavina Blum; two school girls, Eugenia Phares and Laura Ward; and the Jacobsons' youngest son.

The illnesses, plus the extra burden of providing long hours of nursing care, took their toll on the stamina of the boarding school teachers, a number of whom were forced to give up their work entirely or for long periods. As a result, the room companies were reduced from eight to seven. Also: "As was to be expected to be sure the report of the sickness of the last years had spread and as a result of this several of our pupils have been taken home."[12] By the close of 1844, the enrollment had dropped to 122.

In many ways, these past years had been as difficult for Jacobson as those earlier years when he was struggling to win the confidence of his teachers and the congregation. But he was a man of deep commitment and, despite his previous problems, apparently had become quite comfortable, and accepted, in Salem. So in the early summer of 1843 when he was offered the position of inspector in the boarding school at Bethlehem, he concurred with the Provincial Helpers in the opinion that he should remain at his post. As the conference reported the decision:

. . . it would not be right for him to make a change in his service immediately, if at all, in view of the present money crisis and the necessity of securing the outstanding debts and also the reduced number of pupils. . . . Since Br. Jacobson and his wife have become entirely accustomed to the ways of our Southern friends and pupils, and this with good results, which are quite different in the institutions of our Northern congregations, he feared it would be difficult for him to adopt the latter at his age. . . .[13]

However, a year later—and for reasons never explained—these arguments against Jacobson's leaving Salem seem to have lost their validity. For in May of 1844, he received a call to become inspector at Nazareth Hall and immediately accepted. So on the afternoon of June 25, 1844, "our Br. and Sr. Jacobson with their sickly [son] Eugen began their journey to Pennsylvania . . . accompanied by our best wishes."[14]

Although he had said that "at his age" it would be difficult for him to adjust to new places and new work, Jacobson actually was only forty-four years old when he left Salem, and many years of fruitful service lay ahead of him. After remaining at Nazareth Hall for five years, he served eighteen years as head of the Provincial Elders' Conference at Bethlehem, retiring in 1867; during that time, in 1854, he was consecrated a Bishop in the Unity of Brethren. Following his retirement, "his strength gradually declined, and on Thanksgiving afternoon of 1870 he received the summons to come home at the ripe age of seventy-five years."[15]

He never again served in Wachovia. But in 1877, his daughter, Mary, who was then the wife of Bishop Edward Rondthaler, came to Salem with her husband and two children, Rondthaler having been called there as pastor. They moved into the "ministers' house," the same brick dwelling which, some thirty-five years before, Mary's father had had built in exchange for the *Gemein Haus*. Edward Rondthaler would later serve four years as principal of Salem Academy, and after the turn of the century, his son and Jacobson's grandson, Howard E. Rondthaler, would enjoy a distinguished forty-year career as president of the same institution, then Salem Academy and College.

Only a few days after Jacobson had accepted the call to Nazareth Hall, the Provincial Helpers' Conference named his successor at Salem Academy: the Reverend Charles Adolphus Blech, who at that time was serving as assistant pastor in Salem and as head of the Boys' School. Blech, who was then forty, was born near Lebanon, Pennsylvania, in 1804, the year the Girls' Boarding School in Salem opened.

Charles Adolphus Blech, Inspector 1844–1848

He was educated at Nazareth Hall and the Moravian Theological Seminary, later teaching at both institutions. Before receiving the call to Salem in 1842, he had organized a Moravian congregation at Camden Valley, New York, and had served a pastorate in New York City. Blech and his wife, the former Sophia Krause, and their five children arrived in Salem on September 22, 1842. From that time until his appointment as inspector of the Academy, he spent much of his time conducting services outside of Salem and visiting Unity members in the outlying areas.

Another child had been born to the Blechs since their arrival in Salem, and in consideration of his large family, the Provincial Helpers' Conference set Blech's salary as inspector at $400 a year. In addition, he would receive free sugar and coffee and clothing for his two oldest daughters and would be allowed to employ two women servants at the school's expense.

Just a week after the Jacobsons left, the Helpers' Conference

had a long interview with Br. Blech concerning the new and important charge which he has received and accepted, in which we wished him and his helpmeet wisdom and grace from the Lord. We discussed both the great honor represented by this activity of educating our own and the non-Moravian children who are entrusted to us, and also the high goal—in addition to giving them faithful instruction in the various scientific departments for their cultural improvement—of training them very particularly for the Saviour, in the accomplishment of which no effort should be spared by means of religious instruction or other attempts. Br. Blech was requested to devote himself quite particularly to the internal affairs of the school and to lighten his load by delegating to his assistant, Br. Joshua Boner, more than the ordinary bookkeeping, duties connected with business activities, the visiting of non-Moravians, etc. . . .[16]

Then—rather surprisingly, as there had been no previous mention of such offenses—the Helpers' Conference reported that "Br. Blech will endeavor gradually to do away with various abuses which have crept in—extravagance, parties that resemble balls, etc. . . ."[17] The conference, as it turned out, had not been altogether happy, either, with the financial accounting during the last years of Jacobson's tenure. At the end of the fiscal year 1842-43, for example, conference members had been dismayed to learn that although the school's income was $5,000 less than the year before, its expenses were nearly $3,000 more. And they had been even more dismayed by Jacobson's explanation: the expenses "included $3,500 actually spent for food, laundry, etc., before the end of May, 1842, but by oversight not entered in the account for 1841–42. . . ."[18]

So Blech was duly advised "that all outlays due to craftsmen and others which should be reported for the (fiscal) year should be entered in the appropriate accounts before the year's end, even though they should not have been paid in cash."[19] But, as is so often the case with advice, this was more easily given than taken. For, as instructed, Blech had left much of the bookkeeping to Joshua Boner, only to report the following summer that he was having trouble keeping Boner at his books; Boner, it seems, had recently opened a store, which was taking most of his time, and had "as good as given Blech to understand that he—Br. Bl.—should not count much on his continuing his work."[20] The school's accounts remained in a somewhat muddled state for several years—much to the distress of members of the Helpers' Conference, who were, by nature, orderly men and who, more to the point, counted on at least $1,000 a year out of the school's surplus to help pay the community's bills.

Meanwhile, Blech was submerged in other problems. It was about this time that the congregation leaders, disturbed by the dancing and drinking at the Salem Tavern during the annual public Examination of the Academy, were seriously questioning whether the Examination should be continued. As head of the school, Blech could hardly overlook the publicity value carried by this annual extravaganza—not to say the pleasure it afforded most parents and all pupils—and so declined to be drawn into committing himself on one side or the other of the matter.

Like so many of his predecessors, he also at about that time was struggling to find enough qualified teachers and, on occasion, was forced to fill vacancies with Sisters who were barely older than their pupils. In this scarcity of experienced teachers, Blech himself taught some of the classes for the more advanced students; obviously he was a good teacher, especially in the natural sciences, in which, it was said, he "succeeded in arousing enthusiastic interest where many teachers find simple indifference."[21] But there were so many other demands on his time that he had difficulty fitting classes into his busy schedule. The only time he could hear the girls recite their French lessons, for instance, was at seven o'clock in the morning!

Though it was the best the school could do at the moment, Blech was well aware that there were a number of pupils who deserved better opportunities for advanced work than were being offered them. Then in 1847, the widowed Sister Maria Steiner Denke returned to Salem after spending two years in France as chaperone for two former Academy girls who had been studying at a Moravian school there. She, of course, was a splendid teacher, and her willingness to serve again in the Academy enabled Blech to establish a "Select Class" of some eight or ten of the more advanced students. As one recalled years later:

Our classroom was the front room of the north end of the old Gemein Haus. There we sat around her [Sister Denke] in a square on benches without backs but the hours seemed short while we listened to the words of wisdom and instruction and experience that fell from her lips. Many of us owe our aspirations and their higher forms and nobler aims to her wise admonitions and intellectual attainments. . . .[22]

The Examination program for 1849 showed that by that time the school's curriculum included grammar, history, geography, botany, natural philosophy, Latin, French, arithmetic, and astronomy. The program for 1851 indicates that algebra had been added, and a year later, chemistry.

Such academic advances, however, were wrought during and after a personal traumatic experience which eventually forced Blech to give up the inspectorship. Within a year after they had come to the Academy, Blech's wife contracted consumption. As she grew weaker and less able to care for their six children, the obligations at home plus those at the school became too heavy for Blech, and he called his sister, Carolina, from Bethlehem to come to Salem to help him. Realizing that if he did not have such assistance, Blech could not continue as inspector, the Provincial Helpers' Conference agreed that the school would pay Carolina $10 a month and absorb the cost of her board. Then on March 7, 1846:

There died very gently and blessedly as a result of a slow consumption at the age of 35 years our married Sister Sophia Louisa Blech, wife of our

Br. Carl Adolph Blech, Inspector of the Girls Boarding School here, whose loss, both on account of his numerous family of children still not grown, and his heavy duties of office claimed our painful and great sympathy.[23]

Because it was a firmly held conviction that a wife was an essential requisite for an inspector, Sister Blech's death created a dilemma for the Provincial Helpers' Conference. Realizing the Helpers' position, Blech offered to resign, or if not that, he expressed his willingness to work with some Sister of the conference's choice who might be appointed temporarily as supervisor in his office. His own sister, Carolina, he said, could take care of his children "and of the sale of items to the school children carried on hitherto in his house."[24] The suggestion raised a question of propriety, however. The Helpers felt it not quite proper for a widowed Brother to be associated so closely with a Single Sister, even one of the older Sisters. So members of the conference—and Blech, too, as it turned out—were greatly relieved when Carolina Blech offered "to assist her brother in his duties as the Inspector until the examination."[25]

This solution was only temporary, of course, and the conference immediately wrote to Bethlehem for help. If a place could be found for Blech in the Northern Province, the conference reasoned, then the way would be clear to obtain a new inspector for the Academy—one with the necessary credential, a wife. The man the Helpers had in mind was the Reverend Henry A. Schulz, the same whom many in Salem had wanted when Jacobson was appointed inspector. But Bethlehem's answer was prompt and blunt: Brother Schulz was not available.

Meanwhile, Salem faced the forthcoming Examination of the boarding school with apprehension. Some of the residents suggested that elimination of the band concerts customarily presented during Examination week might forestall the disorders experienced in previous years. The Elders' Conference declined to go quite that far, but it did recommend "to the musicians that, instead of playing the customary military music to play more subdued pieces."[26] The *Aufseher Collegium*, being more realistic, disagreed, believing that "music was not to blame for the disorders of examination week, rather, too free use of strong drink."[27] Besides, the *Collegium* said, visitors liked military music, and as the concerts were "the only means for the musicians to earn something towards the purchase of new instruments, music, etc.," the band should be permitted to play its usual program. The sale of strong drink, however, was prohibited during the week. Whether word of this had spread or whether there were other reasons, the number of outsiders attending the Examination was smaller than usual, and the event "went off this time without disturbance."[28]

A few days afterwards, Blech left for a short vacation in Bethlehem. His earlier uncertainty about being able to continue as inspector apparently had disappeared. And upon his return to Salem in the summer of 1846, he proceeded to administer the school's affairs with a confidence that, in one instance, seemed to the Provincial Helpers' Conference to smack of arrogance. Without notifying the Helpers, much less asking their advice, he sent out a notice to the women who had been doing the laundry for the boarding school girls that forthwith he was reducing the payment from one dollar per week per child to eighty cents. As might have been expected, the women protested immediately and vehemently. And the Helpers' Conference itself was dismayed. To be sure, it conceded, it had urged Blech

to observe every possible economy in the expenditures of the Inspector's office. . . . Nevertheless it was with the proviso that he exercise moderation in doing this and observe the good of the place where we dwell, and also with the comment regarding laundry wages that these had been set at *such* a rate for a number of years and this at a time when children's laundry had been less burdensome in many respects than now, and that subsequently table linen and blankets had been added to it. We therefore regretted very much that despite this Br. Blech had instituted this change without having given us prior indication; we deplore it all the more, because it affects poor widows among the rest who should more properly receive help rather than a reduction; and the outcome may deprive us of blessing. Therefore we do not consider this reduction justifiable but expect Br. Blech to take other action.[29]

But Blech stood his ground. Only if the laundry women "could convince him that they were unable to do the laundry at 80 cents per child per week"[30] would he rescind the action, he said. There is no record of the outcome of this squabble, but, whatever the result, Blech hardly endeared himself to many in the congregation.

Less than a year later, his teachers appealed to the Provincial Helpers' Conference for an increase in salary. By this time, the Academy enrollment had begun to climb, necessitating the addition of an eighth room company and several new teachers. After checking on salaries and benefits at the Bethlehem Female Seminary, the conference decided to adjust those in Salem to the Bethlehem level: six dollars a month, a bonus of ten dollars semiannually, free laundry, board, medicine, and postage and, for those with sixteen years of service, an annual pension of fifty dollars for life.

Blech apparently was in accord with the increases. The Helpers' Conference nevertheless was still concerned about Blech himself, "for he cannot well continue in the Inspector's office as a widower, and his relationship in general with the townspeople is *such* that we would be glad for him to have some other position."[31] Consequently in the early summer of 1847, another letter was dispatched to Pennsylvania, in which the Provincial leaders again were asked to find a place there for Blech and to send someone for the inspector's post in Salem. But the answer was discouraging; any changes in assignments in Pennsylvania that might have created an opening for Blech would have to be postponed until after the church synod, which apparently was some time hence.

Desperate now, the Provincial Helpers could see only one solution: "Br. Van Vleck was requested to interview Br. Blech in the name of the P.H.C. and make him understand that he should now give earnest consideration to his remarriage."[32]

19

A Controversial Marriage

To THE PROVINCIAL HELPERS' DISMAY, BLECH absolutely refused to entertain the thought of remarrying. Nor was he willing to accept the preaching post in East Florida which at the moment was the only suitable position open for a widowed minister. So there was nothing the Helpers could do but let him continue as inspector of the Academy. But with each passing day, their uneasiness mounted, "partly because of the precedent, partly on account of various unfavorable consequences which might ensue and could be expected."[1]

The summer of 1847 turned into fall and then fall into winter; still nothing transpired to relieve the school's predicament. Again the Helpers dispatched an urgent appeal to the Northern Province "for a fitting appointment for our Widowed Br. C. A. Blech in some suitable charge there since he *positively* refuses to be remarried."[2] But again the response was disappointing; the North had no place for him. All through the spring of 1848, the awkward situation simmered; through the hot summer and past the turning of leaves in the fall. It was not until November that, in a thoroughly shocking development, the Blech affair finally boiled over.

Actually, although the Helpers had no inkling of it at the time, the build-up for this somewhat explosive denouement had been going on for more than a year—ever since one of the first heart-to-heart talks which Bishop William Henry Van Vleck, president of the Provincial Helpers, had had with Blech on the subject of the inspector's remarriage. In the course of their rather strained conversation that day, Blech had asked what would happen if he "were to decide to marry a non-Moravian person." And in what seems an offhand sort of way, Van Vleck had replied, "She would have to unite with the church, wouldn't she?"[3] Just why Van Vleck chose to answer as he did is not explained in later reports of the conversation. In all probability, the kindly Bishop, thinking Blech was too upset at the moment to realize what he was saying, simply had not taken the question seriously; surely Blech, being himself a minister, knew as well as anyone that in the practice of their church, ministers *always* chose their wives from within the Moravian membership.

Whatever Van Vleck's reason, though, his answer definitely had been a mistake. For now in this November of 1848, it was painfully clear that not only had Inspector Blech been fully conscious of what he was asking that day; he also had taken Van Vleck's offhand answer totally at face value. Whether he had had a specific "non-Moravian person" in mind at the time is a matter of conjecture. But if not, he evidently set out almost at once to explore the field beyond Moravian boundaries. By July of 1848—and with the Salem Brethren still believing him to be obstinately resisting remarriage—he had made his choice of a second wife, had proposed to the chosen lady, and had had his proposal accepted.

In a confidential letter to Van Vleck, dated July 10, 1848, he happily announced his plans to marry Mary Jane Harrison of Green County, Alabama. The letter reached Van Vleck in Herrnhut (Germany), where he was attending a Unity synod. And we can imagine the consternation with which the good Bishop, thousands of miles across the Atlantic, read the shocking news from home. For, as he knew all too well, Miss Harrison was not a Moravian; furthermore, and equally as distressing, she had been a student at Salem Academy as recently as the spring of 1847. To be sure, she had been considerably older than the other pupils in school at that time.* And while she was in his charge, Blech apparently had given no indication that his interest in her was any different from the paternal concern exhibited toward all

---

*The Academy's registration book cites Mary Jane Harrison's birth year as 1818, which would mean that she was twenty-eight or twenty-nine years old when she left the school in 1847. There is no explanation as to why a woman of that age was attending a girls' boarding school.

his pupils. Even so, the mere fact that he was marrying one of his own pupils would inevitably give rise to rumors and questions that could harm the school's reputation.

Fortunately Van Vleck was in Herrnhut, seat of the Unity of Brethren, when he received the disturbing news and so was able to seek counsel directly from the Unity Elders' Conference, the church's highest authority in such matters. Consequently he returned to Salem in November with a clear-cut directive for the Provincial Helpers: the Unity Elders had ruled unanimously "that under these circumstances Br. Blech could not remain in service here [Salem] any longer, especially in the position he has held in the past."[4]

In handing down the severe judgment, the Elders had shown brotherly consideration for Blech's feelings by agreeing "to say a good word to the Pennsylvania H. Confz. [Helpers' Conference] relative to the future employment of the aforesaid brother in the northern district."[5] And on his way home from Herrnhut, Van Vleck had stopped in Bethlehem to try to arrange a place for Blech, hoping that the offer of a new position would soften the blow of dismissal. But the Pennsylvania conference would make no promises. So it was only bad news that Van Vleck could bring home. And shortly after his arrival in Salem, he privately informed Blech of the Unity Elders' decision. The information, as the Helpers later noted, was "ill-received"; what he had done, Blech insisted, was altogether justified by the answer Van Vleck had given to his question the summer before, and no amount of explanation could convince him otherwise.

All of this was reported on November 7 to the Provincial Helpers' Conference, which recorded that it "could not but learn with pain and also with amazement that a brother, whom one could certainly expect to be familiar with our regulations, should resort to a misinterpretation of an answer based upon them."[6] The conference nevertheless could not bring itself to take final action without conferring with members of the Salem Elders' Conference. The meeting with the Elders took place that same afternoon. Obviously the Salem Elders concurred with the Unity Elders, for, convening again the next day, the Helpers discussed at some length both a list of candidates for the position of inspector of the Academy and interim arrangements "should he [Blech] be unwilling to serve until the coming of his successor."[7] Later in the day, Blech was called in and formally notified of the termination of his service at the school. He again brought up Van Vleck's answer to his question about marrying a non-Moravian "and added that it not only had never been his intention to marry his present fiancee *before* she had become a member of the Moravian Church through her reception, but that he had assured himself regarding this *before* he had proposed marriage."[8] But the Helpers stood firm.

In consideration of Blech's former service, however, they voted to grant him an annual subsidy of $160 "effective until his re-employment and for as long a time as the responsibility for the support of his 2 youngest children rests on him alone."[9] The conference further agreed to provide for the education "of the children of his first marriage"[10] when they reached the prescribed age, or, if Blech preferred to keep the children near him rather than to send them back to Salem, it would grant each an annual subsidy of not less than $50. It was only fair also, the Helpers felt, that the Academy bear the expenses of Blech's move from Salem.

Ten days after his dismissal, Blech set out for Alabama, where on December 1, 1848, he was united in marriage with Mary Jane Harrison. There is nothing in the records to indicate his frame of mind as he rode out of Salem, but in a letter to Van Vleck on the day before his departure, he presented his fiancee's request to become a member of the Moravian Church. So if he did harbor any resentment, it was not serious enough to dilute his commitment to the church.

Meanwhile, the tensions of these past few weeks were bound to have seeped through the walls of the old *Gemein Haus* and into the living rooms and classrooms of the Academy. And we can imagine the excited whisperings that went on, especially among the teachers who, as a student there at the time recalled years later, were indignant at Blech's behavior.[11]

Before leaving for Alabama, Blech had made temporary arrangements for the operation of the Academy until his successor could assume the duties: his sister, Carolina, would continue in the responsibilities she had been carrying since his first wife's death; Thomas Pfohl would handle financial matters; and Sister Maria Denke would conduct Blech's French classes. The interim plan already drawn up by the Provincial Helpers was similar, except that Sister Denke would be asked to act as "Directress" of the school. And being the most experienced and respected teacher, she no doubt did more or less take charge.

Already, however, the procedures for acquiring a new inspector were well under way, having begun when Van Vleck stopped in Bethlehem en route home from Herrnhut. Knowing then, of course, that Blech's dismissal was imminent, he had met with the Helpers' Conference in Bethlehem and, as a result of that meeting, had arrived in Salem with the names of five Brethren of the Northern Province to be considered. And at their meetings on November 8 and November 10—the same at which they agonized over Blech's attitude—the Helpers in Salem had examined the qualifications of these five candidates, as well as those of a Brother in the Southern Province who had been nominated. "Following mature deliberation,"[12] the conference had voted to ask the Helpers in Pennsylvania to submit the names of two of the Northern candidates—Emil Adolphus de Schweinitz* and his brother, Robert William de Schweinitz—to the Lot, and a letter to that effect had been dispatched.

On November 26, 1848—just a week and a day after Blech's departure for Alabama—came the reply from Pennsylvania:

... in accordance with a directive from our dear Lord Br. Emil A. von Schweinitz, hitherto the pastor in Nazareth, has received and, relying upon His support, has accepted the call to take over the Inspectorship of the local Girls Boarding School with his dear wife.[13]

His appointment was announced that evening to the congregation and to the teachers and pupils of the Academy. And in the aftermath of the recent unpleasantness, the news must have been welcomed with joyful relief throughout the town. For both Emil de Schweinitz and his wife, Sophia, not only were themselves known and beloved in Salem but also came of families long prominent in the Unity of Brethren; de Schweinitz, in fact, was the great-great-grandson of Count Zinzendorf and was said to have borne "a striking resemblance to Zinzendorf both in face and bearing."[14]

De Schweinitz' father, Lewis David de Schweinitz, was a Moravian

---

*The name is variously written as "de Schweinitz," "von Schweinitz" or "Schweinitz." Because members of the family most closely associated with Salem Academy preferred "de Schweinitz," that form is used here except in direct quotations.

Emil Adolphus de Schweinitz, Inspector 1848–1853

minister who served the Unity in various responsible capacities and whose lifelong interest in botany earned him the title of "Father of American Mycology." Emil had been born in Salem on October 26, 1816, while his father was serving as administrator of Wachovia, but when he was five, he had moved with his family to Bethlehem, where his father became minister of the congregation and principal of the girls' school. He attended Nazareth Hall and the theological seminary at Nazareth, later studying at the theological seminary at Gnaden-feld, Germany. Upon his return to America, he taught at Nazareth Hall for four years and then was placed in charge of the Unity's finan-cial affairs in Nazareth.

On June 28, 1842, he was married to Sophia Herman, who had even stronger ties with Salem. Her father, Bishop Johann Gottlieb Her-man, had taught in the Boys' School in Salem, and in 1821, shortly after accepting a call as pastor of the Moravian congregation at New-port, Rhode Island, had married Anna Paulina Schober of Salem. Although Sophia had been reared in the Northern Province, she had visited Salem frequently and had a number of uncles, aunts, and cousins there. Especially after she began teaching at the Bethlehem Female Academy, she had carried on a lively correspondence with several of her cousins who were then teaching at Salem Academy (Chapter 17). It was one of her teacher-cousins, Henrietta Schober, who, upon hearing of Sophia's engagement to Emil de Schweinitz, had written with a touch of prophecy: "Who knows but what you may some day come to Salem?"[15] Now, only six years later, Sophia was indeed coming not only to Salem but also to the Academy itself.

Upon receiving word of de Schweinitz' acceptance, the Provincial Helpers lost no time in spreading it abroad, hoping that by so doing they could reassure parents who probably had been hearing all sorts of rumors about the recent happenings. A printed circular, dated December 20, 1848, and signed by Bishop Van Vleck, thus was widely distributed:

The Friends and Patrons of the Female Academy at Salem, North Carolina, are respectfully informed, that, agreeable to an arrangement on the part of the Trustees, the Rev'd E. A. de Schweinitz, late of Nazareth, Pennsylvania, has received and accepted an appointment as Principal of the above Institution; the Rev'd C. A. Bleck [sic], being about to remove with his family from this place. The new Principal and his Lady are ex-

pected to enter upon their official duties at the commencement of the ensuing year, and are hereby affectionately recommended to the confidence
of the Parents and Friends of our pupils, and the public in general. No
change will take place in the principles, upon which this Institution is conducted, or the regulations hitherto established for its government.[16]

The circular went on to explain that all debts and notes payable to
the former inspector were now transferred to his successor.

The de Schweinitzes arrived in Salem on December 23, 1848. On
the day after Christmas, de Schweinitz met with the Provincial Helpers' Conference, and at four o'clock that afternoon he and his wife
were introduced to the pupils and teachers of the school. Two days
later, Blech returned from Alabama with his bride, creating a rather
awkward situation, which he did nothing to ease. As the obviously
irritated Provincial Helpers later reported it:

He [Blech] returned here from Alabama with his wife on December 28.
Thereupon on the 29th written notice was given him by the P.H.C. that
his successor, Br. Emil A. v. Schweinitz, had arrived here on the 23rd and
was ready to take over the Inspectorship of the Girls Boarding School,
and that he should turn over to him, without needless delay, the books,
the monies, and all the other effects of the school. Since nothing happened
as a result of this, P.H.C. decided on January 4 to request Br. Blech in
writing to name a day on which he would be ready to make the transfer,
and to offer him at the same time to have the accounts which might not
yet be completed entered by Br. Thos. Pfohl. In a written reply to this
communication, received on the 6th, Br. Blech declined the assistance
offered him as not being needed, and stated that he was unable to name a
definite day for the transfer of the Boarding School and its effects to Br.
Schweinitz. But he promised to have this take place as soon as possible.
But this was delayed until the 15th. Thereupon the departure of Br. Blech
and his family for Bethlehem followed on the 16th.[17]

Blech, his young wife, and his six children remained in Bethlehem
until August, when he was appointed to take charge of the Moravian
congregation at Gnadenhütten and Sharon, Ohio. But his return to
ministerial service would be short-lived; the family had been in Ohio
less than a year when Blech became acutely ill one evening during a
meeting of the congregation, and about ten o'clock the next morning,
January 17, 1850—just a year and a day after he left Salem—"he gently

breathed his last."[18] In those few months in Ohio, however, he must have earned the respect not only of his congregation but of others as well, for it was reported that his funeral was attended by "a large congregation of persons, a great number of whom were friends & neighbors from the country around."[19]

Emil de Schweinitz was only thirty-two years old when he assumed the inspectorship of the Academy. But unlike Jacobson, who had had to overcome open animosity, de Schweinitz had been a popular choice in Salem and thus, despite his youth, was able to enjoy the full confidence and cooperation of both teachers and townspeople from the beginning of his term. And unlike Blech, who tended to be abrasive, he was a man of quiet dignity, who easily inspired admiration and affection. "How kind yet dignified was our dear principal," a teacher later wrote of him, "and how proud we all were of him and his handsome wife, especially on public occasions when they both occupied prominent positions."[20] So, under these favorable circumstances, began a period of stability in the inspector's office—one blessedly free of the internal dissensions and personal crises that had plagued the inspectorship since Abraham Steiner's time.

Using his experience in handling the financial affairs at Nazareth, de Schweinitz set out at once to bring some order to the Academy's somewhat confused bookkeeping with the result that, to the Provincial Helpers' "grateful joy,"[21] the accounts for the fiscal year ending May 31, 1849, showed a surplus of $6,513.83, which meant that for the first time in three years the community would receive a subsidy from the boarding school. And using his experience as a teacher at Nazareth Hall, he took firm control of the classroom work, paying particular attention to the progress of the pupils as shown in the annual private and public Examinations. For these, he kept a small record book in which he recorded the performance of each class as "tol" (tolerable), "pr. good" (pretty good), "good," or "poor."[22] And it was he who instituted a printed program for the public Examination. The story goes that at one of the Examinations during de Schweinitz' administration a gentleman in the audience

thought he had discovered an error in the solution of an algebraic problem, and sent a written notice to the Principal. But he, stepping forward, quickly proved the girls to be entirely correct, and the gentleman acknowledged the fact and highly commended the thoroughness of the instruction the class had received.[23]

De Schweinitz also requested and received from the Provincial Helpers' Conference more definite regulations governing the town girls who attended classes in the boarding school. It was agreed that, as a rule, the town girls would remain in school until they had been received into the Older Girls' Choir (about fourteen years of age), but if their parents wished them to remain longer, a special application had to be entered and arrangements made relative to school fees.

The more dramatic changes during these years, however, occurred in Salem itself. Plank roads had begun to criss-cross North Carolina, providing noisy but all-weather access for farmers to the market places and faster passenger transportation between communities. The longest of these roads—in fact, "the longest plank road ever built anywhere in the world"[14]—stretched from Fayetteville to Bethania, passing through Salem. And by 1854, stagecoaches were arriving in town every Tuesday, Thursday, and Saturday.

Of far greater impact on the once-isolated old congregation town was an act ratified by the General Assembly of North Carolina on January 16, 1849, in which Stokes County was divided. The southern portion, which included the Moravian settlements, became a new county named "Forsyth" in honor of Colonel Benjamin Forsyth, a Stokes County native who had lost his life in the War of 1812. Salem was situated in almost the exact center of this new county. Furthermore, the Salem congregation owned about three thousand acres of land around the town. So when the new county commissioners began their search for the site of Forsyth's county seat, their eyes inevitably fell on Moravian land, and they requested that the congregation sell them fifty acres just north of Salem for the location of a courthouse and other necessary county buildings.

As would be expected, such a request was considerably less than welcomed by many in the congregation, especially the more conservative members, who feared that the unruly crowds often drawn to courthouses would spill over into peaceable Salem. Also, as whipping was still being used as punishment in those days, they objected to the prospect of having a whipping post so close by. On the other hand, argued more progressive members of the congregation, if the Moravians refused to sell this land, the county would locate its courthouse several miles away, and this could hurt Salem economically, as the new town that would surely grow up around the courthouse could seriously drain off Salem's trade. In the end, the economic argument won out; the Salem congregation sold Forsyth County 51¼ acres of land, the southern boundary of which was only five hundred feet from the northern end of Salem.

The deed for the tract was dated May 12, 1849, but it was not until almost two years later that a name was given to the county seat of Forsyth: "Winston," in honor of Major Joseph Winston, Revolutionary War hero who had fought at Kings Mountain and Guilford Courthouse. As the progressives had foreseen, Winston did grow into a new town. And in the years to come, it grew in population and industry until in 1913 the two towns were merged to become the city of Winston-Salem. But for more than half a century, Winston and Salem lived side by side as separate municipalities.

Even so, the founding and growth of Winston brought resident non-Moravians practically to the doorstep of Salem, which for so long not only had been reserved for Moravians alone but also had been separated from others by the breadth of the congregation-owned land. And this proximity to new people and new ways rapidly had its effect on the people and ways of Salem. As the editor of *The People's Press*, Salem's newspaper, put it:

At the opening of the present year [1853] our country is prosperous and happy, at peace with all the world. Our beloved state is marching with rapid strides towards a conspicuous place among her more fortunate sister states, and our village is gradually doffing her ancient garb and putting on more modern airs "a la mode" all the world and the rest of mankind.[25]

By 1856, the basic regulations of a congregation town—church control of land ownership, residency, and businesses—had become so unenforceable that they were abolished. Home owners could now own the land on which their houses stood; non-Moravians could now live in Salem; tradesmen and craftsmen were no longer subject to congregation control of their businesses. In short, Salem ceased to function as a congregation town, and in December of 1856, at the Salem citizens' request, the General Assembly passed an act establishing Salem as a duly incorporated municipality.

20

A Doric
Portico

I N LATE 1852, JUST FOUR YEARS AFTER HE HAD COME
to the Academy, Emil de Schweinitz was appointed to the higher position of administrator of Wachovia, the office held by his father
some thirty years before. Though his term as inspector was relatively
short, it had not been entirely without problems. A severe epidemic
of measles struck the school in 1849, in the course of which more than
forty girls were abed at the same time. Then at the public Examination in 1852, some of the non-Moravian visitors "became intoxicated
. . . and behaved shamefully."[1] Also, like his predecessors, Emil de
Schweinitz struggled with the perennial space shortage.

On the whole, though, he was leaving the school on solid footing:
faculty morale was high, the teachers having just received a dollar-a-
month raise; the financial condition was sound; the school's reputation
was spreading, with girls now in attendance from North Carolina,
South Carolina, Georgia, Virginia, Alabama, Mississippi, Louisiana, Tennessee, and Texas. The Provincial Helpers' Conference, determined to preserve such stability and conceding that "there is no
brother in our district who seems fully qualified for this office,"[2] once
more appealed to the Northern Province for an inspector. Four names
were suggested for submission to the Lot: Robert W. de Schweinitz,
Julius T. Bechler, William T. Roepper, and Henry A. Schulz. On
December 19, 1852, word was received from Bethlehem that Robert
de Schweinitz, then pastor at Lancaster and Emil's younger brother,
had received and accepted the call.

Like Emil, Robert had been born in Salem (on September 20, 1819) while their father, Lewis David de Schweinitz, was serving as administrator of Wachovia. But he had been only two years old when the family moved to Pennsylvania, and he had not lived in Salem since that time, although, both personally and by family connections, he was well known and respected there. He entered Nazareth Hall in 1830, later studying at the Moravian Theological Seminary. After completing his education, he taught at Nazareth Hall for six years. In 1845, he left for a visit to relatives in Europe, and it was while he was in Germany that he met and subsequently (on July 26, 1846) married Maria Louise von Tschirschky, who came of an old Silesian family and who is said to have been quite a beauty. That fall the couple embarked on what unfortunately turned out to be a long and stormy voyage to America. But they reached its shores safely, and, back in Pennsylvania, de Schweinitz soon became a professor at the Theological Seminary. Following his ordination shortly thereafter, he entered the active ministry, serving a pastorate first at Graceham, Maryland, and later at Lancaster, Pennsylvania, where he was living when he received the call to succeed his brother as inspector of Salem Academy.

By this time, the de Schweinitzes had two children—Helen Louise, five years old, and Louis Alexander, who was not yet four—and another was on the way. The prospect of making the long journey to North Carolina with two small children and a pregnant wife could not have been a welcome one for the new inspector. But all accounts describe Robert de Schweinitz as a genial, outgoing man who—as would be demonstrated time and time again during the Civil War years—tended to meet adversity with cheerful aplomb. So if he had any serious qualms about either the trip itself or leaving the area in which he had lived for most of his thirty-three years, there was no evidence of them in his letter to Bishop Johann Gottlieb Herman, dated January 5, 1853:

My Dear Br. Herman

In an official letter from Brother Emil, received yesterday, he suggests that it would be proper for me to direct my answer to yourself, as President of the P.H.C. in the South. This I do with no little pleasure, responding at the same time most cordially to the kind greetings which your

Conference has sent me in view of my contemplated removal into your midst as Inspector of the Salem Academy.

It was not without the most serious misgiving as regards our capacity to take charge of this Institution, that Sr. Schw. & myself did at last resolve to accept the appointment. Now that we have done so may our reliance be cast on the Lord & may He grant us His blessing & support. It is very cheering for us to be well assured, that we are coming among Brethren & old friends who will receive us with love & no doubt do all in their power to assist & direct us.

As regards the details of our journey to Salem, we shall cheerfully follow the suggestions of my Brother's letter. To travel private from Henderson to Salem will I think be absolutely necessary. In the present situation of Sr. Schw. stage travelling over North Carolina roads would be dangerous.

The precise time of our departure from here I can not as yet fix but will write as soon as I can say with certainty when it will be possible for us to leave here. The forwarding of our effects I will attend to according to the directions transmitted—Would they were already packed & off!

With kindest greetings to yourself family & colleagues

I remain affectionately
ROBERT DE SCHWEINITZ[3]

On the same day that Robert wrote his official letter of acceptance, Emil issued a circular directed to "the friends and patrons of Salem Female Academy,"[4] in which he announced his brother's appointment, recommended "the new Principal* and his lady . . . to the confidence of the parents and friends of the pupils and the public in general," assured patrons that there would be no change in either the principles or the regulations of the Academy, and served notice that all debts to the school were now payable to the new principal.

The de Schweinitzes arrived in Salem on February 23, 1853, and on March 2, Robert William de Schweinitz was formally installed as the seventh inspector of the Girls' Boarding School. So began a thirteen-year tenure that would encompass one of the most trying periods in the school's history, "a time requiring more than ordinary

---

*By this time, the terms "inspector" and "principal" had come to be used interchangeably in reference to the chief administrator of Salem Female Academy; the congregation records usually clung to the traditional "inspector," while most public references used the more common "principal."

ability and good judgment."[5] At the same time, Robert's brother and predecessor assumed responsibilities that, too, would become inordinately heavy during the Civil War and its aftermath. As administrator of Wachovia, Emil de Schweinitz was entrusted with the financial affairs of the entire Southern Province of the Moravian Church, a responsibility which he discharged, despite the crucial economic position of the South of that period, with "clear insight and sound judgment."[6] Although he had been ordained before coming to Salem, it was not until after the war that circumstances and his own desires led him into the active ministry. He was consecrated Bishop in 1874, and, by his own choosing, resigned the highest office in the province to become pastor of the small congregation at New Philadelphia, west of Salem. Within only a few years, however, his health began to fail. He was able to make one more trip to Europe, but in the fall of 1879, he returned to Salem and died there on November 3 at the age of sixty-three.

He was still a vigorous man of thirty-seven, though, in that early spring of 1853 when his younger brother took over his work at the Academy. And while Robert was unquestionably able to stand on his own feet at all times, it must have been a comfort to him nevertheless, especially during the difficult war years, to have the advice and support of his brother so close at hand.

Robert had been in office only two days when the school's bookkeeper, Joshua Boner, insisted on an increase in salary. Boner had asked for a raise in January, but the Provincial Helpers had concluded that the $200 a year, plus a gratuity of at least $25, then being paid him "seemed to them adequate in view of his services."[7] Now with a new inspector in the school, Boner realized that he was in a better bargaining position and quickly took advantage of the opening. The Helpers still didn't think an increase was warranted.

Nevertheless due mainly to the consideration that the new Inspector, having just assumed office, could not at that time dispense with the services of a brother who was so familiar with the external affairs of the boarding school except with the greatest inconvenience, it was induced to approve Br. Joshua Boner's receiving a remuneration of at least $250 for the coming year in addition to the gratuity hitherto customary.[8]

In April, the school again was beset by a measles epidemic, which

Robert William de Schweinitz, Inspector (title changed to
President during his term) 1853–1866

struck more than a hundred girls before it ended. But de Schweinitz seems to have slipped easily into the driver's seat, and, according to the local newspaper, the Examination over which he presided in June "gave general satisfaction to all interested in the school."[9] By August, he had met the problem of overcrowding head-on by proceeding with a plan of construction that would not only meet the space needs but also markedly change the face of Salem Square. According to this plan, the old stone and half-timbered *Gemein Haus*, built in 1771 and given over to the school in 1841, would be torn down, and in its place would be constructed a massive new brick building in the neoclassical style popular at that time, towering four full stories and featuring a Doric portico.

There must have been more than a few in Salem that summer who heard these plans with sentimental sadness. For nearly three quarters of a century, the *Gemein Haus* had been central to the life of Salem. It had served as the congregation's first house of worship; far-reaching decisions had been made in its conference rooms; Frederic William Marshall, Carl Gotthold Reichel, and others prominent in the early years of Salem had made their homes there; it was in the house's *saal* that the congregation had gathered on July 4, 1783, to give thanks in song and lovefeast for the peace following the American Revolution; Sister Oesterlein's first school for little girls had occupied one of its rooms; indeed, the Girls' Boarding School itself had had its beginning in this sturdy old house. But if anyone voiced serious objections to the destruction of such a landmark, his protest went unrecorded. On the contrary, according to the records, the Provincial Helpers—obviously with unanimity—hailed the removal of the old building and the construction of a new one as a "desirable undertaking," expressing happiness that the plans "could soon be realized" and noting with satisfaction that a major portion of the funds for meeting the estimated $20,000–$30,000 cost was already in reserve.[10]

Demolition of the *Gemein Haus* would not begin until the following summer, but during the intervening fall and winter months there was much preliminary work to be done. De Schweinitz himself apparently had worked out the basic plan for the building, but a contract was negotiated with Francis Fries of Salem, under the terms of which Fries agreed, for the sum of $1,000, "to act as builder for the entire edifice, to negotiate all contracts, to procure all necessary materials, and to devote his time to the construction until its completion, as though it were his own."[11] Because the north and south wings of the new building would extend farther east than the *Gemein Haus*, the *Aufseher Collegium* agreed to make additional land available to the school and to remove a number of sheds that then stood on the site. In his turn, de Schweinitz began to make arrangements for the temporary quartering of the school girls while the construction was in progress.

Meanwhile, the day-by-day operation of the Academy continued without interruption. According to its catalogue of 1853–54, the faculty now numbered twenty-nine, including the first male (other than the inspector) ever to teach at the school: the Reverend Francis Florentine Hagen, composer of the beloved Moravian Christmas hymn *Morning Star*, who, for lack of music teachers among the Single Sisters, had been engaged to give music lessons at the school twice a week. The enrollment stood at 329—277 boarders and 52 day pupils. In addition to an entrance fee of $5, parents or guardians paid $30 a quarter for a student's board, lodging, and instruction in the basic courses: reading, writing, arithmetic, grammar, history, geography, composition, globes, natural philosophy, chemistry, botany, algebra, plain needlework, and Latin. For extra fees, ranging from $3 to $5 per subject, girls could be given piano, guitar, and melodeon lessons and instruction in German, French, drawing and painting, and ornamental needlework.

In early February, 1854, the town girls' school was moved from the *Gemein Haus* to temporary quarters across the square in the old Single Brothers' House (then called the Widows' House). And in April, the town school for boys moved to the concert hall in the old pottery building two blocks up Main Street in order that the Boys' School building, which faced the northwest corner of the square, could be used by the Academy during the construction of the new building. Work on the project itself, however, was postponed until after the public Examination in June, which, despite the fact that some visitors "made merry with dancing"[12] at one of the hotels, went off very well. The Examination closed the fiftieth session of the Girls' Boarding School in Salem, a milestone which prompted the local newspaper editor to note: "Our flourishing Female Institution . . . has secured for itself a standing among Southern institutions of learning, and a home in the affections of Southern people, of which it may be justly proud."[13]

Because space in the next two years would be more limited than ever, de Schweinitz placed a notice in a number of Southern newspapers, informing the public that "no more scholars can be received at the present time" and that for some time hence "parents and others, desiring to place their daughters, relatives or wards under our care are requested . . . not to set out with them for Salem without having first ascertained by application in writing, to the subscribers whether or not they can be received."[14]

With the Examination over, workmen began removing the heavy timbers and stones of the *Gemein Haus*. On June 20, they came upon the lead capsule that had been sealed in the cornerstone with such ceremony eighty-four years before. In memory of the hallowed old house, Francis Hagen composed and set to music an ode, entitled "Alma Mater." Within six weeks, the *Gemein Haus* was gone, and on its site the foundations of the large brick building, later to be known as "Main Hall," had begun to rise. At 7:30 on the evening of August 9, 1854,

the solemn cornerstone laying of the new academy building was held, at which a throng of people was present. Following an anthem by the choir and the singing of a number of stanzas, Br. Rob. Schweinitz delivered a suitable address and placed various items in a capsule which then was sealed and inserted in the cornerstone prior to prayer by Br. [George Frederick] Bahnson. The evening hour contributed to the solemnity of the whole ceremony.[15]

The building would not be ready for occupancy for nearly two years, but the school kept on operating—if not as usual, at least with admirable resourcefulness. One room company was lodged in the Single Sisters' House, the Sisters having given up their sleep hall and turned their chapel into a dormitory for themselves. The two youngest companies lived in the Boys' School, and others were quartered in the 1805 Girls' Boarding School building (South Hall). As classes were held in both the Boys' School and the 1805 building,

it was great fun to the girls to cross the Square in a great living stream at the opening and close of the various houses. It was especially interesting to them in rainy weather, for which purpose great stands of umbrellas were placed inside the doors of South Hall and the Boys School house.[16]

For the teachers, the inconveniences were not exactly "great fun." As one recalled, "Many a night we were compelled (for want of room in the dormitory) to trudge through rain and snow to our sleeping apartment in the second story of the principal's house." But, she went on, "we were a happy family and the ties of friendship thus formed are still strong and enduring."[17]

In September, 1854, de Schweinitz submitted a financial report which, to the unconcealed delight of the Provincial Helpers, showed a surplus of $11,689.85. Even after allocating $1,000 each to the Wachovia treasury, a reserve for losses of the cotton factory, and a reserve for questionable debts, there remained substantial funds to be applied to the new building: $260 "for 2 new horses and a dray, recently acquired because of the building," $200 reserved for beds, $1,129.85 reserved "for the furniture account, in view of the need of getting new furniture for the new building," and $7,100 reserved for the building account itself.[18]

On August 29, 1855, de Schweinitz submitted another report. The surplus was slightly less—$9,881.34¼; even so, $1,200 was allocated for furniture for the new building, $400 for beds, and $6,581.34¼ for the building account. And de Schweinitz was able to announce "that the school's new building, in its present state of completion, has been almost completely paid for."[19] At the same time, de Schweinitz proposed and the Provincial Helpers' Conference approved an increase in rates: from $30 to $35 for board and tuition, from $5 to $6 for piano lessons, and from $3 to $5 for instruction in French.

Throughout the fall of 1855 and into the new year, de Schweinitz and his teachers coped with the headaches of makeshift facilities. As the inspector recalled, "No easy undertaking it was to tear down and build up, and yet, at the same time, keep a school of more than 200 boarders in full operation."[20] But by March, 1856, the main part of the new building and the north wing were virtually complete, and in its issue of March 7, The People's Press of Salem reproduced an engraving of the imposing new structure together with de Schweinitz's detailed description of it:

The new house occupies the site of the old church and parsonage, immediately adjoining the original school building.

The dimensions of the main building are 100 feet front by 52 feet deep with a wing at the north 70½ feet in length and 34½ feet in depth. The wing on the south end will be 77 by 44 feet. The main building, as well as the wing, are four stories high on the front, and at the rear (on account of the descent of the ground) five stories, including the basement. The fronts of the houses are of pressed brick, expressly manufactured for our buildings, and are probably some of the finest of the kind made in the State.

The front is ornamented by a large Doric portico, 50 feet in length and 13 feet in width. It has four Doric columns, with two pilasters resting against the house. The height of the whole, including bases, columns and entablatures, is between 30 and 40 feet—the cornice of the entablature extending three feet above the sills of the third story windows.

The whole is built strictly in accordance with the classic Doric order of architecture. The columns are of brick, stuccoed with hydraulic cement, in imitation of brown sandstone, as is also the rest of the portico, excepting the bases and steps, which are of hewn granite.

The roof of the house has but one inclination, from front to rear—and is covered with tin. The front elevation is formed and crowned by a very heavy cornice of blockwork, over six feet in height. In the centre there rises above this, a pediment of over fifty feet in length of base by about eighteen feet elevation.

The first and second stories of the main house are divided into 18 dwelling and school rooms, with smaller side rooms attached to each. These side rooms are fitted up with small closets, wardrobes &c. All the rooms are lined to a height of three feet from the floor, with panel-work grained in imitation of walnut. Passages of 12 feet wide extend through the whole length of the house, in each story, and wide staircases run up on both ends of the main house, from the basement to the fourth story. The entrance hall on the first floor, into which the large front door opens, is about 20 feet square, connecting with the main passage, by an elliptical archway of about twenty feet span. On the south end the passage connects by a closed and covered way with the old buildings. The whole third floor forms one dormitory. This is a very large room, extending over the entire house from wall to wall, without any partitions, the ceiling and fourth floor being supported by a colonnade of 16 pillars. The fourth story is divided into 10 rooms—those on the front being fine and airy, intended for smaller classes and music rooms. Those on the rear are roughly finished and only intended for trunk and store-rooms.

The north wing is divided into a large number of rooms, to be used for various purposes.—The whole of the second story of this wing is devoted to the so-called "sick-rooms," with every convenience attached. From the wing there is also a covered and closed way, leading directly into our church, and by this passage our scholars can enter the church under cover at all times.

The whole rear part of the basement story is taken up by "wash" or "dressing rooms." There are 18 such wash-rooms, each being furnished with three stationary basins. Through all these apartments the water, both hot and cold, is conducted in pipes. In addition to these rooms there are a number of bath-rooms, with tub and shower baths. The head of water is obtained from large water tanks, located in the building at the end of the north wing. The supply of water is procured from a well and spring at the foot of the hill upon which the building stands, being drawn up an elevation of some 140 feet by forcing-pumps, which are worked by water-power. The hot water is generated in a large circulatory boiler, located in the cellar of the front house. This boiler was made expressly for our establishment at Auburn, New York.

There are porches of 12 feet-width, running along the rear of the house, two stories high on the main house, and three on the wing. We have introduced a very complete system of ventilation throughout the whole building. Four main trunk ventilators run up from the lower floor extending above the roof. With these main trunks the different rooms are connected by branches. The south wing has not yet been built, as we shall have to take down some of the back buildings of the old house before we can commence. The lower floor of this wing will contain a dining room, large enough to seat some 250 persons. On the second floor, which will be supported by iron pillars, our chapel will be located.

In addition to these new buildings, we shall thoroughly repair the old ones, and keep them in occupancy, —at least so much of them as at present accommodate about 130 boarders.

R. DE S.

This massive brick structure—with its columned portico, covered passageways, ventilating system, and hot-and-cold running water—

1856 Academy building (Main Hall) and 1805 Girls' Boarding
School building with 1837 renovations

was the first building to be constructed on Salem Square for a full
half-century. And a far cry it was from the plain Germanic architecture of its neighbors. Eyes surely must have popped and tongues
wagged not only in the old Moravian community but in neighboring
Winston as well.

As de Schweinitz had indicated, work would begin soon on the
south wing. But with the completion of the main section and the
north wing, the basic facilities—dormitory, infirmary, and classrooms
—were ready for occupancy. So it was that on Easter Monday (March
24, 1856), the temporarily exiled school girls and teachers began to
return home—from the Sisters' House and the Boys' School, from the
Widows' House and the old school building next door. No special
religious services marked the opening of the new building; those
would come later with the dedication of the chapel. And no formal
ceremonies accompanied the move itself. Throughout that week,

room company after room company simply packed up its books and its ink bottles, its embroidery hoops and watercolor brushes and piano exercises, its clothing and other personal belongings, and toted them up the street or across the square to its assigned quarters in the spanking new building.

One can well imagine, though, that the move was not made in silence—not with two hundred or more excitable school girls involved. And there must have been squeals aplenty when they first saw all the "luxuries" that now would be theirs. As one teacher would recall some forty years later,[21] their washrooms were in the depths of the basement "and we had neither carpets on the floor, pictures on the wall, the privacy of curtained alcoves nor the many additions to comfort and appearances that now improve and adorn our old and honored institution." But, she said, "When we moved back into the new and handsome building, we all thought we had everything to make us happy and comfortable."

Main Hall 1858 (Robert de Schweinitz and his wife standing on the portico)

21

Measles and
Morale

THE SOUTH WING OF THE NEW BUILDING WAS
not completed until the spring of 1857. In the meantime, de
Schweinitz was occupied with other matters, including the morale
of his teachers and the health of his pupils. From the beginning of
his term at the Academy, "his genial, kindly manner made him greatly beloved by all who came in contact with him,"[1] especially the school
girls for whom he represented, as Abraham Steiner had before him,
the affectionate image of their own fathers. As one of them recalled:

I can see him now walking through the Academy yard with a bevy of
little girls clinging to him, up in his arms, hanging onto his coat while we
big girls stood aloof with our mouths watering because we didn't have the
privilege. Love him? next to my own father.[2]

And miffed as the teachers were in the salary dispute that erupted
in the fall of 1856, they made it clear that their quarrel was not with
"our highly esteemed, and most respected Principal"[3] but with the
trustees of the school.

The salary controversy started on October 10, 1856, when a group
of Academy teachers dispatched a letter in which they asked for a
raise in pay, pointing out that their duties had increased appreciably
because of the large enrollment. The Provincial Helpers' Conference, trustees of the school, deemed the request valid and asked de
Schweinitz to notify the teachers that, as of the next pay day, their

salaries would be increased from $8 to $9 every four weeks. But instead of placating them, as the trustees obviously expected, the dollar
raise—"trifling," they called it—only fanned their discontent. And
in another—longer and angrier—letter, they felt themselves "constrained to enter into some details concerning our present situation,
believing that all the circumstances of the case have not been fully
understood."[4]

The sorest point seemed to be the comparison of the salaries of the
Academy teachers and those of the teachers in the Moravian schools
for girls in Bethlehem and Lititz. Evidently the trustees had noted
that, with the dollar increase, Academy salaries were now on a level
with those in Pennsylvania. And from that the disgruntled teachers
somehow had arrived at the assumption that salaries in Salem would
never be set higher than those in the Northern Province. To that
issue, they addressed themselves with vehemence:

Why, then, did *we* so long receive *less*? Is it unjust that the scales should
for once turn in *our* favor? We should think not, when we consider that
our Academy, no doubt, yields a much greater income than either of the
others, and that this is owing to its flourishing condition, the burden of
which falls next to the Inspector upon the Teachers. We consider that 25
pupils in a room, give the Teachers more trouble than 16 or 18, which is
probably the highest number placed in one room in the Northern schools;
—especially as in the North, the pupils are generally supplied with clothing
from home, the Teachers having nothing to do with providing for them
in that respect; whereas here, the general outfit in spring and autumn
requires a large amount of time and care of many of us.[5]

The letter went on to cite the higher cost of clothing in Salem than
that in the North, especially shoes—"and, we would remark, that the
immense building in which we now reside, in no way conduces to
the saving of shoes!"[6] Did the trustees consider the Academy teachers
"more extravagant in dress than our Northern sisters"? Moreover:

They live within a few hours ride of our largest cities, and can, at a comparatively trifling expenditure, visit various places of interest, while *we*
must take a long and expensive journey, requiring nearly half a year's
salary, before arriving where *they* are *now*. We are told that certainly
with $9's salary we can manage "to support ourselves and keep out of

debt!" It is therefore, not taken for granted that we would wish to lay by something, either for an occasional trip elsewhere, or for a future day, when our strength will be spent. We are considered as being in the service of the church; but there is no regular annuity to be expected by a teacher no longer in the service, as is the case with the other servants of the church. . . . Is it right and suitable, that any of us should be obliged, as has been the case, to endeavor to add to our income in some other way, laboring in spare hours, to obtain the sum required for a long anticipated journey to a neighboring state.[7]

After expanding on the "dreary future" that would be theirs if they had no savings for trips or for their old age, the teachers asked that their salaries be increased to $10 for four weeks of work—a dollar more than had been granted them. Then, "hoping that this somewhat lengthy and tedious exposition of affairs, as they appear to us, will meet with a lenient, nay kindly reception,"[8] they signed it, each using only the initial of her first name. The signatures were those of Henrietta Schnall, Elizabeth Siewers, Hermina Benzien, Maria Vogler, Theophila Welfare, Sophia Kremer, Louisa Herman, Caroline Siewers, Emma Leinbach, Gertrude Fant, Adelaide Herman, Jane Welfare, Charlotte Pfohl, Elizabeth Chitty, Louisa Belo, Ernestine Reichel, and Lisetta Brietz.[9] Notably missing were the names of several of the older teachers, such as Sophia Zevely and the venerated Maria Steiner Denke.

Within about a week, the teachers had their answer. Written by Emil de Schweinitz[10] in the name of the Provincial Helpers' Conference, the trustees' response[11] did indeed, up to a point, reflect the "lenient, nay kindly" attitude for which the teachers had hoped:

The Trustees are ready, at all times, to entertain propositions emanating from the Teachers of the Academy, as a body, with due consideration, especially if it includes, as in this case, many whose faithful service entitle them to address the Board on a subject of this kind. They fully appreciate the importance of the services rendered by the teachers, & readily admit that their duties have been increased & rendered more onerous, in various ways, during the last year or two. Therefore they have acceded to the request contained in the communication, & fixed the Salary, at the very considerable sum of $10 for every lunar month. The Board trusts that those teachers who have rendered faithful services in time past, will consider this addition an acknowledgment of their labors & expect that those who are as apt at the beginning of their career, will regard it as an incentive to increased exertion in the path of duty.

But having said that, the trustees, on their part, felt constrained not only to set a few facts straight but also to put in a pointed word or two regarding certain misguided grievances set forth in the teachers' letter. There was never any agreement relative to the equality of salaries in the North and South, they said; "hence the arguments based on this supposition fall to the ground." And as to the expense of trips to distant places, they reminded the teachers that "there are many places & regions of interest & great natural beauty, within the borders of our own & neighboring states, which can be visited, at a very moderate expense." Certainly, said the trustees, they did not want the teachers to use their spare time to supplement their income. On the contrary, "the Board most earnestly desires & confidently expects, that after devoting a sufficient time for exercise & recreation, they spend their 'spare hours' in profitable study & necessary preparation for their classes, as the only way in which they can hope to discharge efficiently & with success, the duties devolving upon them." Finally:

It is the earnest wish of the Board that the Teachers of our Academy may not only "be considered" as in the service of the Church, but that they may all *consider themselves* in that light, engaged, as they are, in one of the most important callings, for the faithful discharge of the duties of which they are not only accountable to fellow creatures, but to the Lord Himself who is the true & only Head & Master of his Church & those engaged in His services.

And that apparently was that. Some of the trustees' rebukes may have stung a little, but having won their pay raise, the teachers most probably were more than willing to bow out of the squabble. Although the trustees had consulted de Schweinitz in the matter, there is no evidence that he became personally involved in the dispute, and so he was able to attend to the business of running the school without emotional distractions. But with the large number of pupils then enrolled and with the south wing still under construction, his administrative duties were now so heavy that often he could not meet the classes which he was scheduled to teach. Consequently in February, 1857, the Provincial Helpers decided to employ an assistant for him, their choice for the position being the Reverend Maximilian E. Grunert, then pastor at Bethania.

Grunert would not begin his work until June. Meanwhile, on February 11, the large dining hall on the first floor of the new south wing was formally opened with a dinner attended by ministers of the province and their wives, a number of special guests, and all the Academy teachers and pupils—about two hundred and fifty. According to the Salem diarist, the large number "sat down with great ease & comfort at 10 tables" and enjoyed "a substantial & well prepared dinner" in what he claimed without equivocation was "the largest dining hall in any of our Moravian institutions either this side the Atlantic or the other."[12]

Salem's mood of celebration was to be short-lived, however, for already the winds of a measles epidemic had begun to swirl and rapidly gather force. Before the contagion subsided late that spring, it had cut a wider swath and taken a more tragic toll than any before or since in the Academy's history. No one there at the time would ever forget it—"dreadful" was the way de Schweinitz and a former pupil would write of it years later.[13] At one point during the epidemic's course, as many as a hundred and fifty girls were ill, most of them seriously so. The new sick rooms could not begin to accommodate all who needed nursing care. And to compound the ravages of measles, whooping cough also cropped up. Five girls died at the school, deaths coming in such quick succession that one day the funerals of two were conducted in a single service. Another pupil died after having been taken home by her parents. And still another died at Butner's Hotel in Salem, where her parents were caring for her. "May these mysterious dealings of our Lord & Sav' make a dire impression upon us all,"[14] intoned the Salem diarist.

Because so many girls had been taken home during the epidemic, "rendering it impossible to have anything like a fair examination,"[15] school authorities decided to dispense with the annual public Examination that year, presenting in its stead a musical entertainment to close the session. As it turned out, the class-by-class Examination, which had attracted so many for so many years, would never be resumed; closing exercises in subsequent years consisted principally of songs, piano selections, recitations, and cantatas, with only an occasional question-and-answer interlude to exhibit the girls' knowledge.

The measles epidemic also had so retarded construction of the south wing that it was late May before the chapel on the second floor was completed. The dedication ceremony was held in the afternoon of May 21, 1857. Bishop George Frederick Bahnson "preached a stirring sermon on the words, 'In Salem is His Tabernacle,' " and Inspector de Schweinitz "offered a beautiful and touching prayer."[16] A chorus made up of Academy girls and a number of singers from the town provided music for the occasion—directed by Edward W. Leinbach, who had been employed earlier in the term as the Academy's first full-time male professor of music.

In October, de Schweinitz presented the school's accounts as of May 31, 1857. The balance sheet showed a surplus of $16,672.79, out of which $11,200 was allocated to the building fund. With this installment, the new building, with the exception of a few minor items, was now fully paid for—truly a remarkable achievement for that, or any, time.

When the site was excavated for the new building's basement, the dirt was carried down the slope at the rear and dumped near the bottom—a precarious task for horse and cart, one horse losing its footing and "cart and all went rolling to the bottom."[17] Then stones from the *Gemein Haus* were used to build a wall at the edge of the slope and thus create a level yard immediately at the rear of the building. Finally, "The piece of woods lying back of the Academy [below the wall] was metamorphosed into a beautiful park with alternations of hill and valley, of winding walks and cozy nooks and arbors."[18] Laid out by de Schweinitz, who added pavilions and a rose garden, the park was known to generations of Academy girls as the "Playground" or "Pleasure Ground."

The terrible measles epidemic, it was reported,[19] had done nothing to shake the public's belief "in the healthfulness of our town" or "in the care taken of pupils." And following the vacation in 1857, the boarding school filled with students more quickly than ever.

For all the Academy's modern facilities and despite the changing character of Salem itself, the educational concept of the institution, its moral code and religious emphasis, its disciplinary structure, and even its residential arrangements remained basically unaltered. The pupils were still divided, according to age, into room companies, each with its own sitting and dressing room and each under the constant supervision of two "tutoresses." There still was no privacy for either teachers or students in the dormitories, all sleeping in large open halls.

By this arrangement strict attention to the morale of the pupils is secured, their studies are duly supervised, regular exercise cared for, and every exertion used to cultivate correct personal and social habits, as well as to instill the principles of early piety.[20]

Parents and guardians were "earnestly requested not to supply their daughters and wards with expensive dress, but rather to help us maintain our system of simplicity and economy in this respect."[21] And the girls were still expected to mend and often to make their own clothes. Visiting and visitors were strictly limited; correspondence was subject to the inspection of either the principal or a designated teacher; "system, regularity and punctuality in all things is enforced."[22]

In their school work, the girls were still assigned to classes on the basis of individual aptitude in individual subjects:

Taking the pupil as we find her, we seek to place her into that class of each particular branch of instruction to which she appears to belong by proficiency, and her more or less rapid promotion depends upon her own efforts and progress *in each study separately*.[23]

On the fringes of these fundamentals, though, the effects of the times in which the Academy was then operating and the demands of circumstances within the framework of the institution itself were bringing gradual changes. With the coming of more and better roads and more commodious means of transportation, the Academy had been able to dispense with the haphazard enterings and departures of students and to arrange the school year on a regular schedule of two sessions, one beginning the last Monday in July and continuing until Christmas and the other running from the first of the year until the end of May. There was a recess between Christmas and New Year's Day, and the summer vacation was set for June and July. Also, although the majority of Academy teachers still came from the ranks of the Single Sisters in Salem, qualified women from other places and other denominations were being occasionally accepted. Then on January 15, 1859, the Academy buildings "were lighted with gas for the first time."[24]

Perhaps the most marked change came in the means of providing meals for the school. Since the institution opened in 1804, meals for the Academy students and teachers had been catered by the Single Sisters, who prepared the food in a kitchen at the rear of their house and carried it to the school's dining hall. It had been a profitable enterprise for the Sisters but, with the steadily increasing enrollment at the school, a back-breaking job, and it was becoming harder and harder to find a Sister able and willing to head the operation. As early as December, 1850, the Provincial Helpers, faced with recurring vacancies in the position, mentioned the possibility of the school's taking over the responsibility for meals. But they conceded that "a considerable number of arrangements would have to be made before such a measure could be carried out,"[25] and no concrete action had been taken at that time. The suggestion came up again the following summer, this time in the *Aufseher Collegium*, but the immediate problem was solved later that year with the employment of a married couple, Brother and Sister Allen Spach, to supervise the Single Sisters' kitchen.

With the change in the inspectorship in 1853 and the subsequent preoccupation with the construction of the new building, the question of a possible change in the meal arrangements was laid aside. It was not until August of 1859 that, the situation now in desperate need of attention, the Provincial Elders' Conference* took action:

Br. Robert Schweinitz stated in his capacity of Inspector of the Girls Boarding School that the meals provided the Boarding School by the Single Srs' Diac. had been very poor for a long time past. Especially more recently the meals have deteriorated more and more. The Boarding School has suffered considerable damage thereby, and even greater injury had probably been avoided most recently only by the assurance given to parents and scholars that a complete change was to be made in the arrangements for meals. There could be no other way of bringing about an improvement than by the Boarding School itself taking over the kitchen. The P.A.C.

---

*At the Wachovia Provincial Synod in February, 1858, the name of the Provincial Helpers' Conference was officially changed to "Provinzial Aeltesten Conferenz" (Provincial Elders' Conference), and that body became the executive board of the province.

could raise no objection to this proposal, since it had long been evident that under the existing conditions this would be the only means of improving the meals.[26]

By this time, the *Aufseher Collegium* had been re-christened the "Board of Trustees of the Salem Congregation," and it was with this board that the Provincial Elders worked out the physical and financial details of the changeover. The Academy would buy a portion of the town lot assigned to the Single Sisters—the part lying generally at the northern and northeastern sides of the Sisters' House and including the kitchen building at the rear. It would also purchase (from the Sisters) the barn, pigsties, cowsheds, and other dependencies, together with "the entire inventory belonging to the kitchen and domestic establishment."[27] In addition, the Academy would rent certain other of the Sisters' facilities: the lower floor at the north end of the Sisters' House itself for the use of the kitchen staff, the cellar of the house, a woodshed, a granary, an ice house, a spring house, and "the garden, field and meadows."[28]

With the release of the food operation came the end of the Single Sisters' joint industries—and, in effect, the end of an institution. As individuals, Sisters continued to teach at the school and work in its kitchen and laundry. And for several years "one or two little shops were conducted in the House where Sisters sold knitting needles, edging, thread, etc., and small articles of china."[29] But gone now was the unified strength and prosperity of the choir itself. Gone essentially, too, was the unquestioning acceptance of the tightly-controlled, communal form of living in which there was no place for privacy—much less, individual will and ambition. Within a year or so, the old room company system in the Sisters' House would be abandoned and partitions installed to give each resident a separate room.

But in the formative years of the Girls' Boarding School and for nearly half a century thereafter, the Single Sisters' Choir in Salem was virtually the sole source of its teachers, its domestic services, and the tender care given its pupils—staples without which the institution could not have functioned, or certainly not so responsibly and so well. As a later president, Dr. Dale H. Gramley, often said, the Single Sisters were, in a very real sense, the school's "first endowment."

22

A Refuge
in War

DURING ITS YEARS AS A SELF-CONTAINED CON-
gregation town, Salem had generally held itself aloof from
politics. And even now, with loosened church authority and closer
commerce with the rest of the state, there seemed little inclination on
the part of Salem residents to become embroiled. But as the 1850s
drew to a close, the rumble of mounting differences within the nation
was by no means lost on the old Moravian town:

There is plainly a weight lying on the spirit of all good men, & a dread
of judgment coming upon the land. Our prayers have been joined to those
of our fellow Christians in the north & south, that the Lord in mercy
would stay the madness of sectional strife, & make of those who are
brethren by a common origin & history, & by every consideration of interest, duty, patriotism, & religion a truly united & happy people.[1]

The issues roiling the South at that time were, within themselves,
of little moment to the Moravians. For reasons of their own, they had
always been lukewarm to the practice of slavery. And as for states'
rights, the old Germanic acceptance of existing authority—in this
case, the federal government—still held strong; as late as February,
1861, *The People's Press* in Salem was ardently opposing secession.
Besides—and perhaps key to the Moravians' position—the continual
interchange of personnel between the Northern and Southern prov-
inces of the church and the common bond of the faith itself precluded
any feelings of sectional bias.

So, although there was an underlying uneasiness over storm clouds in the distance, both Salem and the Salem Female Academy assumed a business-as-usual posture during most of 1860. The streets of the town were lighted by gas. Joshua Boner asked for and was given another raise in salary for his work as the Academy's bookkeeper. The congregation trustees voted funds "towards the erection of a new church for the colored people."[2] At the Academy's closing exercises in early June, attended by a large number of visitors, the enrollment stood at 340—62 girls from Salem and 278 boarders representing all of the states in the soon-to-be-formed Confederacy, plus Kentucky, Missouri, and the Indian Territory. And when the school reopened later that summer, the number entering was "equal to former years."[3]

As the presidential election of 1860 approached, *The People's Press* strongly endorsed John Bell of Tennessee, the Southern candidate committed to preserving the Union, and called on "all who love their country and the institutions of their fathers better than they do party to go to the polls . . . and make one united rally for the constitution and the union."[4] But the electoral majority went to the Northern Republican, Abraham Lincoln, and before the year ended, neighboring South Carolina had seceded from the Union. On New Year's Eve, members of the Salem congregation gathered as always at the church for the Watch Night service and the traditional reading of the Memorabilia. But the words they heard held little of the joy and none of the promise of years past:

. . . we cannot conceal from ourselves the mournful fact that we are now through the madness of political strife between two different sections of our country, in the most fearful & perilous crisis which has occurred in our history as a nation. The triumph of a sectional majority in the election of their candidate to the presidency has strained to the utmost the cords which during three fourths of a century have bound together our growing republic—if indeed it has not already caused them to part asunder forever. Like a ship laboring in the storm & suddenly grounded upon some dangerous shoal, every timber of this vast confederacy strains & groans under the pressure. . . .[5]

For a few months, the Academy managed to maintain a semblance of normality. But by the end of February, six more of the school girls' home states had seceded, and after the firing on Fort Sumter on April

12, pupils departed in growing numbers, "the present unsettled &
alarming condition of the country having caused many persons living
at a distance to prefer having their daughters at home."[6]

With President Lincoln's call for troops in April and North Carolina's secession in May, Salem sorrowfully accepted the inevitable
and aligned itself with the cause of the South—to the point of amend-
ing "the prayers in the church litany which refer to the government
of our country, and also the prayer in times of war, that they would
be consistent with our present circumstances."[7] Forsaking its earlier
position, though declaring that its conscience was clear for having
tried to save the Union, *The People's Press* called on all farmers in
the area to plant corn and raise stock: "If we act the part of prudent
and wise men and prepare for this emergency, with the blessing of
God we will at least have provisions in abundance and to spare."[8]

On June 21, 1861, two volunteer companies from Forsyth County,
including men from Salem and the other Moravian communities,
left for Danville, Virginia, where they would join others for the
formation of a North Carolina regiment. Before marching out of
town, they halted in front of the Academy, where, "in the presence
of a large concourse of people"[9] and with the Doric portico serving as
a platform for the ministers, they were given a prayerful farewell. A
third Forsyth company left three days later. In less than a month came
word that the young men of Salem and vicinity had participated in the
battle at Manassas Junction. In time, Salem also would hear the story
of how, in that same battle, a Confederate officer, Thomas J. Jackson,
so stubbornly held his ground that he would be known thereafter as
"Stonewall." And especially those close to the Academy would remember that Jackson's wife, the former Mary Anna Morrison of
Lincoln County, had been a student in Salem not many years before
(1847–49).*

During the late summer and fall of 1861, many of the men from
Forsyth, still encamped in the area of Virginia around Manassas
Junction and Centreville, were among the hundreds in their regiment
stricken with one or the other of the serious illnesses—typhoid fever,

---

*The wife of another prominent Confederate officer, Major General William Dorsey Pen-
der, also had been an Academy student (Mary Frances Shepherd, 1849–55). And there could
be no counting of the other women scattered all over the South whose school days had been
spent in Salem and whose husbands now wore the Confederate gray.

measles, dysentery—then rampaging through the camps. Responding to the regiment's desperate need for nursing care, six women—including one Academy teacher, Margaret Clewell, and a former Academy teacher, Eliza Vierling Kremer—left Salem in September and spent two months working at Blantyre Hospital. Their dedicated service inspired a special order of commendation and gratitude from the regiment's commanding officer.

Although the drop in enrollment had not been as great as expected, the Academy reopened after the summer vacation in 1861 with space to spare for the first time in many years. Anticipating not only further decreases after the Christmas recess but also difficulties in obtaining payment of school fees because of war conditions, de Schweinitz moved during the fall to tighten the Academy's belt. Heretofore parents of the town girls attending the school had paid the tuition fees directly to the Salem congregation trustees, who in turn had paid the school a lump sum of $130 a year, retaining any surplus for congregation needs. As the annual payment no longer covered the cost of instruction for the town girls, de Schweinitz asked that these fees now be paid directly to the school, and the trustees agreed. Late in the year, it was decided that, with the beginning of the new term, the ten room companies would be reduced to nine. This meant that two teachers would have to be dropped from the staff. One teacher, Adelaide Lange, had planned to return to Pennsylvania anyway; thus one of the two layoffs could be taken care of painlessly. As to the other, de Schweinitz and the Provincial Elders agreed that the last to come should be the first to go. But it happened that the last to come was not one but two; Margaret Clewell and Sophia Butner had joined the staff on the same day. "Since the Inspector could express no preference between them," the Elders reported, "they will have to draw lots to see which must leave."[10]

As it turned out, neither was forced to leave. For in the early months of 1862, girls began to stream into Salem from Mobile, Alabama, and Macon, Georgia, Petersburg, Virginia, Hawkins, Tennessee, and San Felipe, Texas—all parts of the war-torn South—parents now believing that their young daughters would be safer at the school than in their own homes. And from then until the end of the war, the Academy was filled to overflowing: ". . . every day brought new applications until the message was sent abroad, 'there is no more room, but if you will bring beds we will try to board you,' and when even that resource failed a few became 'out boarders.' "[11]

One father, G. W. Malone of Franklin County, Alabama, gathered his four daughters around him, divulged where he had buried the family's gold and silver, and then dispatched the girls to Salem, where they arrived safely on April 11, 1862. As one of them told it later:

Many months had passed in 1862, with only a shadowy report of where Father was, or what he was doing until late one afternoon . . . the Malone 4 were notified that the principal Mr. De Schweinitz wished them at this office. The kindliest of men, his word was ever obeyed, and we appeared to see him so joyously . . . holding our dear Father by the arm!![12]

Malone—attended by his servant, Billy—settled in at the Salem hotel and remained there for more than two years. During the Academy's summer vacation in 1864, he rented a small house on Main Street so that, for a short time anyway, he and the girls could be together. They did not return to Alabama until the war was over.

Few of the girls in school at that time were as fortunate as the Malone sisters; for most of them, long months often passed without any word from their families, much less an opportunity to see them. But de Schweinitz and his teachers made every effort to maintain as normal an atmosphere as possible, and, as Adelaide Fries later wrote, "Those long years in the sheltered nest, while the storm raged around and beyond, ripened in those girlish hearts a never-to-be-forgotten love for their Alma Mater."[13] As their parents had hoped, the school girls were spared not only the horrors and pillages of the war itself but also many of the privations experienced by their contemporaries elsewhere in the South. There was always food on their tables, clothing on their backs, warmth in their rooms, the security of constant loving care. And not for one day in the course of those difficult years were classes suspended.

The burden of sustaining the school—of providing for the hundreds of girls entrusted to it—fell, of course, squarely on the shoulders of Robert de Schweinitz. "It was a task of no little difficulty to supply and protect three hundred souls in those trying times," his son, Paul, would recall, "and many were the makeshifts that had to be resorted to both for food and clothing."[14] But the task would have been harder still had de Schweinitz not had the assistance of Augustus Fogle, who had been appointed steward of the Academy in 1861, and the warm friendship of North Carolina's wartime Governor, Zebulon B. Vance.

Fogle, a one-time cabinetmaker, had had little formal education, but he was a faithful member of the congregation and "was favored with a physical frame which seemed capable of bearing every form of fatigue and exposure."[15] His physical stamina would stand him in good stead during those Civil War years when, with food supplies so scarce, he was obliged to be constantly on the move, scouring the countryside for fresh vegetables or grain, a few cattle here or a few hogs there—anything to stock the Academy's lean cupboard. "On one occasion the Steward returned from such an expedition to Salisbury, reaching home about 10 P.M., only to be met by the news that some hogs were for sale up the country, and by 3 A.M., he was again in the saddle."[16]

Governor Vance had issued written permission for Fogle and de Schweinitz, who sometimes also made these forays, to pass through Confederate lines in their search for food, and on one occasion he himself sent to the Academy two barrels of sugar from captured supplies. The Governor's close ties with Salem stemmed from earlier in the war when Vance, then commander of the Twenty-Sixth North Carolina Regiment, engaged the Salem band as regimental musicians. The band had been popular with the men of the Twenty-Sixth, playing for guard mounts and dress parades and entertaining in the evenings with special concerts. And in the fall of 1862 when Vance became Governor, it was given the honor of playing at his inauguration—the official inaugural march having been composed and arranged by the Academy's professor of music, Edward Leinbach. After the ceremonies, the band returned to its regiment, and Vance assumed the awesome burden of leading his state in a time of war. But the personal bond between him and the Moravians of Salem remained strong. Recognizing the service that the Academy was rendering in caring for girls from throughout the Confederate States, Vance time and again went out of his way to come to the school's aid. De Schweinitz would often recount one instance in particular:

On a certain occasion I had secured, in Eastern Carolina, a large and costly consignment of perishable food supply for the Academy, which, however, was hopelessly detained at Goldsboro on account of the impossibility of obtaining transportation. A messenger was sent by me to Raleigh, who arrived there long after midnight,—nevertheless, he forthwith went to the Governor's private residence, and pitilessly rousing him out of bed, begged him to issue an order for State transportation. Governor Vance, although at first not a little astounded at the audacity of such a demand, and that made in the dead of night, no sooner heard from whom the request came than he promptly issued the order for State transportation, and thus saved the Academy from grievous loss.[17]

Today in the south wing of Main Hall, a stained glass window, a gift of the Class of 1894, still honors the memory of Zebulon B. Vance, whose friendship had meant so much, as de Schweinitz later said, "during those years of never-to-be-forgotten trial."[18]

The pinch of the Civil War was by no means confined to the Academy's food supply, of course. Classroom materials became equally as scarce, and de Schweinitz advertised for old textbooks, "even if the books are somewhat injured."[19] As the war wore on, most of what little cloth and leather were available in Salem went to clothe the fighting men. And it was not uncommon to see strips of cloth tacked to the fences in town and being painted to make "oilcloth" for keeping the soldiers dry. Pupils in the Academy simply "made do" with what clothing they had or what little the school or their parents could provide, many clattering around the halls in shoes made with wooden soles. With the inflationary costs of that time, Fogle was paying $48 for twelve chickens, a like amount for six pounds of potatoes, $15 for three pounds of butter, $5 for thirty eggs, and $60 for a stack of hay.[20] Time after time, de Schweinitz was forced to raise the quarterly school fees; by February, 1864, the cost per quarter had risen to $200. Payment for the students' board and tuition, if it was made at all, was made in Confederate money, which was becoming more and more worthless. Even so, the school managed to come up with a small surplus each year until 1865, when the accounts showed a deficit of $3,978.69—virtually all of its investments now being grimly conceded "a complete loss."[21]

At that, though, the Academy was blessed in that neither its plant nor its pupils were ever in any actual physical danger. Salem was somewhat remote from the battlefront, and even the path of General William Tecumseh Sherman's devastating march through Georgia and the Carolinas lay well to the east of the old town. "No footprint of an enemy has been seen in these parts," the Salem minister had noted in the Memorabilia of 1863,[22] and that report would stand up until the surrender at Appomattox on April 9, 1865. It was on the day after the surrender that Salem, not yet having heard the news, encountered the dreaded Yankees for the first time.[23]

Ten days earlier, word had come that General George Stoneman's Raiders, galloping from eastern Tennessee toward the Confederate stores and railroad at Greensboro, were approaching the Yadkin River and could be expected to pass through Salem. De Schweinitz and Fogle, out in the countryside in search of wheat, heard the news as they were returning home. Upon arrival at the Academy, they hurriedly cached valuable papers under the stone flooring in the cellar of the Inspector's House and the school's money under the sitting room floor boards. The Academy's two fine black horses were hidden in the basement of Main Hall. And all night long, wagons rumbled up and down the streets as others in Salem secreted valuables and provisions.

For more than a week, though, the only soldiers Salem saw were companies of Confederates, who were either scouting the approaching enemy or moving into position to try to protect the railroad, which at that time was the lifeline to General Robert E. Lee's army. During the week, news trickling into Salem was a little more encouraging: Stoneman's forces, having crossed the Yadkin, appeared to be heading for Mount Airy, in which event they would bypass Salem to the north. So it was in an atmosphere of somewhat lessened tension that the Salem congregation and the Academy girls participated in the Palm Sunday services on the morning of April 9. But that evening rumors began to make their rounds: the Raiders were at Danbury in the neighboring county of Stokes. As some of these reports were conflicting but still persistent the next morning, a small reconnoitering party set out about noon in the direction of Danbury. The scouts met the enemy sooner than they had expected and were forced to scatter, but about four o'clock that afternoon they managed to sound the alarm in Winston and in Salem: the Raiders were just three miles away and approaching fast.

At the courthouse in Winston, John Blackburn, Clerk of the Court, frantically scooped up the county's valuable papers, stuffed them into sacks, and distributed them either in nearby homes or to passing friends. Then, in his own words:

I locked up the office and started down street to hear the news in Salem. Met Robert De Schweinitz principal of the Female Academy in Salem, Joshua Boner Mayor of Salem, Thos. J. Wilson, Mayor of Winston and R. L. Patterson, Esq. who was on a visit to Salem, on their way up street to meet the Yankee Army. They invited me to accompany them and we went up street into Liberty [now North Winston] in front of the house then occupied by Mr. Alexander Bevel and halted there & waited the arrival of the army which was about or near sundown. . . .[24]

Between five and six o'clock, some ten or fifteen Yankees on horseback galloped in, brandishing pistols, but the "reception committee," waving white handkerchiefs, managed to convince them that there were no Confederate troops thereabouts and that the town was totally defenseless. Within a short time, the commanding officer, Colonel W. J. Palmer,* and his staff rode up.

The Inspector tied his white handkerchief to his cane and waved it as a flag of truce, but the soldiers paid no attention to him, and he impulsively grasped the rein of the horse on which the General was riding. The General reached for his pistol, and (he never knew why) the Inspector exclaimed: "I am de Schweinitz!" In utter surprise the General put his pistol back into the holster, and said, "I had a teacher of that name when I was in school in Lititz."[25]

It has generally been surmised that Palmer's earlier, and apparently pleasant, association with the Moravians was at least partially responsible for his sparing Salem from the ruthless destruction suffered by other towns in the Raiders' path. Whatever the reason, Palmer heard with sympathy the plea for protection of Salem "not only on our own account, but also of our large female boarding school,"[26] and, except for minor incidents, Salem was unmolested.

Soon after the confrontation at the edge of town, Palmer established headquarters in Joshua Boner's house on the main street [now the official home of the president of Salem Academy and College]. Then:

In very great, comparative, silence about 3000 cavalry passed through our town, pitching their tents on the high ground beyond the creek. Had it not been for the noise their horses & swords made, it would have been

---

*Most local accounts confer on Palmer the rank of general.

hardly noticed that so large a number of, at the time, hostile troops were passing through our streets. The strictest discipline was enforced, guards rode up & down every street and very few indeed comparatively were the violations of proper & becoming conduct on the part of the soldiers. . . .[27]

When the troops passed the Salem Female Academy, it is said that a hotheaded student from Alabama (probably one of the Malone sisters) waved a Confederate flag from a third-story window of Main Hall and gave the Rebel yell but was quickly suppressed by her teacher before the Yankees could respond. Although local accounts make no mention of it, the reaction of Salem to the passing soldiers, as told from the Yankee viewpoint, was altogether different: "The ladies cheered us, and brought out bread, pies and cakes. . . . The people showed much enthusiasm at the sight of the flag we carried, and many were the touching remarks made about it."[28] And indeed in her reminiscences, Eliza Vierling Kremer did recall that "the night they [the Yankees] came in I baked panful after panful of biscuits. . . ."[29]

Palmer stationed one of his aides and another guard at the Academy. The aide confided to Fogle that he had not slept for six nights. Whereupon the Academy's kindly steward suggested that he take over the guard duty and let both the aide and the other guard get a good night's sleep. Surprisingly the weary aide agreed, but not before cautioning Fogle to wake him if certain signals were heard from the camp south of town.

At midnight a horseman came up, inquired for the sentinels and, suspecting foul play, at first flatly refused the invitation to go into the room where they were, but finally plucked up courage to follow Mr. Fogle and his lighted candle through the Steward's office into the room beyond. There he paused, utterly amazed, and with sundry superlatives, exclaimed: "A soldier in an enemy's country, in the dead hours of night asleep in an enemy's bed! Was the like ever heard in the annals of history!!" One jerk landed the nearer sleeper on his back, but discovering that it was the aide-de-camp, of higher rank than himself, the man desisted, and contented himself with carrying off the other sentinel, while the aide finished the night in comfort. Next morning a passing soldier discovered and took possession of one of the Academy horses, but the aide, learning of it, forced him to return it.[30]

Upon arriving in Salem with Colonel Palmer on the evening of April 10, a portion of the command had been sent immediately to burn the railroad bridge at Jamestown. And the next day Palmer himself made a reconnaissance of the vicinity to determine the Confederate strength. He gained no definite information but concluded (erroneously) that Salem was surrounded by Confederate scouts. So that evening when the party detailed to destroy the railroad bridge returned with a report of having encountered resistance, Palmer decided to regroup with the rest of Stoneman's forces then moving toward the Shallowford of the Yadkin River en route to Salisbury. Abandoning the camp south of town, the Yankees again marched through Salem—past the Academy and up Cedar Avenue beside God's Acre. And as they passed the rows of flat gravestones, dating back to 1771, each man silently removed his hat.

23

End of an Era

THREE DAYS AFTER COLONEL PALMER AND HIS men left Salem, Abraham Lincoln was assassinated, and North Carolina-born Andrew Johnson became President. Just when Salem heard the tragic news is not known; *The People's Press* did not carry an account of it until May 20, 1865. And there is nothing in the somewhat sketchy records of that time to indicate Salem's reaction either to Lincoln's death or to the man who succeeded him in office. In later years, the Academy would note with pride that President Johnson's daughter, Martha (Mrs. David Patterson), who served as his official hostess at the White House, had been one of its students. But her name does not appear in the Academy's registration books, and sources close to the Johnson family records[1] have yet to uncover any evidence that Martha attended school in Salem. So unless and until facts emerge to support the claim, the often-told story, like that of the courtship of James and Sarah Polk at the Academy, will have to be confined to the realm of legend.

When Colonel Palmer departed Salem on April 11, 1865, he left three wounded men to be cared for until they were fit to resume duty. They remained four weeks and upon their leaving issued a statement "expressing to the citizens our warmest thanks for the kind attentions and many acts of kindness shown us during our stay among them."[2] Actually, it wasn't the conquering foe that harassed Salem in those weeks following Lee's surrender; what troubles there were came from the South's own men:

On the 20th of April a number of Confederates made their appearance, pretending to be in search of government cloth, to find which they had intended to search individual houses. As had been agreed upon, the different bells were at once rung & in a very short time, a by no means inconsiderable number of men, many of them soldiers themselves, who had come back on parole, assembled near the square, armed as well as circumstances permitted & fully determined to resist the entrance into private houses. Our unbidden visitors soon changed their language & withdrew after a short time without offering any molestation at all.[3]

With such turmoil going on practically under the Academy's windows, the teachers must have had their hands full calming their excitable charges. But by late May, 1865, the Stars and Stripes again flew atop the Forsyth County courthouse; fewer and fewer paroled Confederates straggled through Salem on their way home; and the Academy focused its attention on the approaching close of the term. For most of the girls, the end of the school year meant going home—perhaps for the first time in several years—though all too many of them would find little more than remnants of the comfortable homes they had left. The Malone family departed in early June aboard a salt wagon going to Virginia, thence by rail, mule car, and freight train to their home and buried treasure in Alabama.[4] By June 12, only thirty or forty girls remained at the Academy; some would leave within the new few weeks, but others would have to wait until the long-lost contact with their families could be re-established.

Realizing that the shattered economy of the South offered little prospect of a healthy enrollment for the next term, de Schweinitz and the Provincial Elders' Conference early in the summer came to grips with a hard choice: "to close the Boarding School for a time, or to arrange to reduce it substantially and carry it on with the Lord's help."[5] But deep down in the good Brethren's hearts there was never any real dilemma: the school would go on, though with necessarily stringent economies. The number of room companies would be reduced to five, with a commensurate reduction in the teaching staff. The kitchen and servants' staffs would be pared drastically, and the Academy would rid itself of all but two of its horses.

Meanwhile in that summer of 1865, Salem began to pick up the pieces of normal community life. *The People's Press* would later complain that the community, along with the rest of the South, was "in a state of betweenity, bearing all the burdens of taxation without representation."[6] But as it had borne none of the property damage suffered by other areas and as most of its residents had never been rabid secessionists, Salem could, and did, adjust more quickly and less bitterly to Reconstruction than did many Southern towns. Governor Vance's old friends, the Salem band, came home on July 2—just in time to play for a gala Fourth of July celebration in the town square, which attracted some three or four thousand people "embracing all colors, ages, sexes and conditions."[7] And later that month, the congregation rejoiced in receiving, for the first time in four years, letters from the Unity Elders' Conference in Europe.

There is no record of how many students enrolled at the Academy at the end of July, but the school also seems to have settled into its customary routine. Though reports of the war years made little mention of the assistant principal, Maximilian Grunert, he undoubtedly had shared the heavy duties with de Schweinitz, probably minding academic affairs while the principal scavenged for food. And just before the war ended, criminal tragedy had come to Grunert's home:

An attempt to poison the wife of Rev. M. E. Grunert of this place was made a few days since by her servant girl. The poison was put in a bowl of soup of which Mrs. Grunert being unwell partook sparingly causing only vomiting. A little daughter, however, partook freely of the soup which caused her death in a short time. The girl admits that this is the third attempt of poisoning her mistress and has implicated others in procuring the poison for her. The wretch has been committed to jail and richly deserves the fate which awaits her. Two Negro men have been committed for trial as her accessories and others may yet be implicated.[8]

The Academy closed the term in December, 1865, with two programs: a musical entertainment attended by a large audience and one of the old-style dialogues that had been so popular in Inspector Reichel's time. Then, to the delight of everyone, the term opening with the new year brought a larger enrollment than had been anticipated, an average of five girls a day arriving during January, with more trickling in during the weeks following. By the end of the term, the enrollment stood at 244: 116 from North Carolina, 28 from Georgia, 11 from Virginia, 12 from Tennessee, 10 from Mississippi, 9 from

South Carolina, 3 from Arkansas, 1 from Texas and 43 from Salem.

So in a numerical sense, the Salem Female Academy was almost back to normal. But as the nature of Salem had changed after it ceased to function as a congregation town, and as the South was never the same following the Civil War, events of 1866 brought changes and presages of change to the Academy, which, in the light of historical perspective, would mark the beginning of the end of an era at the school as well.

As early as the spring of 1865, the Provincial Elders, acting as trustees of the Academy, had decided that, particularly from a tax standpoint, it would be wise to establish the school as a corporate entity—separate from the financial structure of the church. Consequently steps were taken to obtain an act of incorporation from the General Assembly of North Carolina, but it was not until February 3, 1866, that the act passed its final reading and was written into state law.

The act of incorporation[9] altered in no way the church's control of the institution. The first section simply noted that the Right Reverend George F. Bahnson, the Reverend Emil A. de Schweinitz, and the Reverend Lewis Rights had been elected by the synod of the Southern Province of the church to direct the ecclesiastical affairs of the province and that by virtue of their office were the trustees of Salem Female Academy. So hereinafter these men or their duly elected successors would constitute "a body politic and corporate," empowered to hold the Academy property and to act in all legal transactions relative to it. The second vested in these trustees the power to operate the Academy and to make such by-laws and establish such regulations as were needed for its care and management. In future years, the number of trustees holding these powers would be increased, but the controlling voice would remain in the Moravian Church.

Even so, the conversion of the boarding school into a separate corporate unit marked the beginning of evolutionary changes in the church-school relationship. These changes would come gradually; it would be more than eighty years, for example, before a man other than an ordained Moravian minister was chosen as administrative head of the institution.[10] But as the years passed, the school would become less and less parochial in nature, always retaining close ties with the Moravian Church but at the same time assuming an identity and a certain independence of its own.

The third section of the act of incorporation empowered the faculty, with the consent of the trustees, to confer "all such marks of literary distinction, or diplomas, as are usually conferred in colleges and seminaries of learning." It would be more than a quarter of a century before such degrees were actually conferred and forty-one years before the name of the institution would be changed (to Salem Academy and College) to signify this expanded academic scope. But, here again, the act presaged a significant change in the nature of the institution—one in which, as time went on, the college would become the dominant arm.

In referring to the faculty, this section of the act spells out that term to mean "the president and professors and teachers." Nowhere is it explained whether the author of the act had been requested to confer the title of "president" on the administrative head of the Academy or whether he had simply done so of his own accord. But since Samuel Kramsch was engaged in 1802, the title of the position, at least in the church records, had been "inspector." So in yet another area, the act represented a change for the Academy. And the by-laws adopted by the Provincial Elders on July 5, 1866, include note of it:

Section 1. The president of S.F.A. (the new title given the Inspector in the charter) shall manage and conduct the internal & outward business of the Academy as the principal of the institution heretofore conducted the same, according to existing rules & such other regulations as may be, from time to time, laid down by the Board of Trustees for the government of the institution.

Section 2. In the management of the affairs of the S.F.A., the president of the same shall in all respects be subject, in accordance with the principles of the Moravian church, to the supervision of the Board of Trustees and responsible to the same for his official acts.[11]

The first "president" of Salem Female Academy thus was Robert William de Schweinitz. But he would not hold that title long, for on May 21, 1866, came a letter from Bishop John Christian Jacobson, former inspector of the Academy and now head of the Provincial Elders' Conference in Pennsylvania, notifying the Provincial Elders in Salem that de Schweinitz had been called to become the inspector of Nazareth Hall. The news was far from welcome; de Schweinitz was one of the most capable and certainly one of the most popular administrators the Academy had ever had, and the Elders did not relish the task of finding a replacement. But they did not hesitate to inform de Schweinitz of the call, little doubting that it would be accepted. Not only was the post at Nazareth Hall a prestigious one in the church but also it would be only natural that de Schweinitz, having spent most of his life in the North, would want to return when an attractive opportunity arose.

Within the week, de Schweinitz had accepted the call. And because the Provincial Elders had expected that he would, they already had unanimously agreed to offer the presidency of the Academy to the man who had been assistant inspector since 1857 and who now held the title of "vice president," the Reverend Maximilian Eugene Grunert. So on the same day—May 28, 1866—the Elders reported that de Schweinitz would leave and that Grunert had accepted the offer to replace him.

Two days later, the Academy closed its term with an elaborate musical entertainment in the flower-decked chapel which de Schweinitz had had such a major hand in planning and building. It was both a joyous and a sad occasion for the Academy and for Salem itself. And in reporting the event, *The People's Press* took the opportunity to pay editorial tribute to the departing president:

Mr. de Schweinitz was deservedly one of the most popular and highly esteemed principals who has ever presided over the destinies of Salem's time honored institution of learning. Under his administration it has advanced in public favor beyond precedent. The present magnificent academic structure was erected in his supervision and will ever remain a monument to his good taste, enterprise and liberality. He and his worthy lady enjoyed the love, respect and esteem of the pupils and the parental training and wholesome admonitions imparted to the large number of young ladies will ever have a place in their memories.[12]

De Schweinitz remained at Nazareth Hall only a year, having been elected in 1867 to the higher position of president of the Provincial Elders' Conference in the North. He held that post for eleven years and served in other positions of trust until ill health forced his retirement in 1899. But he continued to keep in close touch with Salem,

Maximilian Eugene Grunert, President 1866–1877

and it is said that his presence at the Academy commencement in 1886 was "a magnetic force in the organization of the Alumnae Association."[13] As the nineteenth century drew to a close, though, "The feebleness of advancing age grew upon him, bowing his tall, commanding figure, and he became totally blind."[14] He died on October 29, 1901, at the age of eighty-two.

Robert de Schweinitz had occupied a special place in the affections of the Academy's teachers and pupils. And the building that had been called a "monument" to his talents still stands. But neither affections nor buildings are immune to the erasures of time. In the end, perhaps the one indelible mark de Schweinitz left on the history of Salem Academy and College was the stupendous feat of keeping the school's doors open at a time when so many other institutions of learning were forced to close and when the future of the nation itself lay in jeopardy. Without that extraordinary legacy, there might not be a Salem Academy and College today—with a proud history to tell.

Notes

Because of the frequency with which a number of the reference sources occur in these notes, the following abbreviations will be used:

RM — *Records of the Moravians in North Carolina.* 11 vols. The name of the editor of the volume cited is followed by *RM* and the volume and page number
AC — *Aufseher Collegium* minutes
CC — Congregation Council minutes
EC — Elders' Conference minutes
LB — Letter Books of the girls' school
MAN — Archives of the Moravian Church in America, Northern Province, Bethlehem, Pa.
MAS — Archives of the Moravian Church in America, Southern Province, Winston-Salem, N. C.
SCL — Grace Siewers Room, Salem College Library

CHAPTER 1

1. *North Carolina Journal* (Halifax, N.C.), Dec. 11, 1793.
2. S. S. Laurie, *Life and Works of Comenius*, p. 133.
3. Frantisik Kozik, *The Sorrowful and Heroic Life of John Amos Comenius*, p. 64.
4. Vladimir Jelinik, Introduction to his translation of *The Analytical Didactic of Comenius*, p. 8.
5. J. Taylor Hamilton, *A History of the Church Known as the Moravian Church*, pp. 104–5.
6. Adelaide L. Fries, ed., *RM* I, 323.
7. *Ibid.*, II, 589.
8. *Ibid.*, II, 618.

CHAPTER 2

1. Adelaide L. Fries, "Sesquicentennial of Salem Academy and College," May 29, 1922, unpublished paper, SCL.
2. Fries, ed., *RM*, II, 899.
3. *Ibid.*, III, 1086.
4. *Ibid.*, p. 1329.
5. *Ibid.*, I, 23.
6. *Ibid.*, II, 878.
7. *Ibid.*, IV, 1910.
8. *Ibid.*, III, 1308.
9. *Ibid.*, II, 879.

10. *Ibid.*, IV, 1594.
11. *Ibid.*, V, 2235.
12. Memoir of Catharine Sehner Steiner, MAS.
13. Fries, ed., *RM*, V, 2369.
14. *Ibid.*, VI, 2669.
15. CC, Feb. 19, 1801, MAS.

CHAPTER 3

1. AC, June 5, 1787, MAS.
2. Fries, ed., *RM*, VI, 2959.
3. *Ibid.*, V, 2403.
4. *Ibid.*, p. 2350.
5. William C. Reichel, *Bethlehem Seminary Souvenir*, p. 83.
6. EC, Nov. 1, 1802, MAS.
7. Adelaide L. Fries, *Historical Sketch of Salem Female Academy*, p. 6.
8. CC, Sept. 1, 1803, MAS.
9. Fries, ed., *RM*, VI, 2958–64.
10. *Ibid.*, p. 2960.
11. *Ibid.*, p. 2961.
12. *Ibid.*, p. 2963.
13. MAS.
14. EC, March 7, 1804, MAS.
15. *Ibid.*, April 4, 1804, MAS.
16. *Ibid.*
17. House Conference minutes, April 26, 1804, MAS.
18. Fries, ed., *RM*, VI, 2766.

CHAPTER 4

1. House Conference minutes, May 21, 1804, MAS.
2. *Ibid.*, June 13, 1804, MAS.
3. *Ibid.*
4. Fries, ed., *RM*, VI, 2767.
5. Douglas L. Rights, ed., *RM*, VIII, 4175.
6. Fries, ed., *RM*, VI, 2771.
7. House Conference minutes, Dec. 5, 1804, MAS.
8. Small account book (in English), dated May 30, 1804, MAS.
9. Fries, ed., *RM*, VI, 2967–71.
10. Eliza Vierling Kremer, "Bits of Old Salem Gossip," SCL.
11. House Conference minutes, Sept. 2, 1805, MAS.

CHAPTER 5

1. Fries, ed., *RM*, VI, 2809.

2., *Ibid.*, p. 2812.

3. *Ibid.*

4. House Conference minutes, Aug. 19, 1805, MAS.

5. *Ibid.*, Sept. 16, 1805, MAS.

6. *Ibid.*

7. *Ibid.*, Oct. 19, 1805, MAS.

8. *Ibid.*

9. Fries, ed., *RM*, VI, 2818.

10. Provincial Helpers' Conference minutes, Nov. 14, 1815, translated by Kenneth G. Hamilton, MAS.

11. *Ibid.*, Nov. 20, 1805, MAS.

12. *Ibid.*, Nov. 14, 1805, MAS.

13. AC, Nov. 19, 1805, MAS.

14. *Ibid.*

15. Provincial Helpers' Conference minutes, Nov. 20, 1805, translated by Kenneth G. Hamilton, MAS.

16. Fries, ed., *RM*, VII, 3123.

17. CC, Nov. 4, 1813, MAS.

18. Rights, ed., *RM*, VIII, 3628.

19. House Conference minutes, Nov. 25, 1805, MAS.

20. Fries, ed., *RM*, VI, 2815.

21. Letter, Dec. 6, 1805, translated by Frank P. Albright, MAN.

22. Memoir of Abraham Steiner, MAS.

23. *Ibid.*

24. *Ibid.*

CHAPTER 6

1. Letter, April 11, 1806, translated by Erika Huber, MAN.

2. House Conference minutes, Nov. 18, 1806, MAS.

3. *Ibid.*, Dec. 15, 1807, MAS.

4. Student Accounts, SCL.

5. *Ibid.*

6. Letter from Nancy Youngblood, Edgefield, S.C., April 10, 1809, LB, SCL.

7. Nov. 7, 1808, LB, SCL.

8. House Conference minutes, Dec. 15, 1807, MAS.

9. Letter to James B. White, Columbus County, N.C., June 9, 1809, LB, SCL.

10. Jan. 19, 1811, LB, SCL.

11. May 24, 1809, LB, SCL.

12. Oct. 19, 1808, LB, SCL.

13. Letter from Sarah Mills, Rockingham, N.C., April 8, 1809, LB, SCL.

14. Letter from Richard Jones, Pittsylvania County, Va., Oct. 16, 1809, LB, SCL.

15. Letter to James R. Baird, Abbeville District, S.C., July 29, 1814, LB, SCL.

16. Fries, ed., *RM*, VII, 3096.

17. House Conference minutes, Aug. 24, 1807, MAS.

18. Fries, ed., *RM*, VI, 2474.

19. *Ibid.*, p. 2866.

20. *Ibid.*

21. *Ibid.*, p. 2898.

22. *Ibid.*

23. Letter to Jonathan Maxey, Columbia, S.C., Jan. 9, 1807, LB, SCL.

24. Letter to General William R. Davie, Lancaster Courthouse, S.C., April 23, 1807, LB, SCL.

25. Letter to James B. White, June 9, 1809, LB, SCL.

26. Letter to General William R. Davie, Jan. 11, 1807, LB, SCL.

27. Letter to Dr. Elijah Gillett, Barnwell District, S.C., May 31, 1813, LB, SCL.

28. Letter to Joseph Beckley, Abbeville District, S.C., Jan. 23, 1812, LB, SCL.

29. Letter to Samuel Pannill, Campbell County, Va., June 26, 1809, LB, SCL.

30. Letter to Walter Leigh, Augusta, Ga., March 8, 1811, LB, SCL.

31. Letter to Dr. Whitmel Pugh, Bertie County, N.C., May 2, 1814, LB, SCL.

32. Fries, ed., *RM*, VII, 3174.

33. Letter from Samuel Pannill, April 24, 1809, LB, SCL.

34. *Ibid.*, May 9, 1810, LB, SCL.

35. Letter from Walter Leigh, Feb. 11, 1811, LB, SCL.

36. Letter from Gilbert Hay, Washington, Ga., April 30, 1812, LB, SCL.

37. Letter from William L. Morton, Prince Edward, Va., Jan. 19, 1813, LB, SCL.

38. Letter from General William R. Davie, Sept. 30, 1808, LB, SCL.

39. Letter from William H. Hill, Dec. 5, 1808, LB, SCL.

40. Letter from Thomas Hill, Dec. 13, 1808, LB, SCL.

41. Letter from Louisa C. Blickensderfer, *The Academy*, Vol. II, No. 2 (April, 1879).

42. Evidently the rough draft of a letter that Steiner wrote to Sarah Guyther's guardian, SCL.

43. *The Academy*, Vol. II, No. 2 (April, 1879).

44. *Ibid.*

45. Fries, ed., *RM*, VI, 2890.

46. Draft of letter, SCL.
47. *The Academy*, Vol. II, No. 2 (April, 1879).

CHAPTER 7

1. MAS.
2. Appended to copy of rules, SCL.
3. Dialogues, SCL.
4. Letter from Eliza Safford Fannin to Thomas S. N. King, Sept. 16, 1830, Houston Public Library.
5. LB, SCL.
6. Letter of July 18, 1808, LB, SCL.
7. Letter of Aug. 19, 1808, LB, SCL.
8. Fries, ed., *RM*, V, 2148.
9. *Ibid.*, VII, 3240.
10. Letter of April 28, 1811, LB, SCL.
11. Article by the Rev. Dr. J. E. Edwards, *The Academy*, Vol. VI, No. 46 (Dec., 1883).

CHAPTER 8

1. House Conference minutes, Jan. 19, 1807, MAS.
2. *Ibid.*
3. Inventories, SCL.
4. "Classing of the Schools in Salem Boarding School," Feb. 23, 1807, SCL.
5. Eliza Vierling Kremer, "Bits of Old Salem Gossip," SCL.
6. Candace Wheeler, *The Development of Embroidery in America*, p. 67.
7. Inventories, SCL.
8. Student Accounts, SCL.
9. Fries, ed., *RM*, VII, 3123.
10. *Ibid.*
11. Exercises in Writing, MAS.
12. *The Academy*, Vol. VII, No. 52 (Jan., 1885).
13. Fries, ed., *RM*, VI, 2919.
14. Examination Questions, SCL.
15. *Ibid.*
16. *Ibid.*
17. *Ibid.*
18. *Ibid.*
19. *Ibid.*
20. *Ibid.*
21. *Ibid.*
22. *Ibid.*

23. *Ibid.*
24. *Ibid.*
25. *Ibid.*
26. *Ibid.*
27. Minnie J. Smith, ed., *RM*, IX, 4827.

CHAPTER 9

1. Fries, ed., *RM*, VII, 3096.
2. MAS.
3. AC, March 26, 1811, MAS.
4. Fries, ed., *RM*, VII, 3137.
5. *Ibid.*, p. 3205.
6. *Ibid.*, p. 3234.
7. *Ibid.*, p. 3226.
8. Letter to William Logan, Halifax County, Va., Jan. 13, 1814, LB, SCL.
9. Letter to John S. Maner, Robertville, S.C., Feb. 18, 1814, LB, SCL.
10. Letter to Nathaniel Peoples, Rowan County, N.C., Aug. 26, 1814, LB, SCL.
11. EC, Aug. 24, 1814, MAS.
12. *Ibid.*
13. AC, Sept. 28, 1813, MAS.
14. Letter, Nov. 1, 1813, translated by Erika Huber, MAN.
15. EC, May 15, 1800, MAS.
16. Fries, ed., *RM*, VI, 2675.
17. *The Academy*, Vol. VII, No. 53 (Feb., 1885).
18. *Ibid.*
19. AC, July 9, 1827, MAS.
20. Fries, ed., *RM*, VII, 3191.
21. Letter from George Hariston, Sassafras Grove, Va., Feb. 26, 1814, LB, SCL.
22. Letter from Isaac Medley, Halifax County, Va., Aug. 15, 1814, LB, SCL.
23. Fries, ed., *RM*, VII, 3255.
24. *Ibid.*, p. 3257.
25. *Ibid.*, p. 3273.
26. EC, Jan. 17, 1816, MAS.

CHAPTER 10

1. Fries, ed., *RM*, VII, 3273.
2. *Ibid.*, p. 3301.
3. *Ibid.*, p. 3295.
4. *Ibid.*

5. *Ibid.*, p. 3286.
6. EC, Aug. 28, 1816, MAS.
7. *The Academy*, Vol. VII, No. 52 (Jan., 1885).
8. *Ibid.*
9. Fries, ed., *RM*, VII, 3347.
10. AC, May 19, 1817, MAS.
11. *Ibid.*, June 2, 1817, MAS.
12. Fries, ed., *RM*, VII, 3347.
13. *Ibid.*, p. 3328.
14. Charles Grier Sellers, Jr., *James K. Polk, Jacksonian*, p. 75.
15. *Ibid.*
16. Ledgers, SCL.
17. Student Register, SCL.
18. Marianne Means, *The Woman in the White House*, p. 64.
19. Milton Lomask, *This Slender Reed*, p. 64.
20. Means, *The Woman in the White House*, p. 80.
21. *The Academy*, Vol. VIII, No. 66 (June, 1886).
22. Fries, ed., *RM*, VIII, 3329.
23. *Ibid.*, pp. 3321 and 3325.
24. *Ibid.*, p. 3325.
25. Letter to Major Robert Crockett, Wythe Courthouse, Va., Oct. 26, 1817, SCL.

CHAPTER 11

1. AC, Feb. 9, 1818, MAS.
2. *Ibid.*
3. *Ibid.*
4. Circulars, SCL.
5. Diary of Juliana Margaret Connor, Southern Historical Collection, University of North Carolina Library, Chapel Hill, N.C.
6. Letter from Bishop Jacob Van Vleck to the Rev. Christian Friedrich Schaaf, June 22, 1818, translated by Erika Huber, MAN.
7. EC, July 8, 1818, MAS.
8. Circulars, SCL.
9. Memoir of Gotthold Benjamin Reichel, MAS.
10. Fries, ed., *RM*, VII, 3378.
11. EC, April 21, 1819, MAS.
12. *Ibid.*
13. AC, March 27, 1820, MAS.
14. Fries, ed., *RM*, VII, 3516.
15. EC, May 28, 1823, MAS.
16. Adelaide L. Fries, "History of the Single Sisters House," MAS.

17. Memoir of Maria Steiner Denke, MAS.

18. Letter from Maria Crockett to Major Robert Crockett, Wythe County, Va., Jan. 13, 1818, SCL.

19. Article by the Rev. F. R. Holland, *The Academy*, Vol. VIII, No. 64 (March, 1886).

20. EC, Nov. 5, 1823, MAS.

21. *Ibid.*

22. AC, March 22, 1824, MAS.

23. *Ibid.*

24. EC, Sept. 29, 1824, MAS.

25. Memoir of Maria Steiner Denke, MAS.

CHAPTER 12

1. Accounts, 1820, SCL.

2. AC, Dec. 15, 1823, MAS.

3. EC, March 29, 1820, MAS.

4. Fries, ed., *RM*, VII, 3450.

5. Eliza Vierling Kremer, "Bits of Old Salem Gossip," SCL.

6. *Ibid.*

7. *Ibid.*

8. Fries, ed., *RM*, VII, 3450.

9. AC, Dec. 15, 1823, MAS.

10. *Ibid.*

11. AC, March 2, 1824, MAS.

12. Rights, ed., *RM*, VIII, 3696.

13. *Ibid.*, p. 3687.

14. *Ibid.*

15. *Ibid.*, p. 3688.

16. *Ibid.*

17. *Ibid.*

18. *Ibid.*

19. *Ibid.*, p. 3689.

20. *Ibid.*

21. *Ibid.*, p. 3690.

22. *Ibid.*, p. 3691.

23. *Ibid.*, p. 3692.

24. Letter from Amelia Roe Woodward, *The Academy*, Vol. X, No. 88 (Sept., 1888).

25. AC, May 31, 1824, MAS.

26. *Ibid.*, June 9, 1823, MAS.

27. Rights, ed., *RM*, VIII, 3810.

28. Fries, ed., *RM*, VII, 3544–45.

29. *Ibid.*, p. 3544.

30. AC, Dec. 29, 1823, MAS.

31. EC, Aug. 14, 1824, MAS.

CHAPTER 13

1. Eliza Vierling Kremer, "Bits of Old Salem Gossip," SCL.

2. *Ibid.*

3. *Ibid.*

4. *Ibid.*

5. William D. Martin, *The Journal of William D. Martin: A Journey from South Carolina to Connecticut in the Year 1809*, p. 13.

6. Eliza Vierling Kremer, reminiscences, MAS.

7. Letter from Mrs. Mary Phillips, *The Academy*, Vol. VII, No. 49 (Oct., 1884).

8. Diary of Juliana Margaret Connor, Southern Historical Collection, Chapel Hill, N.C.

9. Rights, ed., *RM*, VIII, 3804.

10. AC, April 15, 1827, MAS.

11. Rights, ed., *RM*, VIII, 3797.

12. Letter from Louisa Lenoir to Mrs. Louisa Lenoir, Fort Defiance, N.C., Dec. 7, 1829, Southern Historical Collection, Chapel Hill, N.C.

13. *Ibid.*

14. Diary of George Frederick Bahnson, Jan. 1, 1835, Evangeline B. Smith Collection, Winston-Salem, N.C.

15. Thurman Wilkins, *Cherokee Tragedy*, p. 144.

16. *Ibid.*, p. 347.

17. Eliza Vierling Kremer, "Bits of Old Salem Gossip," SCL.

18. *Ibid.*

19. Diary of Juliana Margaret Connor, June 23, 1827, Southern Historical Collection, Chapel Hill, N.C.

20. Eliza Vierling Kremer, "Bits of Old Salem Gossip," SCL.

CHAPTER 14

1. Rights, ed., *RM*, VIII, 3839.

2. *Ibid.*, p. 3831.

3. *Ibid.*, p. 3849.

4. *The Weekly Gleaner* (Salem, N.C.,) June 2, 1829.

5. Rights, ed., *RM*, VIII, 3911.

6. *The Weekly Gleaner*, June 2, 1829.

7. Donald M. McCorkle, "The Collegium Musicum Salem," *North Carolina Historical Review*, Vol. XXXIII, No. 4 (Oct., 1956).

8. *Ibid.*

9. *The Weekly Gleaner*, June 23, 1829.

10. Letter from M. L. Springs to Miss Sophia Harris, Charlotte, N.C., July 6, 1829, SCL.

11. Journal of John Henry Leinbach, July 4, 1831, MAS.

12. Rights, ed., *RM*, VIII, 3972.

13. Adelaide L. Fries, *Historical Sketch of Salem Female Academy*, p. 15.

14. *The Weekly Gleaner*, March 24, 1829.

15. Letter from the Rev. Johann Christian Bechler to Bishop John Daniel Anders, July 25, 1829, translated by Frank P. Albright, MAN.

16. EC, July 29, 1829, MAS.

17. Letter from Bechler to Anders, July 25, 1829, translated by Frank P. Albright, MAN.

18. *Ibid.*

19. Letter from Bechler to Anders, Aug. 29, 1829, translated by Frank P. Albright, MAN.

20. *Ibid.*, Nov. 24, 1829.

21. *Ibid.*

22. *Ibid.*

23. *Ibid.*

24. Rights, ed., *RM*, VIII, 3915.

25. Journal of John Henry Leinbach, May 16, 1830.

26. *Ibid.*, June 27, 1830.

27. John Henry Clewell, *History of Wachovia in North Carolina*, p. 321.

28. Rights, ed., *RM*, VIII, 4061.

29. *Ibid.*, p. 4068.

CHAPTER 15

1. Provincial Helpers' Conference minutes, Jan. 20, 1834, translated by Mary Creech, MAS.

2. *Ibid.*, March 24, 1834.

3. Letter from the Rev. Johann Christian Bechler to Bishop John Daniel Anders, April 22, 1834, translated by Frank P. Albright, MAN.

4. Diary of George Frederick Bahnson, June 29, 1834, Evangeline B. Smith Collection, Winston-Salem, N.C.

5. *Ibid.*

6. *Ibid.*

7. *Ibid.*

8. Letter from Bechler to Anders, April 22, 1834, MAN.

9. *Ibid.*

10. Diary of George Frederick Bahnson, June 29, 1834.

11. *Ibid.*, April 1, 1835.

12. John Henry Clewell, *History of Wachovia in North Carolina*, p. 322.

13. Address by Mrs. Ann Sturdivant delivered c. 1900, MAS.

14. Paper by Mrs. Sophia K. Kernan, *The Academy*, Vol. XIII, No. 110 (Nov., 1890).

15. Diary of George Frederick Bahnson, Nov. 6, 1834.

16. *Ibid.*, July 2, 1835.

17. *The Farmer's Reporter and Rural Repository*, May 23, 1835.

18. *Ibid.*

19. Journal of John Henry Leinbach, Jan. 4, 1834, MAS.

20. Diary of George Frederick Bahnson, July 2, 1835.

21. *Ibid.*

22. Smith, ed., *RM*, IX, 4768.

23. MAS.

24. Rights, ed., *RM*, VIII, 4185.

25. AC, Aug. 3, 1835, MAS.

26. Letter from John H. Wimbish, Halifax County, N.C., Jan. 27, 1836, SCL.

27. Letter from W. B. Carter, Caswell County, N.C., Sept. 16, 1836, SCL.

28. Lithograph by Gustavus Grunewald, MAS.

29. Letter from Henrietta Schober to Sophia A. Herman, Bethlehem, Pa., Sept. 27, 1837, SCL.

30. *Ibid.*

31. *Ibid.*

Chapter 16

1. Diary of George Frederick Bahnson, May 21, 1835, Evangeline B. Smith Collection, Winston-Salem, N.C.

2. *The Farmer's Reporter and Rural Repository*, May 30, 1835.

3. Adelaide L. Fries, *Historical Sketch of Salem Female Academy*, p. 17.

4. Public Examinations, 1812–1814, SCL.

5. Fries, *Historical Sketch*, p. 17.

6. Diary of George Frederick Bahnson, May 21, 1835.

7. *Ibid.*, May 22, 1835.

8. Fries, *Historical Sketch*, p. 17.

9. Letter from R. H. Morrison, Cottage Home, N.C., May 24, 1841, SCL.

10. Article by the Rev. Dr. J. E. Edwards, *The Academy*, Vol. VI, No. 46 (Dec., 1883).

11. AC, April 30, 1832, translated by Edmund Schwarze, MAS.

12. Journal of John Henry Leinbach, May 27, 1830, MAS.

13. Diary of George Frederick Bahnson, May 21, 1835.

14. Journal of John Henry Leinbach, May 20, 1831.

15. EC, June 11, 1845, MAS.

16. Kenneth G. Hamilton, ed. *RM*, X, 5147.

17. Letter from Jane Crawford, Gladdens Grove, S.C., Feb. 17, 1842, SCL.

18. Letter from Missouri Alston to Mrs. Sarah Alston, Halifax County, N.C., Feb. 8, 1841, SCL.

19. Eliza Vierling Kremer, "Bits of Old Salem Gossip," SCL.

20. "The Academy from 1834 to 1844," *The Academy*, Vol. VII, No. 54 (March, 1885).

21. Letter from Eliza Safford Fannin to Thomas S. N. King, Sept. 16, 1830, Houston Public Library.

22. Letter from Louisa Lenoir to Mrs. J. L. Lenoir, Fort Defiance, N.C., Aug. 13, 1829, Southern Historical Collection, Chapel Hill, N.C.

23. *Ibid.*, Sept. 19, 1829.

24. Letter from Heziah I. Sullivan to James N. Sullivan, Tumbling Shoals, S.C., May 2, 1838, SCL.

25. *Ibid.*

26. Letter from Sarah S. Davis to Jasper W. Davis, July 27, 1838, Jasper Davis Papers, Duke University, Durham, N.C.

27. *Ibid.*, Dec. 17, 1838.

28. Letter from Whitney & Sanford, Boston, to J. C. Jacobson, April 11, 1836, SCL.

29. Letter from A. G. Hughes, Mecklenburg County, Va., 1836, SCL.

30. Letter from Ann McDowell, Quaker Meadows, Feb. 9, 1837, SCL.

31. Letter from Archibald Yarbrough, Franklin City, N.C., Jan. 31, 1837, SCL.

32. Letter from Daniel Murray, Raleigh, N.C., July 7, 1837, SCL.

33. Letter from Alexander Gray, Randolph County, N.C., May 8, 1837, SCL.

34. Letter from T. T. Napier, Macon, Ga., March 29, 1837, SCL.

35. Diary of George Frederick Bahnson, Sept. 24, 1836.

36. Rights, ed., *RM*, VIII, 4230.

37. *Ibid.*, p. 4229.

CHAPTER 17

1. Charles Grier Sellers, Jr., *James K. Polk, Jacksonian*, p. 75.

2. Rights, ed., *RM*, VIII, 4226.

3. Adelaide L. Fries, "One Hundred Years of Textiles in Salem," *North Carolina Historical Review*, Vol. XXVII, No. 1 (Jan., 1950).

4. CC, July 8, 1836, MAS.

5. *Ibid.*

6. EC, Nov. 1, 1837, MAS.

7. AC, July 31, 1838, MAS.

8. EC, March 2, 1836, MAS.

9. Smith, ed., *RM*, IX, 4477.

10. Letter from I. D. Erwin, Ervinton, S.C., Jan. 23, 1836, SCL.

11. Letter from Mary Williams, Panther Creek, N.C., Oct. 8, 1837, SCL.

12. Letter from Joseph Medley, Beverly, N.C., Sept. 17, 1837, SCL.

13. Letter from Rachel M. Maner, Tallahassee, Fla., Dec. 28, 1836, SCL.

14. Letter from William Moore, Chucky Bend, E. Tenn., Dec. 25, 1840, SCL.

15. Letter from John W. Headen, Floyd County, Va., June 21, 1836, SCL.

16. Letter from Rachel M. Maner, Tallahassee, Fla., Dec. 28, 1836, SCL.

17. Letter from H. W. Williams, Jr., Yorkville, S.C., Oct. 5, 1836, SCL.

18. Rights, ed., *RM*, VIII, 4178.

19. SCL.

20. Diary of George Frederick Bahnson, July 2, 1835, Evangeline B. Smith Collection, Winston-Salem, N.C.

21. Letter from Aurelia Herbst to Julia A. Conrad, Bethania, N.C., Feb. 26, 1841, SCL.

22. Letter from Henrietta Schober to Sophia Herman, Bethlehem, Pa., Nov. 28, 1841, SCL.

23. Letter from Lavinia Blum to Sophia Herman, Aug. 1, 1841, SCL.

24. Letter from Lucinda Blum to Sophia Herman, July 15, 1840, SCL.

25. Letter from Henrietta Schober to Sophia Herman, Nov. 28, 1841, SCL.

26. Smith, ed., *RM*, IX, 4453.

CHAPTER 18

1. EC, Nov. 4, 1840, MAS.

2. AC, Nov. 20, 1840, MAS.

3. *Ibid.*, Dec. 14, 1840.

4. Hamilton, ed., *RM*, X, 5076.

5. *Ibid.*, p. 5074.

6. *Ibid.*

7. *Ibid.*, p. 5088.

8. *Ibid.*

9. *Ibid.*

10. Letter from Susanna Columbia Thomas, *The Academy*, Vol. XV, No. 136 (May, 1893).

11. Smith, ed., *RM*, IX, 4706.

12. *Ibid.*, p. 4760.

13. Hamilton, ed., *RM*, X, 5098.

14. *Ibid.*, p. 5124.

15. John Henry Clewell, *History of Wachovia in North Carolina*, p. 324.

16. Hamilton, ed., *RM*, X, 5124–25.

17. *Ibid.*

18. *Ibid.*, p. 5102.

19. *Ibid.*, p. 5125.

20. *Ibid.*, p. 5146.

21. Clewell, *History of Wachovia*, p. 324.

22. Paper by Sophia K. Kernan, *The Academy*, Vol. XIII, No. 110 (Nov., 1890).

23. Smith, ed., *RM*, IX, 4890.

24. Hamilton, ed., *RM*, X, 5158.

25. *Ibid.*, p. 5159.

26. EC, April 15, 1846, MAS.

27. *Ibid.*

28. Smith, ed., *RM*, IX, 4892.

29. Hamilton, ed., *RM*, X, 5166.

30. *Ibid.*, p. 5167.

31. Hamilton, ed., *RM*, X, 5182.

32. *Ibid.*, p. 5189.

CHAPTER 19

1. Hamilton, ed., *RM*, X, 5189.

2. *Ibid.*, p. 5199.

3. *Ibid.*, p. 5208.

4. *Ibid.*

5. *Ibid.*

6. *Ibid.*

7. *Ibid.*, p. 5210.

8. *Ibid.*

9. *Ibid.*, p. 5211.

10. *Ibid.*

11. Letter from Susanna Columbia Thomas, *The Academy*, Vol. XV, No. 136 (May, 1893).

12. Hamilton, ed., *RM*, X, 5210.

13. *Ibid.*, p. 5212.

14. Funeral sermon for de Schweinitz by Edward Rondthaler, Nov. 5, 1879, MAS.

15. Letter from Henrietta Schober to Sophia Herman, May 15, 1842, SCL.

16. SCL.

17. Hamilton, ed., *RM*, X, 5203.

18. Obituary of Charles Adolphus Blech, records of the Moravian congregation, Gnadenhutten, Ohio.

19. *Ibid.*

20. Paper read by Sophia K. Kernan, *The Academy*, Vol. XIII, No. 110 (Nov., 1890).

21. Hamilton, ed., *RM*, X, 5323.

22. SCL.

23. Adelaide L. Fries, *Historical Sketch of Salem Female Academy*, p. 17.

24. Hugh Talmage Lefler and Albert Ray Newsome, *North Carolina: The History of a Southern State*, p. 381.

25. *The People's Press* (Salem, N.C.), Jan. 1, 1853.

CHAPTER 20

1. Hamilton, ed., *RM*, XI, 5735.

2. *Ibid.*, p. 5700.

3. MAS.

4. SCL.

5. Obituary of Robert de Schweinitz, *The Academy*, Vol. XXV, No. 215 (Oct., 1901).

6. John Henry Clewell, *History of Wachovia in North Carolina*, p. 326.

7. Hamilton, ed., *RM*, XI, 5778.

8. *Ibid.*, p. 5780.

9. *The People's Press* (Salem, N.C.), June 4, 1853.

10. Hamilton, ed., *RM*, XI, 5788.

11. *Ibid.*, p. 5789.

12. Hamilton, ed., *RM*, XI, 5896.

13. *The People's Press,* June 10, 1854.

14. *Ibid.*, June 24, 1854.

15. Hamilton, ed., *RM*, XI, 5897.

16. *The Academy*, Vol. XVII, No. 177 (May, 1897).

17. Paper by Sophia K. Kernan, *The Academy*, Vol. XIII, No. 110 (Nov., 1890).

18. Hamilton, ed., *RM*, XI, 5860.

19. *Ibid.*, p. 5926.

20. Letter from Robert de Schweinitz, *The Academy*, Vol. VII, No. 55 (April, 1885).

21. Paper by Sophia K. Kernan, *The Academy*, Vol. XIII, No. 110 (Nov., 1890).

CHAPTER 21

1. Obituary of Robert de Schweinitz, *The Academy*, Vol. XXV, No. 215 (Oct., 1901).

2. Letter from Lizzie Reeves Wiley, *The Academy*, Vol. IX, No. 77 (June, 1887).

3. Letter "To the Trustees of Salem F. Academy from the Teachers of the same," MAS. The letter is undated, but all of the teachers whose signatures it bears were at the Academy in 1856. Also, the references to this letter in the de Schweinitz response of Nov. 11, 1856, indicate that the teachers registered their complaints in early November of that year.

4. *Ibid*.

5. *Ibid*.

6. *Ibid*.

7. *Ibid*.

8. *Ibid*.

9. From a listing of Academy teachers and the dates of their service in John Henry Clewell's *History of Wachovia in North Carolina*, the first names of the teachers could be matched easily with their initialed signatures except in the case of "M. Herman." Clewell lists only an "Adelaide Herman" during that period, but a certificate in the Moravian Archives (Winston-Salem) filed with other material relating to Adelaide Herman gives her full name as "Adelaide Mathilda Herman." The conclusion thus is drawn that "M. Herman" and "Adelaide Herman" were one and the same person.

10. Hamilton, ed., *RM*, XI, 5975.

11. Letter, "To the Teachers of Salem Female Academy," signed by Levin T. Reichel, Nov. 11, 1856, MAS.

12. Salem Diary, Feb. 11, 1857, MAS.

13. Letter from Robert de Schweinitz, *The Academy*, Vol. VII, No. 55 (April, 1885); letter from Mrs. John Sullivant, *The Academy*, Vol. VII, No. 57 (June, 1885).

14. Salem Diary, May 7, 1857, MAS.

15. *The People's Press* (Salem, N.C.), June 5, 1857.

16. *The Academy*, Vol. IX, No. 74 (March, 1887).

17. Reminiscences of Augustus Fogle, SCL.

18. *The Academy*, Vol. VII, No. 56 (May, 1885).

19. Memorabilia of 1857, MAS.

20. *Catalogue of the Teachers and Scholars of Salem Female Academy, 1858–59*, SCL.

21. *Ibid*.

22. *Ibid*.

23. *Ibid*.

24. *The People's Press*, Jan. 21, 1859.

25. Hamilton, ed., *RM*, X, 5456.

26. *Ibid.*, IX, 6048.

27. *Ibid.*, p. 6050.

28. Adelaide L. Fries, "History of the Single Sisters House," MAS.

29. *Ibid.*

CHAPTER 22

1. Memorabilia of 1859, MAS.

2. Salem Diary, Aug. 3, 1860, MAS.

3. *The People's Press* (Salem, N.C.), Sept. 7, 1860.

4. *Ibid.*, Nov. 2, 1860.

5. Memorabilia of 1860, MAS.

6. Salem Diary, May 29, 1861, MAS.

7. Hamilton, ed., *RM*, XI, 6062.

8. *The People's Press*, May 3, 1861.

9. *Ibid.*, June 21, 1861.

10. Hamilton, ed., *RM*, XI, 6065.

11. Adelaide L. Fries, *Historical Sketch of Salem Female Academy*, p. 20.

12. Autobiography of Lucie Malone Thompson, Southern Historical Collection, Chapel Hill, N.C.

13. Fries, *Historical Sketch*, p. 20.

14. Dorothea de Schweinitz, *Summary History of the Schweinitz Family*.

15. Memoir of Augustus Gottlieb Fogle, MAS.

16. Fries, *Historical Sketch*, p. 21.

17. Letter from Robert de Schweinitz, *The Academy*, Vol. XVIII, No. 161 (Nov., 1895).

18. *Ibid.*

19. *The People's Press*, Aug. 22, 1862.

20. Account book of Augustus Fogle, SCL.

21. Hamilton, ed., *RM*, XI, 6082.

22. MAS.

23. This account of Stoneman's brief stay in Salem is a compilation of material from the following sources: Douglas L. Rights, "Salem in the War Between the States," *North Carolina Historical Review*, Vol. XXVII, No. 3, (July, 1950); Adelaide L. Fries et als, *Forsyth: A County on the March*; Adelaide L. Fries, *Forsyth County*; Charles H. Kirk, *History of the Fifteenth Pennsylvania Volunteer Cavalry*; *The People's Press*, April 14, 1866; Memorabilia of 1865, MAS; Eliza Vierling Kremer, "Bits of Old Salem Gossip," SCL. Only direct quotations are specifically attributed.

24. Statement by John Blackburn in Adelaide L. Fries, *Forsyth County*, p. 98.

25. *Forsyth: A County on the March*, from which this incident is quoted, does not cite its source. However, in a letter to Dr. John H. Chandler,

former president of Salem Academy and College, dated Aug. 16, 1974, Dorothea de Schweinitz, granddaughter of Robert de Schweinitz, verified the story as she had heard it.

26. Memorabilia of 1865, MAS.

27. *Ibid.*

28. Charles H. Kirk, *History of the Fifteenth Pennsylvania Cavalry,* p. 501.

29. Eliza Vierling Kremer, "Bits of Old Salem Gossip," SCL.

30. Adelaide L. Fries, *Historical Sketch of Salem Female Academy,* p. 22–23.

CHAPTER 23

1. Letter to the author from Mrs. Patricia Clark, assistant editor, The Papers of Andrew Johnson, the University of Tennessee, Knoxville, March 27, 1972: "We have never uncovered any evidence of Martha Johnson's attending school in Salem, and it seems rather doubtful to me that Johnson would have sent his daughter so far from home."

2. *The People's Press* (Salem, N.C.), May 27, 1865.

3. Memorabilia of 1865, MAS.

4. Autobiography of Lucie Malone Thompson, Southern Historical Collection, Chapel Hill, N.C.

5. Hamilton, ed., *RM,* XI, 6079.

6. *The People's Press,* March 24, 1866.

7. *Ibid.,* July 8, 1865.

8. *Ibid.,* March 9, 1865.

9. An Act to Incorporate Salem Female Academy, at Salem, in the County of Forsythe [sic], Session Laws of ———, Chapter 31.

10. Dr. Dale H. Gramley, a newspaper editor of Bethlehem, Pa., and a non-Moravian at the time, was elected president in 1949.

11. Hamilton, ed., *RM,* XI, 6089.

12. *The People's Press,* June 2, 1866.

13. Obituary of Robert de Schweinitz, *The Academy,* Vol. XXV, No. 215 (Oct., 1901).

14. John Henry Clewell, *History of Wachovia in North Carolina,* p. 327.

Bibliography

MANUSCRIPT SOURCES

Archives of the Moravian Church in America, Northern Province, Bethlehem, Pa.
  Letters, translated by Erika Huber and Frank P. Albright
  Provincial Helpers' Conference minutes, translated by Vernon H. Nelson
Archives of the Moravian Church in America, Southern Province, Winston-Salem, N.C.
  Aufseher Collegium minutes, translated by Erika Huber
  Congregation Council minutes, translated by Erika Huber
  Elders' Conference minutes, translated by Edmund Schwarze
  House Conference minutes, translated by Kenneth G. Hamilton
  Journal of John Henry Leinbach
  Memoirs
  Memorabilia of the Salem Congregation
  Miscellaneous letters, rules, class schedules, reminiscences
  Provincial Helpers' Conference minutes, translated by Mary Creech and
     Kenneth G. Hamilton
  Salem Diary
Duke University, William R. Perkins Library, Durham, N.C.
  Jasper Davis Papers
Houston Public Library
  Fannin Letters, Small Collections, Houston Metropolitan Research
     Center
Salem College Library, Grace Siewers Room, Winston-Salem, N.C.
  Bulletins and circulars
  Day Books
  Dialogues
  Examination questions
  Inventories
  Ledgers
  Letter Books and miscellaneous letters
  Miscellaneous student accounts, class schedules, programs
  Student register
Smith, Evangeline B.
  Diary of George Frederick Bahnson
University of North Carolina at Chapel Hill Library, Southern Historical
Collection
  Juliana Margaret Connor Diary, #174
  Lenoir Family Papers, #426
  Thompson Family Papers, #1460

BOOKS AND ARTICLES

Academy, The. 25 vols. (March, 1878—Summer, 1912). A monthly journal of Salem Female Academy. Salem, N.C.: Academy Alumnae Association.

Africa, Philip. "Slaveholding in the Salem Community 1771–1851," *North Carolina Historical Review*, Vol. LIV, No. 3 (July, 1977).

Albright, Frank P. and Horton, Frank L. "History of Properties in Old Salem." Unpublished paper. Old Salem, Inc., Winston-Salem, N.C.

Barzman, Sol. *The First Ladies.* New York: Cowles Book Company, 1970.

Beard, Charles A. and Mary R. *A Basic History of the United States.* New York: Doubleday, Doran & Company, 1944.

Brown, Dee. "The Trail of Tears," *American History Illustrated*, Vol. VII, No. 3 (June, 1972).

Clewell, John Henry. *History of Wachovia in North Carolina.* New York: Doubleday, Page & Company, 1902.

Crabtree, Beth G. *North Carolina Governors 1585–1958.* Raleigh: State Department of Archives and History, 1958.

Farmer's Reporter and Rural Repository, The. Salem, N.C., 1835.

Fries, Adelaide L. *Customs and Practices of the Moravian Church.* Rev. ed. Winston-Salem: Board of Christian Education and Evangelism, 1962.

——— et al. *Forsyth: A County on the March.* Chapel Hill: The University of North Carolina Press, 1949.

———. *Forsyth County.* Winston, N.C.: Stewart's Printing House, 1898.

———. *Historical Sketch of Salem Female Academy.* Salem, N.C.: Crist & Keehln, Printers, 1902.

———. "History of the Single Sisters House, Salem, N.C." 1914. Unpublished paper. Moravian Archives, Winston-Salem, N.C.

———, trans. and ed. *Records of the Moravians in North Carolina.* Vols. I–VI. Raleigh: North Carolina Historical Commission, 1927–1943; Vol. VII. Raleigh: State Department of Archives and History, 1947.

———. "One Hundred Years of Textiles in Salem," *The North Carolina Historical Review*, Vol. XXVII, No. 1 (Jan., 1950).

Hall, Harry H. *A Johnny Reb Band from Salem.* Raleigh: North Carolina Confederate Centennial Commission, 1963.

Haller, Mabel. *Early Moravian Education in Pennsylvania.* Nazareth, Pa.: Moravian Historical Society, 1953.

Hamilton, J. Taylor. *A History of the Church Known as the Moravian Church or The Unitas Fratrum.* Bethlehem, Pa.: Times Publishing Co., 1900.

Hamilton, Kenneth G. "Minutes of the Mission Conference Held in Springplace," *Atlanta Historical Bulletin*, Vol. XV, No. 4 (Winter, 1970).

————. *Records of the Moravians in North Carolina*, Vols. X–XI. Raleigh: State Department of Archives and History, 1966 and 1969.

Harbeson, Georgiana Brown. *American Needlework*. New York: Bonanza Books, 1938.

Jelinik, Vladimir, trans. *The Analytical Didactic of Comenius*. Chicago: The University of Chicago Press, 1953.

Kirk, Charles H., comp. and ed. *History of the Fifteenth Pennsylvania Volunteer Company*. Philadelphia: privately printed, 1906.

Kozik, Frantisik. *The Sorrowful and Heroic Life of John Amos Comenius*. Translated by Edith Pargeter. Prague: State Educational Publishing House, 1958.

Kremer, Eliza Vierling. "Bits of Old Salem Gossip." Unpublished paper. Salem College Library.

————. Unpublished reminiscences. Moravian Archives, Winston-Salem, N.C.

Laurie, S. S. *Life and Works of Comenius*. Syracuse: C. W. Bardeen, Pub., 1893.

Lefler, Hugh Talmage and Newsome, Albert Ray. *North Carolina: The History of a Southern State*. 3rd ed. Chapel Hill: The University of North Carolina Press, 1973.

Levering, Joseph Mortimer. *A History of Bethlehem, Pennsylvania 1741–1892*. Bethlehem: Times Publishing Company, 1903.

Lomask; Milton. *This Slender Reed*. New York: Farrar, Strauss and Giroux, 1966.

Martin, William D. *The Journal of William D. Martin: A Journey from South Carolina to Connecticut in the Year 1809*. Prepared by Anna D. Elmore. Charlotte: Heritage House, 1959.

McCorkle, Donald M. "The Collegium Musicum Salem," *North Carolina Historical Review*, Vol. XXXIII, No. 4. (Oct., 1956).

Means, Marianne. *The Woman in The White House*. New York: Random House, 1963.

Parris, John. *The Cherokee Story*. Asheville: The Stephens Press, 1950.

People's Press, The. Salem, N.C. 1854–1866.

Powell, William S. *The North Carolina Colony*. New York: Crowell-Collier Press, 1969.

Preston, Julia Jackson Christian. *Stonewall's Widow*. Winston-Salem: Hunter Publishing Company, 1961.

Reichel, William C. *Bethlehem Seminary Souvenir: A History of the Rise, Progress and Present Condition of the Bethlehem Female Seminary 1785–1858*. Philadelphia: J. B. Lippincott & Co., 1858.

Rights, Douglas L. *The American Indian in North Carolina*. Winston-Salem: John F. Blair, Publisher, 1957.

————. "Salem in the War Between the States," *North Carolina Historical Review*, Vol. XXVII, No. 3 (July, 1950).

————, trans. and ed. *Records of the Moravians in North Carolina*, Vol. VIII. Raleigh: State Department of Archives and History, 1954.

Salem Academy catalogs

Sellers, Charles Grier, Jr. *James K. Polk, Jacksonian 1795–1843*. Princeton: The Princeton University Press, 1957.

de Schweinitz, Dorothea. *Summary History of the Schweinitz Family 1350 to 1975*. Washington: privately printed, 1974.

Smith, Charles Lee. *The History of Education in North Carolina*. Washington: Bureau of Education, 1888.

Smith, Minnie J., trans. and ed. *Records of the Moravians in North Carolina*, Vol. IX. Raleigh: State Department of Archives and History, 1964.

Surratt, Jerry Lee. *From Theocracy to Voluntary Church and Secularized Community: A Study of the Moravians in Salem, North Carolina 1772–1860*. Ann Arbor: University Microfilms, 1968.

Weekly Gleaner, The. Salem, N.C. 1829.

Weinlick, John R. *Count Zinzendorf*. New York—Nashville: Abingdon Press, 1956.

Wheeler, Candace. *The Development of Embroidery in America*. New York: Harper & Brothers Publishers, 1921.

Whitton, Mary Ormsbee. *First First Ladies 1789–1865*. New York: Hastings House, 1948.

Wilkins, Thurman. *Cherokee Tragedy*. New York: The Macmillan Company, 1970.

Woody, Thomas. *A History of Women's Education in the United States*. Vol. 1, New York: Octagon Press, 1929.

Index